The CIO's Guide to Oracle Products and Solutions

Jessica Keyes

CRC Press
Taylor & Francis Group
Boca Raton London New York

CRC Press is an imprint of the
Taylor & Francis Group, an **informa** business

AN AUERBACH BOOK

CRC Press
Taylor & Francis Group
6000 Broken Sound Parkway NW, Suite 300
Boca Raton, FL 33487-2742

First issued in paperback 2019

ISBN-13: 978-1-4822-4994-1 (hbk)
ISBN-13: 978-0-367-37838-7 (pbk)

Library of Congress Cataloging-in-Publication Data

Keyes, Jessica, 1950-
    The CIO's guide to Oracle products and solutions / Jessica Keyes.
      pages cm
    Summary: "This book is the go-to guide for all things Oracle. It provides management level guidance for successfully navigating and managing the Oracle-verse. Coverage includes executive level overviews of the Oracle product line - features and benefits; management best practices; user/developer lessons learned; management considerations; compliance and security considerations, and management metrics"-- Provided by publisher.
    Includes bibliographical references and index.
    ISBN 978-1-4822-4994-1 (hardback)
    1. Oracle (Computer file) 2. Relational databases. I. Title.

QA76.9.D3K358975 2014
005.75'6--dc23
                                                  2014023833

Visit the Taylor & Francis Web site at
http://www.taylorandfrancis.com

and the CRC Press Web site at
http://www.crcpress.com

Contents

Preface

Cloud. Database. Middleware. Applications. Exalogic. Exalytics. Java. Servers. Virtualization. Storage. What do these, and the rest of those products listed in Figure P.1, all have in common? Simple. It's Oracle.

Oracle is just about everywhere, in every category, as shown in Table P.1, and it has the market share to prove it. According to Gartner, Inc., Oracle is number one in worldwide RDBMS (relational database management system) software revenue share, holds a larger revenue share than the four closest competitors combined, and leads the next closest competitor's revenue share by 29%.

So it's a no-brainer that now, or sometime in the near future, most executives will be confronted with having to manage one or more Oracle products. Given the share diversity of the Oracle product line, and the level of complexity of integration, management is quite a daunting prospect.

However, all is not rosy in the Kingdom of Oracle. A recent *Fortune* magazine article asked, "What you do when you're the best company in your industry, but your industry is mired in a slump of mediocre performance?" (Kelleher 2013). This is not really a book about Oracle's financial performance. However, it is important, when making a commitment to Oracle products and services, to understand the ramifications tied to what many consider to be a macroeconomic slowdown in the global market. Many argue, however, that it's not so much the global economics that's the problem. These pundits say that the doldrums the industry is facing are caused by the shift to cloud computing. This is probably the reason that Oracle is placing such an emphasis on its cloud products. We will touch on many of these products in several chapters of this book.

In doing the research for this book, I reviewed many articles written by Oracle experts inside and outside of the company to search for best practices and lessons learned in the use of Oracle products and services. Because this book is focused on the CIO, we're not really going to get into technical lessons learned, e.g., the 10 top ways of handling metadata. Instead, we're going to focus on what the CIO needs to do to orient (or reorient, as the case may be) the organization toward use of Oracle products and services. Toward that end, as I was reviewing the articles written by various experts, I found that the best practices and lessons learned were

FIGURE P.1
Oracle product Wordle (created on http://www.wordle.net).

similar across the board when it comes to strategy. Essentially, there are several axioms to consider:

1. Prepare
2. Educate
3. Keep up with change
4. Mitigate risk
5. Move forward with confidence

The format of this book is really quite simple and in line with the five axioms listed here. Given the great number of Oracle products and services, and the availability of technical information about these products and services on the Oracle website as well as various secondary websites, we are going to focus more on developing a strategic framework for the use of these products and services rather than the specific product or service itself. The strategic framework will assist you in preparing, educating, keeping up with change, mitigating risk, and then implementing with the confidence needed to be successful.

What you will find are chapters focused on particular product lines containing summary information about those products and services. More importantly, you will find specific information about preparing the organization and its assets toward the use of those products and services. We cover the very heart of the Oracle products set. This includes Oracle analytics, enterprise performance management, the Oracle cloud, data management, application development, the social business, and fusion. Aligned with these chapters is a set of appendices available on

TABLE P.1

Oracle's Extensive Product List (as of Winter 2013)

Oracle Cloud	Software as a Service (SaaS)
	Platform as a Service (PaaS)
	Infrastructure as a Service (IaaS)
Applications	Customer Experience
	Enterprise Performance Management
	Enterprise Resource Planning
	Human Capital Management
	Supply Chain Management
	Industry Applications
	Applications Product Lines
Database	Oracle Database
	Real Application Clusters
	Data Warehousing
	Database Security
	MySQL
	Berkeley DB
	TimesTen In-Memory Database
Java	Java Platforms
	Java Embedded
	Java for Mobile
	Oracle Java Cloud Service
Developer Tools	Java
	Business Intelligence
	Oracle Database and PL/SQL
	.NET
Operating Systems	Oracle Solaris
	Oracle Linux
Middleware	Cloud Application Foundation
	Data Integration
	Business Analytics
	Identity Management
	Service-Oriented Architecture
	Business Process Management
	WebCenter
	WebLogic
Enterprise Management	Cloud Management
	Application Management
	Database Management
	Middleware Management

(Continued)

TABLE P.1 (CONTINUED)

Oracle's Extensive Product List (as of Winter 2013)

	Hardware and Virtualization Management
	Heterogeneous Management
	Lifecycle Management
Engineered Systems	Big Data Appliance
	Exadata Database Machine
	Exalogic Elastic Cloud
	Exalytics In-Memory Machine
	Database Appliance
	Oracle SuperCluster
	Oracle Virtual Compute Appliance
	Oracle ZFS Storage Appliance
Servers	SPARC
	x86
	Blade
	Netra
Storage and Tape	SAN Storage
	NAS Storage
	Tape Storage
Networking and Data Center Fabric Products	Virtual Networking
	Ethernet Networking
	InfiniBand Networking
	Storage Networking
Enterprise Communications	Enterprise Session Border Controller
	Enterprise Operation Monitor
	Enterprise Communications Broker
	WebRTC Session Controller
	Application Session Controller
	Interactive Session Recorder
Virtualization	Oracle Secure Global Desktop
	Oracle VM for x86
	Oracle VM for SPARC

the CRC Press website for download (http://www.crcpress.com/product/isbn/9781482249941) that includes cloud procurement questions, best practices and security, cloud migration tips, a sample project procurement plan template, and various glossaries.

I would especially like to thank those who assisted me in putting this book together. As always, my editor, John Wyzalek, was instrumental in getting my project approved and provided great encouragement.

REFERENCE

Kelleher, K. 2013. What kind of problem does Oracle have exactly? *Fortune*, June 28. Retrieved from http://tech.fortune.cnn.com/2013/06/28/what-kind-of-problem-does-oracle-have-exactly/ (accessed March 29, 2014).

About the Author

Jessica Keyes is president of New Art Technologies, Inc., a high-technology and management consultancy and development firm started in New York in 1989.

Keyes has given seminars for such prestigious universities as Carnegie Mellon, Boston University, University of Illinois, James Madison University, and San Francisco State University. She is a frequent keynote speaker on the topics of competitive strategy, productivity, and quality. She is a former adviser for DataPro, McGraw-Hill's computer research arm, as well as a member of the Sprint Business Council. Keyes is also a founding board of director member of the New York Software Industry Association. She completed a two-year term on the Mayor of New York City's Small Business Advisory Council. She currently facilitates doctoral and other courses for the University of Phoenix and the University of Liverpool. She has been the editor for WGL's (Warren, Gorham & Lamont) *Handbook of eBusiness* and CRC Press's *Systems Development Management* and *Information Management*.

Prior to founding New Art, Keyes was managing director of R&D for the New York Stock Exchange and has been an officer with Swiss Bank Co. and Banker's Trust, both in New York City. She holds a Masters of Business Administration from New York University and a doctorate in management.

A noted columnist and correspondent with over 200 articles published, Keyes is the author of the following books:

The New Intelligence: AI in Financial Services, HarperBusiness, 1990
The Handbook of Expert Systems in Manufacturing, McGraw-Hill, 1991
Infotrends: The Competitive Use of Information, McGraw-Hill, 1992
The Software Engineering Productivity Handbook, McGraw-Hill, 1993
The Handbook of Multimedia, McGraw-Hill, 1994
The Productivity Paradox, McGraw-Hill, 1994
Technology Trendlines, Van Nostrand Reinhold, 1995
How to Be a Successful Internet Consultant, McGraw-Hill, 1997
Webcasting, McGraw-Hill, 1997
Datacasting, McGraw-Hill, 1997
The Handbook of Technology in Financial Services, CRC Press, 1998

The Handbook of Internet Management, CRC Press, 1999

The Handbook of eBusiness, Warren, Gorham & Lamont, 2000

The Ultimate Internet Sourcebook, Amacom, 2001

How to Be a Successful Internet Consultant, 2nd ed., Amacom, 2002

Software Engineering Handbook, CRC Press, 2002

Real World Configuration Management, CRC Press, 2003

Balanced Scorecard, CRC Press, 2005

Knowledge Management, Business Intelligence, and Content Management: The IT Practitioner's Guide, CRC Press, 2006

X Internet: The Executable and Extendable Internet, CRC Press, 2007

Leading IT Projects: The IT Manager's Guide, CRC Press, 2008

Marketing IT Products and Services, CRC Press, 2009

Implementing the Project Management Balanced Scorecard, CRC Press, 2010

Social Software Engineering: Development and Collaboration with Social Networking, CRC Press, 2011

Enterprise 2.0: Social Networking Tools to Transform Your Organization, CRC Press, 2012

Bring Your Own Devices (BYOD) Survival Guide, CRC Press, 2013

1

Agile PLM

Oracle's Agile Product Lifecycle Management (PLM) enables the organization to manage the complete life cycle of a product: from the ideation phase through to recycling and retirement. Most importantly, Agile Product Lifecycle Management focuses on process efficiency, rapid innovation, cross-functional collaboration, closed-loop quality control, risk mitigation, and cost effectiveness. As shown in Figure 1.1, Oracle's PLM product line consists of four components.

The core of Oracle's Agile Product Lifecycle Management solution for the complete product value chain, Oracle's Agile Product Collaboration, enables the organization to connect globally dispersed product teams, suppliers, and customers in a collaborative environment to accelerate product launches, as shown in Figure 1.2.

Its functionality includes the ability to:

- Provide secure access to preliminary and released information about any product, part, or document
- Gain visibility into pending and released changes and items affected by these changes
- Establish automated and streamlined change-management processes with intelligent workflow
- Drive efficient product management across global, multitiered supply chains
- Create an environment to manage and control manufacturers and their product content
- Synchronize manufacturing systems with the current product record
- Simplify project and product management with a single integrated view
- Establish best-practice project and resource management capabilities

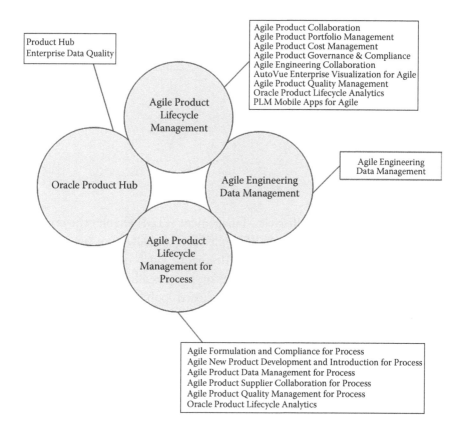

FIGURE 1.1
Agile PLM product line.

- Enhance decision support with cross-project, multienterprise executive dashboards and portfolio analytics
- Accelerate throughput with automated task completion based on product deliverable life cycles

WHAT IS PLM?

In industry, product life-cycle management (PLM) is the process of managing the entire life cycle of a product from inception, through engineering design and manufacture, to service and disposal of manufactured products. PLM integrates people, data, processes, and business systems and provides a product information backbone for companies and their extended enterprise.

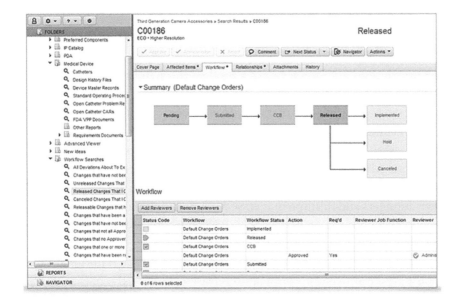

FIGURE 1.2
Oracle's Agile Product Collaboration enables clear and concise tracking of items in review, products in transition, and issues in resolution.

The inspiration for the burgeoning business process now known as PLM came from American Motors Corporation (AMC). The automaker was looking for a way to speed up its product development process to better compete. After introducing its compact Jeep Cherokee (XJ), the vehicle that launched the modern sport utility vehicle (SUV) market, AMC began development of a new model that later came out as the Jeep Grand Cherokee. The first part in its quest for faster product development was a computer-aided design (CAD) software system that made engineers more productive. The second part in this effort was a new communication system that allowed conflicts to be resolved faster while also reducing costly engineering changes, because all drawings and documents were in a central database. The product data management was so effective that after AMC was purchased by Chrysler, the system was expanded throughout the enterprise, connecting everyone involved in designing and building products. By being an early adopter of PLM technology, Chrysler was able to become the auto industry's lowest-cost producer, recording development costs that were half of the industry average by the mid-1990s.

PLM systems help organizations in coping with the increasing complexity and engineering challenges of developing new products for the global competitive markets. However, product life-cycle management (PLM) should be distinguished from product life-cycle management (marketing) (PLCM). PLM describes the engineering aspect of a product, from managing descriptions and properties of a product through its development and useful life, whereas PLCM refers to the commercial management of the life of a product in the business market with respect to costs and sales measures.

Product life-cycle management can be considered as one of the four cornerstones of a manufacturing corporation's information technology (IT) structure. All companies need to manage communications and information with their customers (i.e., CRM, customer relationship management), their suppliers and fulfillment (i.e., SCM, supply chain management), their resources within the enterprise (i.e., ERP, enterprise resource planning), and their product planning and development (PLM).

One form of PLM is called people-centric PLM. While traditional PLM tools have been deployed only upon release or during the release phase, people-centric PLM targets the design phase. The benefits of people-centric PLM include:

- Reduced time to market
- Increase in full-price sales
- Improved product quality and reliability
- Reduced prototyping costs
- More accurate and timely requests for quote generation
- Ability to quickly identify potential sales opportunities and revenue contributions
- Savings through the reuse of original data
- A framework for product optimization
- Reduced waste
- Savings through the complete integration of engineering workflows
- Ability to provide contract manufacturers with access to a centralized product record
- Seasonal fluctuation management, with improved forecasting to reduce material costs
- Maximized supply chain collaboration

Within PLM there are five primary areas:

1. Systems engineering (SE)
2. Product and portfolio management (PPM)

3. Product design (computer-aided technologies, CAx)
4. Manufacturing process management (MPM)
5. Product data management (PDM)

Systems engineering is focused on meeting all requirements, primarily meeting customer needs, and coordinating the systems-design process by involving all relevant disciplines. An important aspect of life-cycle management involves a subset within systems engineering called *reliability engineering*. Product and portfolio management is focused on managing resource allocation, tracking progress vs. plan for new product development projects that are in process (or in a holding status). Portfolio management is a tool that assists management in tracking progress on new products and making trade-off decisions when allocating scarce resources. Product design is the process of creating a new product to be sold by a business to its customers. Manufacturing process management is a collection of technologies and methods used to define how products are to be manufactured. PDM is focused on capturing and maintaining information on products and/or services through their development and useful life. Change management is an important part of PDM/PLM.

The core of PLM is in the creation and central management of all product data and the technology used to access this information and knowledge. PLM as a discipline emerged from tools such as CAD, CAM (computer-aided manufacturing), and PDM, but it can be viewed as the integration of these tools with methods, people, and the processes through all stages of a product's life. It is not just about software technology but is also a business strategy.

The exact order of event and tasks will vary according to the product and industry in question, but the main processes are:

1. Conceive
   a. Specification
   b. Concept design
2. Design
   a. Detailed design
   b. Validation and analysis (simulation)
   c. Tool design

3. Realize
   a. Plan manufacturing
   b. Manufacture
   c. Build/Assemble
   d. Test (quality check)
4. Service
   a. Sell and deliver
   b. Use
   c. Maintain and support
   d. Dispose

The major key-point events are:

1. Order
2. Idea
3. Kickoff
4. Design freeze
5. Launch

However, the reality is more complex. People and departments cannot perform their tasks in isolation, and one activity cannot simply finish and the next activity start. Design is an iterative process, and designs often need to be modified due to manufacturing constraints or conflicting requirements. Where a customer order fits into the time line depends on the industry type and whether the products are, for example, built to order, engineered to order, or assembled to order.

PHASES OF PRODUCT LIFE CYCLE

Many software solutions have developed to organize and integrate the different phases of a product's life cycle. PLM should not be seen as a single software product, but as a collection of software tools and working methods integrated to address single stages of the life cycle, to connect different tasks, or to manage the whole process. Some software providers cover the whole PLM range, while others address a single niche application. Some applications can span many fields of PLM with different modules within the same data model. An overview of the fields within PLM is covered here. It should be noted, however, that the simple classifications do not always fit exactly. Many areas overlap, and many software products cover more than one area or do not fit easily into one category. It should also not be forgotten that one of the main goals of PLM is to collect knowledge that can be reused for other projects and to coordinate simultaneous concurrent development of many products. It is about business processes, people, and methods as much as software application solutions. Although PLM is mainly associated with engineering tasks, it also involves marketing activities such as product portfolio management (PPM), particularly with regards to new product development (NPD).

There are several life-cycle models in industry to consider, but most are rather similar. The following discussion presents one possible life-cycle model. While it emphasizes hardware-oriented products, similar phases would describe any form of product or service, including nontechnical or software-based products:

Phase 1: Conceive—Imagine, Specify, Plan, Innovate

The first stage is the definition of the product requirements based on customer, company, market, and regulatory bodies' viewpoints. From this specification, the product's major technical parameters can be defined. In parallel, the initial concept design work is performed defining the aesthetics of the product together with its main functional aspects. Many different media are used for these processes, from pencil and paper to clay models to 3-D CAID (computer-aided industrial design) software.

In some concepts, the investment of resources into research or the analysis of options may be included in the conception phase, e.g., bringing the technology to a level of maturity sufficient to move to the next phase. However, life-cycle engineering is iterative. It is always possible that something doesn't work well enough in any one phase to back up into a prior phase—perhaps all the way back to conception or research. There are many examples to draw from.

Phase 2: Design—Describe, Define, Develop, Test, Analyze, and Validate

This is where the detailed design and development of the product's form starts, progressing to prototype testing, through pilot release, to full product launch. It can also involve redesign and ramping for improvement to existing products as well as planned obsolescence. The main tool used for design and development is CAD. This can be simple 2-D drawing/drafting or 3-D parametric feature-based solid/surface modeling. Such software includes technology such as hybrid modeling, reverse engineering, KBE (knowledge-based engineering), NDT (nondestructive testing), and assembly construction.

This step covers many engineering disciplines, including mechanical, electrical, electronic, and software (embedded) as well as domain-specific disciplines such as architecture, aerospace, automotive, etc. Along with the actual creation of geometry, there is the analysis of the components and product assemblies. Simulation, validation, and optimization tasks are carried out using CAE (computer-aided engineering) software either integrated in the CAD package or as stand-alone applications. These are used to perform tasks such as stress analysis, FEA (finite-element analysis), kinematics, computational fluid dynamics (CFD), and mechanical event simulation (MES). CAQ (computer-aided quality) is used for tasks such as dimensional tolerance (engineering) analysis. Another task performed at this stage is the sourcing of bought-out components, possibly with the aid of procurement systems.

Phase 3: Realize—Manufacture, Make, Build, Procure, Produce, Sell, and Deliver

Once the design of the product's components is complete, the method of manufacturing is defined. This includes CAD tasks such as tool design, creation of CNC (computer numerical control) machining instructions for the product's parts—as well as tools to manufacture those parts—using integrated or separate CAM software. This will also involve analysis tools for process simulation of operations such as casting, molding, and die-press forming. Once the manufacturing method has been identified, CPM (critical path management) comes into play. This involves CAPE (computer-aided production engineering) or CAP/CAPP (production planning) tools for carrying out factory, plant, and facility layout and production simulation, e.g., press-line simulation, industrial ergonomics, and tool selection management. Once components are manufactured, their geometrical form and size can be checked against the original CAD data with the use of computer-aided inspection equipment and software. Parallel to the engineering tasks, the work of sales product configuration and marketing documentation takes place. This could include transferring engineering data (geometry and part list data) to a web-based sales configurator and other desktop publishing systems.

Phase 4: Service—Use, Operate, Maintain, Support, Sustain, Phase Out, Retire, Recycle, and Dispose

The final phase of the life cycle involves managing of in-service information, providing customers and service engineers with support information for repair and maintenance as well as waste management/recycling information. This involves using tools such as maintenance, repair, and operations (MRO) management software.

There is an end of life to every product. Whether it be disposal or destruction of material objects or information, this needs to be considered, because it may not be free from ramifications.

Cross Phases

None of the previous four phases can be seen in isolation. In reality, a project does not run sequentially or in isolation of other product-development projects. Information is flowing between different people and systems. A major part of PLM is the coordination and management of product-definition data. This includes managing engineering changes and release status of components, configuration of product variations, document management, planning project resources and time scale, and risk assessment.

For these tasks, graphics, text, and metadata such as product bills of materials (BOMs) needs to be managed. At the engineering-departments level, this is the domain of PDM software, and at the corporate level, it is the domain of EDM (enterprise data management) software. Although these two definitions tend to blur, it is typical to see two or more data management systems within an organization. These systems are also linked to other corporate systems such as SCM, CRM, and ERP. Associated with these system are project-management systems for project/program planning.

This central role is covered by numerous collaborative product development tools that run throughout the whole life cycle and across organizations. This requires many technology tools in the areas of conferencing, data sharing, and data translation. The field of product visualization includes technologies such as DMU (digital mock-up), immersive virtual digital prototyping (virtual reality), and photorealistic imaging.

USER SKILLS

The broad array of solutions that make up the tools used within a PLM solution set (e.g., CAD, CAM, CAx) were initially used by dedicated practitioners who invested time and effort to gain the required skills. Designers and engineers worked wonders with CAD systems; manufacturing engineers became highly skilled CAM users; and analysts, administrators, and managers fully mastered their support technologies. However, achieving the full advantages of PLM requires the participation of many people of various skills throughout an extended enterprise, each requiring the ability to access and operate on the inputs and output of other participants.

Despite the increased ease of use of PLM tools, cross-training all personnel on the entire PLM tool set has not proven to be practical. Now, however, advances are being made to address ease of use for all participants within the PLM arena. One such advance is the availability of role-specific user interfaces. Through tailorable user interfaces, the commands that are presented to users are appropriate to their function and expertise.

These techniques include:

- Concurrent engineering workflow
- Industrial design
- Bottom-up design
- Top-down design
- Front-loading design workflow
- Design in context
- Modular design
- NPD new product development
- DFSS design for Six Sigma
- DFMA design for manufacture/assembly
- Digital simulation engineering
- Requirement-driven design
- Specification-managed validation
- Configuration management

Concurrent Engineering

Concurrent engineering (British English: *simultaneous engineering*) is a workflow that, instead of working sequentially through stages, carries out a number of tasks in parallel. For example, it might involve starting tool design as soon as the detailed design has started, even before the detailed designs of the product are finished; or it might entail starting on detailed design of solid models before the concept design of surface models is complete. Although this does not necessarily reduce the amount of manpower required for a project, as more changes are required due to the incomplete and changing information, it does drastically reduce lead times and thus time to market.

Feature-based CAD systems have for many years allowed the simultaneous work on 3-D solid models and the 2-D drawings by means of two separate files, with the drawing looking at the data in the solid model; when the model changes, the drawing will associatively update. Some CAD packages also allow associative copying of geometry between files. This allows, for example, the copying of a part design into the files used by the tooling designer. The manufacturing engineer can then start work on tools before the final design freeze; up to that point, when a design changes size or shape, the tool geometry will then update. Concurrent engineering also has the added benefit of providing better and more immediate communication between departments, reducing the chance of costly, late design changes. It adopts a problem-prevention method as compared to the problem-solving and redesigning method of traditional sequential engineering.

Bottom-Up Design

Bottom-up design occurs where the definition of 3-D models of a product starts with the construction of individual components. These are then virtually brought together in subassemblies of more than one level until the full product is digitally defined. This is sometimes known as the *review structure* showing what the product will look like. The BOM contains all of the physical (solid) components; it may (but not necessarily) contain other items required for the final-product BOM such as paint, glue, oil, and other materials commonly described as bulk items. Bulk items typically have mass and quantities, but they are not usually modeled with geometry.

Bottom-up design tends to focus on the capabilities of available real-world physical technology, implementing those solutions that this technology is most suited to. When these bottom-up solutions have real-world value, bottom-up design can be much more efficient than top-down design. The risk of bottom-up design is that it very efficiently provides solutions to low-value problems. The focus of bottom-up design is "What can we most efficiently do with this technology?" rather than the focus of top-down, which is "What is the most valuable thing to do?"

Top-Down Design

Top-down design is focused on high-level functional requirements, with relatively less focus on existing implementation technology. A top-level spec is decomposed into lower and lower-level structures and specifications, until the physical implementation layer is reached. The risk of a top-down design is that it will not take advantage of the most efficient applications of current physical technology, especially with respect to hardware implementation. Top-down design sometimes results in excessive layers of lower-level abstraction and inefficient performance when the top–down model has followed an abstraction path that does not efficiently fit available physical-level technology. The positive value of top-down design is that it preserves a focus on the optimum solution requirements.

A parts-centric top-down design may eliminate some of the risks of top–down design. This starts with a layout model, often a simple 2-D sketch defining basic sizes and some major defining parameters. Industrial design brings creative ideas to product development. Geometry from this is associatively copied down to the next level, which represents different subsystems of the product. The geometry in the subsystems is then used to define more detail in the levels below. Depending on the complexity of the product, a number of levels of this assembly are created until the basic definition of components can be identified, such as position and principal dimensions. This information is then associatively copied to component files. It is in these files that the components are detailed, and this is where the classic bottom-up assembly starts.

The top-down assembly is sometime known as a *control structure*. If a single file is used to define the layout and parameters for the review structure, it is often known as a *skeleton file*.

Defense engineering traditionally develops the product structure from the top down. The system engineering process prescribes a functional decomposition of requirements and then physical allocation of product structure to the functions. This top-down approach would normally have lower levels of the product structure developed from CAD data as a bottom-up structure or design.

Both-Ends-against-the-Middle Design

Both-ends-against-the-middle (BEATM) design is a design process that endeavors to combine the best features of top-down design and bottom-up design into one process. A BEATM design process flow may begin with an emergent technology which suggests solutions that may have value, or it may begin with a top-down view of an important problem that needs a solution. In either case, the key attribute of BEATM design methodology is to immediately focus at both ends of the design process flow: a top-down view of the solution requirements, and a bottom-up view of the available technology that may offer promise of an efficient solution. The BEATM design process proceeds from both ends in search of an optimum merging somewhere between the top-down requirements and the bottom-up approach that leads to efficient implementation. In this fashion, BEATM has been shown to genuinely offer the best of both methodologies. Indeed some of the best success stories from either top-down or bottom-up have been successful because of an intuitive, yet unconscious use of the BEATM methodology. When employed consciously, BEATM offers even more powerful advantages.

Front Loading

Front loading is taking top-down design to the next stage. The complete control structure and review structure, as well as downstream data such as drawings, tooling development, and CAM models, are constructed before the product has been defined or a project kickoff has been authorized. These assemblies of files constitute a template from which a family of products can be constructed. When the decision has been made to go with a new product, the parameters of the product are entered into the template model, and all the associated data is updated. Obviously, predefined associative models will not be able to predict all possibilities and will require additional work. The main principle is that a lot of the experimental/investigative work has already been completed. A lot of knowledge is built into these templates to be reused on new products. This does require additional resources up front but can drastically reduce the time between project kickoff and launch. Such methods do, however, require organizational changes, as considerable engineering efforts are moved into off-line development departments. It can be seen as an analogy to creating a concept car to test new technology for future products, but in this case the work is directly used for the next product generation.

Design in Context

Individual components cannot be constructed in isolation. CAD and CAID models of components are designed within the context of part or all of the product being developed. This is achieved using assembly-modeling techniques. Other components' geometry can be seen and referenced within the CAD tool being used. The other components within the subassembly may or may not have been constructed in the same system, their geometry being translated from other collaborative product-development (CPD) formats. Some assembly checking such as DMU is also carried out using product-visualization software.

Product and Process Life-Cycle Management

Product and process life-cycle management (PPLM) is an alternate genre of PLM in which the process by which the product is made is just as important as the product itself. Typically, this is the life sciences and advanced specialty chemicals markets. The process behind the manufacture of a given compound is a key element of the regulatory filing for a new drug application. As such, PPLM seeks to manage information around the development of the process in a similar fashion that baseline PLM talks about managing information around development of the product.

One variant of PPLM implementations involves the use of process-development execution systems (PDESs). These typically implement the whole development cycle of high-tech manufacturing technology developments, from initial conception through development and into manufacture. PDESs integrate people with different backgrounds from potentially different legal entities as well as from different data, information and knowledge, and business processes.

PLM RELATED TO INNOVATION MANAGEMENT

Product life-cycle management is very closely aligned to innovation management. Ideas for products and services have to come from somewhere. Thus, it is the senior manager's responsibility to ensure that innovation is promoted and managed. In this last section of this chapter, we will run through techniques that can be used to get those ideas into the product pipeline.

Peter Drucker (2002), a well-known pundit in the field of business, wrote a book on innovation and entrepreneurship more than 20 years ago. Drucker identified seven sources of innovation—four internal to the company and three external:

1. *Unexpected occurrences (internal)*: Drucker considers unexpected successes and failures to be excellent sources of innovation because most businesses usually ignore them. IBM's first accounting machines, ignored by banks but later sold to libraries, is an example.
2. *Incongruities (internal)*: The disconnect between expectations and results often provides opportunities for innovation. The growing market for the steel industry, coupled with falling profit margins, enabled the invention of the minimill.
3. *Process needs (internal)*: Modern advertising permitted the newspaper industry to distribute newspapers at a very low cost, increasing readership (process need) dramatically.
4. *Industry and market changes (internal)*: Deregulation of the telecommunications industry created havoc in the industry but provided ample opportunity for innovation.
5. *Demographic changes (external)*: Japanese businesses surveyed changing demographics and made the determination that the number of people available for blue-collar work is decreasing. As a result, they have taken a leadership position in the area of robotics. However, they are not stopping at robotics for manufacturing.
6. *Changes in perception (external)*: Although Americans are healthier than ever before, according to Drucker they worry more about their health. This change in perception has been exploited for innovative opportunity. An example is the proliferation of web-based health sites, such as webmd.com.

7. *New knowledge (external)*: This is the traditional source of innovation—the first car, the first computer, the printing press. This source of information usually leads to more radical innovation than the other six sources mentioned by Drucker. There are two types of innovation based on new knowledge: incremental and disruptive. An example of incremental innovation is the Pentium IV chip. There was a Pentium III that preceded it. Therefore, the Pentium IV represents just a slight increment of innovation over the III. On the other hand, a radical innovation is something totally new to the world, such as transistor technology. However, technological innovation does have one drawback—it takes much longer to effect. For example, while computing machines were available in the early 1900s, it wasn't until the late 1960s that they were commonly used in business.

Drucker's framework for innovation is quite comprehensive. Most would agree with his assessment, although many would use different categories for the sources. Palmberg (2004) asserts that innovation depends on the characteristics of the market and broader environment in which the firm operates. Palmberg disagrees with Drucker's distinction between internal and external sources, saying that the distinction is artificial, because collaboration and in-house activities are not mutually exclusive.

Palmberg proposes six categories: generic, science based, competitive, customer oriented, regulatory, and technology oriented. The first component, *generic*, stems from the fact that sources of innovation are related to assimilation of generic technologies. The *science-based* component is characterized by scientific breakthroughs and public research programs as the origin of innovation. Great importance is attached to collaboration with universities and research organizations. The *competitive* component is marked by collaboration with competitors. Alternatively, a firm might turn inward in their quest for sources of innovation in the face of competitive markets. The fourth component is referred to as *customer oriented* due to the importance of market niche and customer demand, which spurs innovation. The fifth component is labeled *regulatory* because a variety of environmental, legal, and regulatory issues will suggest sources of innovation. The final component, *technology oriented*, is characterized by sources of innovations related to scientific breakthroughs and new technologies.

Generating Innovation

Whether innovation is demand-led or supply-pushed is a topic of considerable debate, according to the definition of innovation found on Wikipedia (http://en.wikipedia.org/wiki/Innovation). Wikipedia is a good example of innovation that is both. There was a demand in the marketplace for a free, web-based encyclopedia. The technology of the Internet and the concept of the wiki, a web application that lets users add and change content (http://en.wikipedia.org/wiki/Wiki), is an excellent example of supply-pushed innovation. The wiki was conceived and developed by Ward Cunningham in the mid-1990s.

Steve Lipscomb's World Poker Tour (Olmstead 2005) is another example. Poker has taken America by storm, largely because of Lipscomb's innovative approach to the once-seedy concept of the poker tournament.

Both Lipscomb and Cunningham have what Drucker would refer to as entrepreneurial personalities, but they would be more commonly categorized as innovative or creative. Drucker's framework for sources of innovation is worthless without someone seeing these opportunities for what they are.

Drucker's article, therefore, falls short of actually describing how to generate the entrepreneurial or innovative personality. Couger et al. (1991) suggest a process for generating innovation via a series of bottom-up creativity techniques. A brief list of the best of these techniques follow:

1. *Brainstorming*: This technique is perhaps the most familiar of all the techniques discussed here. It is used to generate a large quantity of ideas in a short period of time. My company often brings in consulting experts, partners, and others to brainstorm along with us.
2. *Blue slip*: Ideas are individually generated and recorded on a 3" × 5" sheet of blue paper. When done anonymously to make people feel more at ease, people readily share ideas. Because each idea is on a separate piece of blue paper, the sorting and grouping of like ideas is facilitated.
3. *Extrapolation*: A technique or approach, already used by the organization, is stretched to apply to a new problem.
4. *Progressive abstraction technique*: By moving through progressively higher levels of abstraction, it is possible to generate alternative problem definitions from an original problem. When a problem is enlarged in a systematic way, it is possible to generate many new

definitions that can then be evaluated for their usefulness and feasibility. Once an appropriate level of abstraction is reached, possible solutions are more easily identified.

5. *5Ws and H technique*: This is the traditional, and journalistic, approach of who-what-where-when-why-how. Use of this technique serves to expand a person's view of the problem and to assist in making sure that all related aspects of the problem have been addressed and considered.

6. *Force-field analysis technique*: The name of this technique comes from its ability to identify forces contributing to or hindering a solution to a problem. This technique stimulates creative thinking in three ways: (a) it defines direction, (b) identifies strengths that can be maximized, and (c) identifies weaknesses that can be minimized.

7. *Problem reversal*: Reversing a problem statement often provides a different framework for analysis. For example, in attempting to come up with ways to improve productivity, try considering the opposite, how to decrease productivity.

8. *Associations/Image technique*: Most of us have played the game, at one time or another, where a person names a person, place, or thing and asks for the first thing that pops into the second person's mind. The linking of combining processes is another way of expanding the solution space.

9. *Wishful thinking*: This technique enables people to loosen analytical parameters to consider a larger set of alternatives than they might ordinarily consider. By permitting a degree of fantasy into the process, the result just might be a new and unique approach.

The Harvard Business Essentials guide to *Managing Creativity and Innovation* (2003) refers to idea generation as "opening the Genie's bottle." However, without management support and encouragement, idea generation is simply not possible. The key, then, is in how management interacts with and supports its employees.

Oren Harari (1993), a professor at the University of San Francisco and a management consultant, relates an interesting experience with one of his clients. While he was waiting for an appointment with this particular client, he overheard two of the manager's clerical assistants calling customers and asking them how they liked the company's product. Professor Harari reflected that it was no wonder this manager had such a good reputation. When he finally met with her, he offered his congratulations on her ability to delegate the customer service task to her staff. "What you talking about?" she asked, bewildered. "Why, your secretaries are calling up customers on their own," Harari replied. "Oh, really? Is that what they're doing?" she laughed. "You mean you didn't delegate that task to them?" Harari asked.

"No," she said. "I didn't even know they were doing it. Listen, Oren, my job is to get everyone on my team to think creatively in pursuit of the same goal. So what I do is talk to people regularly about why we exist as a company and as a team. That means we talk straight about our common purpose and the high standards we want to achieve. I call these our goal lines. Then we talk regularly about some broad constraints we have to work with them, like budgets, ethics, policies, and legalities. Those are our sidelines.

"It's like a sport. Once we agree on the goal lines and sidelines, I leave it to my people to figure out how to best get from here to there. I'm available and attentive when they need feedback. Sometimes I praise; sometimes I criticize—but always constructively, I hope. We get together periodically and talk about who's been trying what, and we give constructive feedback to one another. I know that sounds overly simplistic, but I assure you that this is my basic management philosophy.

"And that's why I don't know what my assistants are doing, because it's obviously something they decided to try for the first time this week. I happen to think it's a great idea, because it's within the playing field and helps keep high standards for being number one in our industry. I will tell you something else: I don't even know what they intend to do with the data they're collecting, but I know they'll do the right thing.

"Here's my secret: I don't know what my people are doing, but because I work face to face with them as a coach, I know that whenever it is they're doing is exactly what I'd want them to be doing if I knew what they were doing!"

The Harari story is one of my favorites because it encapsulates into one very brief story exactly what a good manager is supposed to do to encourage innovative thinking in his or her employees.

Harvard Business Essentials (2003) refers to the need to create an ambidextrous organization—one that gets the work done today and also anticipates tomorrow's discontinuities. It goes on to provide a list of seven responsibilities for the organization's leaders. These run from the obvious (e.g., develop a culture that nurtures creativity and innovation and putting the right people in charge) to the less than obvious (e.g., improve the idea-to-commercialization process and think of ideas and projects in terms of a portfolio with distinct risk and return dimensions).

The "obvious" responsibilities are covered in depth by the authors as well as many other authors. It's these less-than-obvious responsibilities that are the most intriguing, for with these, the authors correlate the creativity and innovation to financial goals, all important to me as the CEO.

Computerized Brainstorming

Human performance: That's what it all boils down to! Enabling a person to perform at his or her full potential. In the beginning, we developed technology appliances to make the drudgery of clerical work less burdensome—and even to replace humans. Later, technology began to be used to help humans sort through massive information data stores. The age of the personal productivity appliance, the PC, began in the early '80s, and during that decade, and on into the new millennium, spurred an avalanche of productivity-enhancing tools that nearly boggle the mind. But still, the emphasis was on productivity *enhancing*. What's really needed by companies searching for that elusive silver bullet of competitive leadership is some sort of tool that is productivity *producing*.

Marsh Fisher was the original founder of the Century 21 real-estate empire, unfortunately recently deceased. Any businessperson would take advice from Fisher. After all, his business was worth billions. But Fisher wanted to offer more than advice. He wanted to offer ideas. Actually, he wanted to offer competitive advantage through creativity. Fisher calls this type of software *Human Performance Technology*.

Fisher got the idea for creativity boosting back in the days when computers were large, monolithic mainframes stuck away in the basements of office buildings, providing only a smattering of the functionality that has become available as a matter of course today. In 1964, Fisher was studying comedy writing. He noticed that most of the other students in his class were much better at being faster on their feet than he was. They seemed to ad lib a lot better than he did. So, he started to look for some sort of crutch with which he could at least become competitive.

He began to study the art of ad-libbing, and comedy in general, and found that there is a unique association between the punch line and the setup line. Related to both of these phrases is an assumed word or phrase. It is this word or phrase that associates the setup line to the punch line.

When Fisher retired from Century 21, he began to study cognitive sciences, which is a combination of linguistics and computer science. One of the goals of cognitive science is to determine whether the mind can be mimicked in the mysterious task of problem solving.

Fisher describes problem solving as the three Rs: recording, recall, and reassociate. Recording of information is done spontaneously. Everything we say, hear, smell, or touch is stored in the grandest of all databanks—the human brain. Of course, once it's stored inside, it sometimes is quite difficult to get it back out. This is the task of recall or remembering. We have this massive warehouse of information stored in our subconscious, and trying to find something buried away is usually quite difficult. Once an item of information is recalled, the third R is deployed. We reassociate, or recombine, one or more items of information to produce an original creative idea.

Of course, if we had instant access to everything tucked away in our memories, the road to creativity would be much less arduous. Unfortunately, as we're reminded time and time again as we search in vain for the name of the person that we just met in the hallway, this is usually not the case. Even if all humans were possessed of the gift of instant recall, there's still that third R to contend with: reassociation—the creative R, the R that gives us creative leverage.

In the '60s, Fisher wanted to give humans a creativity shot in the arm by publishing a book of associations. By the time he was ready to do it, the PC had become so ubiquitous that he decided to write it in software. This is when IdeaFisher (now ThoughtOffice: http://www.thoughtrod.com/idea-software/ideafisher-upgrades/) was born.

The heart of IdeaFisher was the IdeaBank. This is where users look up related ideas and concepts. The IdeaBank is an organized storehouse of more than 65,000 ideas, words, phrases, and concepts. The software's cross-referencing capabilities create more than 775,000 associations. Ideas and concepts are organized by grouping related ideas. This method of organization is patterned after the way we naturally store information in the human brain. It explains the common experience of "one idea leading to another." IdeaFisher claims it can help us make something quite novel out of the fragmented, and seemingly useless, bits of information we deal with on a daily basis. Here's how it works:

In this example, we will join the product-planning group of a sock company. They're developing a plan to sell more socks in the summer months. In undertaking a challenge of this nature, it is important that the strategy team understand that this process actually consists of four subprocesses: understanding the goal, defining the strategy, naming the product, and finally identifying the key attributes of the product for advertising and product positioning.

> *Understanding the goal*: Our first step is to fully understand the specific challenge. In order to do this, we normally get a group together to brainstorm to pick the goal—and the resultant ideas—apart and then piece them back together into a solution. Brainstorming relies on a series of questions and answers. But what if you can't come up with the right questions? Fortunately, IdeaFisher comes with some add-ons in the form of various question banks. Questions are categorized along several lines, including developing a story script; developing a new product or service; developing a name, title, theme, or slogan; and developing a marketing strategy or promotional campaign. Because our goal is to develop a new line of socks, we will choose developing a new product service. Here we look through a series of questions and pick the ones most appropriate to our goal. Questions such as: "Does the customer fit a particular category—a distinct type of thought and behavior (a stereotype)?" "What are the customer's relevant physical traits in addition to age and sex?" "List the person's relevant psychographics traits. What product or service characteristics are more important to this customer?"
>
> After each question is selected, the strategy team enters its responses and starts brainstorming. Our team brainstorms answers such as: adult males and females of all ages; people at home and outside; likes to be outdoors, gardening, bird watching; socks should be fashionable; socks should be useful in outside activities; socks should be in a fabric that doesn't hold moisture or is hot. Once all of this is filtered into a series of key concepts, the team is ready to target the most relevant key concepts and move on to the next step.
>
> After much debate, our team finally targets the key concepts of bird watching, color coordination, gardening, moisture, and useful in

outside activities. This, then, is the breakdown of the key elements in the marketing strategy. Defining a specific strategy is the next activity.

Defining the strategy: To develop a feasible strategy to sell more socks in the summer, our team will use IdeaFisher's IdeaBank. Our team wants to begin with the socks key concept. Upon highlighting this word, the program will display all the topical categories that contain the word *socks*. IdeaFisher has multiple topics that deal with socks, including black/gray, cleaning/dirty/clean, clothing/fashion/style, and push/pull/attract/repel. This last topic intrigues one of the members of the team, so it is highlighted to see the section titles on the next level. It turns out that there is close to 1000 idea words or phrases associated with push/pull/attract/repel categorized into groupings such as things/places, things that repel, things that attract, and abstractions/intangibles. The team decides to pursue things that repel. Highlighting this they find some intriguing items such as anti-icer, body armor, car wax, and mosquito repellent. Certainly, these are things that repel.

Marsh Fisher describes the act of creativity as one that involves coming up with new ideas whose revelation excite the creator so much that he or she exclaims, "A-ha!" Our fictitious team experiences this feeling when they realize the interesting possibilities in mosquito-repellent on socks.

Naming the product: Now that the team has decided upon their novel product, they need come up with a good name for it—a good hook. Selecting a name for a product or service has many elements: It must be easily remembered, be descriptive, and tie in with the customer's perceived needs and values.

The team decides to compare two topical categories to create a new unique name for the socks. The idea is to associate two disparate ideas to merge them together into a single word or phrase that creates a novel hook for the new product. Picking stocks as the first key concept to compare, the team is prompted to pick one of many topical categories containing this word. The head of the team recommends that the team pursues limbs/appendages. Outdoors is the second word that the team wants to use in comparison. Again, a list of topical categories containing the word outdoors is displayed. This time the team picks camping/hiking/mountaineering. IdeaFisher takes over at this point and produces a listing of words and phrases found in both of these categories. This list serves as a jog to creativity.

The team looks through the list, bypassing blister, footing, footpath, and 55 other words and phrases. One word jumps out at them as the perfect name for the new line of socks: surefooted.

So far, all in one sitting, the team has brainstormed the meaning of their challenge, defined their strategy, and named their product—in the space of hours, rather than days. All that remains of their task is to identify key attributes for advertising and product positioning. In order to do this, the team decides to explore the key concepts in greater detail.

Identifying key attributes: The team decides that the key attribute they want to emphasize is summer uses of socks. So they select and highlight the word *summer*. Ultimately, the team winds up with a host of summertime activities and hobbies that people in the target market might enjoy more with surefooted socks.

The final results of the IdeaFisher session, which began just a few scant hours before, is as follows:

1. Socks keep bugs away
2. Color coordination with current athletic clothes and incorporation of reflective material in some models
3. Lightweight material that doesn't hold heat or moisture inside
4. An insect-repellent fabric that could be used for clothing, sleeping bags, and tents

When Pabst Brewing Company customers began calling out PBR when ordering Pabst Blue Ribbon Beer, Pabst knew it was onto something hot, but it needed more than just "PBR" to create a hot jingle—it needed some inspiration. That's when it turned to IdeaFisher to assist in writing a jingle that is based on abbreviations. This is what its fishing caught: "I'm gonna give my thirst some TLC, just PBR me ASAP." Pabst is not alone; IdeaFisher has been used to write copy for everything from beer to the Discover card.

Sustainable Innovation

In 2004, Procter & Gamble Co.'s G. Gil Cloyd, chief technology officer, was named *Industry Week*'s Technology Leader of the Year. According to Teresko (2004), Cloyd has successfully shown how any company can contend with the classic innovator's dilemma: Most innovations fail, but companies that don't innovate die. His solution, *innovating innovation*, resulted in P&G exceeding all of its financial goals in fiscal 2004. To do this, Cloyd leveraged a strategy designed to innovate innovation. The focus is on using technology and innovation to compete on multiple fronts simultaneously without spreading the corporate structure too thin. Among his changes were:

1. More collaboration
2. Strengthening of external relationships
3. Expansion of R&D's role to include not only knowledge generation, but knowledge brokering as well
4. Utilizing computational modeling and simulation as the evolving solution for fast-cycle learning

That P&G could achieve such startling financial results is a testament to the fact that changing the way businesses do business can lead to great creativity—and a tidy bottom line.

An interesting twist on reengineering is the one used by Ideo, a company that is on a mission to change the way businesses think. Ideo is actually a design firm, but the dot-com bust forced Ideo's founder, Kelley to adapt his business model. Instead of "cool" products, Kelley began to focus on processes. For example, he streamlined the processes for admission into hospitals and new ways to stock supermarket shelves.

Ideo is now a business consultancy that specializes in reengineering companies to make them more efficient and more innovative. The company uses transformational ideas directly from the design world and applies them to business processes. For example, Ideo once sent the CEO of P&G on a shopping trip in San Francisco's Mission District. Top executives from Kraft were spirited away to a traffic control center to watch cars stop and start to determine whether this experience could influence their supply-chain management. Apparently it did, as Kraft cut in half the time it took to get products to retail.

Some are calling Ideo's ideas revolutionary. Kelley's goal is to merge business, design, and education together to both help the companies and train the next generation of business leaders to use a more innovative and emotional way of doing business. Maybe this is the next big thing. Maybe it's not. Whatever it is or isn't, it's definitely an approach to get those creative and innovative juices flowing within an organization. And that's all that matters.

The S-Curve and Innovation Management

The S-curve, a quantitative trend-extrapolation technique used in forecasting, has long been used in the technology industry. Many argue that this analysis is actually more useful to see where you've been rather than where you should go (Spencer 2005). The S-curve is most often used to compare two competitive products in two dimensions: usually time and performance, as shown in Figure 1.3.

An excellent example of an S-curve can be found in Alexander (2001), in his discussion of the product innovation cycle. He discusses the S-curve of the ubiquitous automobile. In 1900 the automobile was first introduced to the public and became the plaything of the rich. Between 1900 and 1914, the automobile went through the lower curve of the cycle, or the innovation phase, at the end of which Henry Ford introduced the assembly line. Between 1914 and 1928, according to Alexander, the automobile went through its growth phase. It was during this phase that the automobile caught on and was adopted by the general public. By 1928, the automobile was in its maturity phase (the top part of the S-curve), and Ford was seeing leaner, meaner competition.

The S-curve can unleash unparalleled creativity when you realize the time has come for your company to make its entry into the marketplace. It's at this point that you've got to get your product out there in a way that effectively competes with the established giant. This often translates

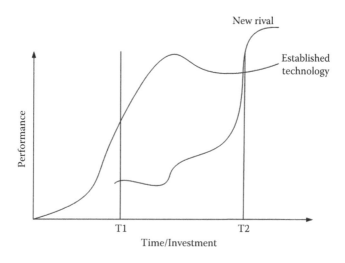

FIGURE 1.3
The S-curve for an established technology and a new rival.

to reverse engineering the competitive product and determining which features to adopt into your own product and then, essentially, one-upping them by adding new and novel features and/or services.

For a company who is a defender of an established technology, the S-curve predicts at what point their leadership position might decline. Avoiding this should become their chief focus. Some companies— Microsoft, for example—practice what I like to call *continuous innovation*. They practice all of the techniques in this chapter and then some, including operating Skunk Works, acquiring small companies that might become rivals (e.g., Hotmail), and leapfrogging the attacker's technology. This last technique is Microsoft's current tactic with the introduction of their new MSN search engine, which nicely rivals the google.com powerhouse. Microsoft, then, makes a good topic for a case history on knowledge and innovation management.

P-Cycle

According to Davenport and Prusak (2003), the idealized life cycle of an idea within an organization is called the P-cycle, so named because each of its five stages starts with the letter P, i.e., progenitor, pilot, project, program, perspective, and pervasiveness, as shown in Figure 1.4.

The authors suggest that successful idea practitioners understand each idea's life cycle so that they can predict where it might move next. There is an internal as well as an external life cycle, and these might differ for many environmental reasons.

The P-cycle is somewhat similar to the traditional SDLC (systems development life cycle) in that both start with someone's bright idea (the progenitor). After a feasibility study has been performed, the next stage that

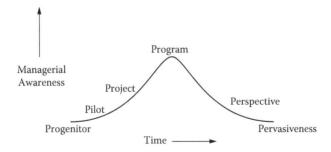

FIGURE 1.4
The P-cycle of a successful business idea.

the idea (or system) enters is the pilot. This is usually a scaled-down version of the grand idea so that stakeholders can determine if the idea is a fit for the company and whether it works. Once this has been proven to be true, we enter the project stage. At this point, a project plan is created and funded, other resources are allocated, and work can begin. If successful, the idea (or system) can be implemented and is now referred to as an ongoing program. The program may spawn additional projects, all related to the original idea. The program is usually part of a strategic plan so that its goals can be cascaded down throughout the organization and, thus, used within many departments. Over time, the program is embedded within the corporate psyche and becomes firmly entrenched within the operating methods and controls of the company. At the beginning of this "rootedness," the idea can be said to be gaining perspective. By the time everyone in the company uses it on a daily basis, we reach the ideal end state for the P-cycle—pervasiveness.

The external P-cycle of an idea is similar to the internal P-cycle. There are usually five stages in the external life cycle of an idea: discovery, wild acceptance, digestion, decline, and hard core. Understandably, the external life cycle of an idea often drives the internal life cycle, sometimes to the detriment of the idea.

Davenport and Wilson (2003) discuss the decline of the business-process reengineering idea because the idea became too popular too soon in the external idea marketplace. Therefore, expectations within companies likely rose too high, and the idea of reengineering never reached pervasiveness.

Davenport and Wilson also provide a framework that idea practitioners can follow to promote their ideas and see them through to implementation. The most salient ideas are summarized here:

1. *Idea identification*: The CEO should be an advocate for continual learning and growth. This means encouraging employees to read the latest, greatest business books, to take courses, and to go to seminars and network. The CEO should also be a supporter of knowledge management (KM), as this provides a collaborative platform and methodology for knowledge and idea sharing. It is from these sources and using these tools that good ideas sprout.

2. *Advocating the idea*: An idea that's not heard is no idea at all. CEOs and other managers need to provide a pulpit for those advocating

these great ideas. This may be through internal meetings, at retreats, or even on the corporate intranet.

3. *Make it happen*: CEOs need to provide a slush fund so that these ideas at least progress to the pilot stage. This may be through a corporate-wide R&D department or through individual departmental budgets. There also needs to be a way for these pilots to be seen and heard. Finally, if the pilot gets selected to move into the pilot stage the CEO must provide the means to drive the idea through to the pervasiveness stage.

What Makes a Business Guru?

Business guru is a difficult term. Wikipedia, the free, edit-your-own-content encyclopedia, which is itself a wonderful idea that has reached the pervasiveness stage, does not provide a formal definition of the term *business guru*, but it does define the term *guru* and its extension from a meaning of "Hindu religious teacher" to more general usage as "an expert of legendary proportions" (http://en.wikipedia.org/wiki/Guru). The term *guru* is nearly synonymous with *wizard* but implies that there is a history of being a knowledge resource for others.

Wikipedia also provided an interesting discussion on why people are attracted to gurus. Although it was written from the religious perspective, I'd like to reprint it here with my annotations modifying the religious construct to the business construct:

> There are several reasons why people in Western cultures are attracted by gurus. The most common is that people look for the meaning of life (*business*) and are disillusioned in traditional religions (*business techniques and ideas*).

Wikipedia states that the gurus who are eloquent are the ones who are more likely to be unreliable and dangerous. Wikipedia quotes the scholar David C. Lane, who wrote that a charlatan who cons people is not as dangerous as a guru who really believes in his delusions, and that the bigger the claims a guru makes, the bigger the chance that he is a charlatan or deluded. Of course, the context of this discussion really involves religious gurus, but I am gleeful to report that I see many parallels here. There is a fine line between business guru and huckster.

Gurus have some common attributes:

1. Creative
2. Tenacious
3. Zealots for their idea
4. Often quirky

According to Goldsmith (2003), innovative or creative personalities are often those who are inflexible and don't deal with others very well. He offers the examples of Ludwig von Beethoven, Thomas Edison, and Winston Churchill as those who have tremendous creativity but were not warm, friendly, accommodating, and cooperative. Creative people have a vision in mind; however, their difficulty is expressing it to others. They frustrate themselves, as well as others, with their inability to effectively communicate.

The key, then, is to find these innovative personalities and then integrate them into the company so that they can be productive and not counterproductive, as their personalities may force them to be. Pollard (2005) suggests that KM has become the organizational ghetto for the most creative minds in the business. So, this would be a wonderful place to nurture these innovative personalities.

Davenport and Wilson's (2003) idea framework, discussed earlier, provides a sound methodology that can be used by these innovators to take a company forward in idea generation and innovation.

Innovation Management at Microsoft

The software industry is hypercompetitive. Therefore, it is important for a software firm to hire only the best and the brightest. However, Microsoft also realizes that knowledge should not be static, so it embarked upon a project to create a competence-based skills profile, known as SPUD, to track and enhance employee competencies.

In the mid-1990s, the head of Microsoft's IT department hired Susan Conway to create the competence program. Conway, who had created similar competence-based programs at Computer Sciences and Texaco, soon created a pilot (personal knowledge). SPUD (skills planning *und* development) focused on those skill sets and competencies required to stay at the edge of an extremely competitive industry.

The five major components of SPUD consisted of:

1. Developing a structure of competence types and levels
2. Defining the competencies or skills
3. Rating the performance or individuals based on the defined competencies
4. Implementing the knowledge competencies in an online system
5. Linking the competence model to training

Within each of the four competence types—entry level or foundation, local or unique, global, and universal—are two separate skill categories: explicit, which involves expertise in specific tools or methods, and implicit, which involves abstract thinking and reasoning skills. For example, knowledge of Microsoft Access is an explicit competence, while problem solving can be considered implicit. Going into the pilot, Microsoft identified 137 implicit competencies and 200 explicit competencies.

Within each competence, there were also four defined skill levels: Level 1, basic; Level 2, working; Level 3, leadership; and Level 4, expert. A sample competence description is shown in Table 1.1.

There are a variety of benefits to the competence model. These include:

1. Provides a better fit of employee to specific job
2. Enables managers to find the right employee more quickly
3. Provides an organizational view of knowledge assets that is a valuable input into strategic planning
4. Enables creation of detailed job descriptions so that #1 can be more easily achieved
5. Enhances ability to match employee to training offerings (Training can now be targeted at specific skill gaps.)
6. Improves general overall competencies of the entire firm (Theoretically, an improvement in the skill levels of individual employees should lead to an improvement of skill levels within the firm as a whole.)

TABLE 1.1

Sample Competence Description

T430 Data Administration/Repository Management

Definition: Development and maintenance of a flexible, efficient, shared data environment utilizing facilities such as data models, data definitions, common codes, reference databases, and data toolsets

Level 1:

- Basic knowledge of data administration and repository management
- Basic knowledge of the principles and practices employed in the management of data and repositories
- Familiar with information models and modeling
- Understands the rationale behind maintaining a centralized, reusable library of the business and enterprise models of a corporation

Level 2:

- Working knowledge of data administration and repository management
- Working knowledge of the principles, practices, and tools associated with the access to and updating of local repositories

Level 3:

- Mastery of data administration and repository management
- Knowledge of and demonstrated expertise in data management
- Can assess the impact of functional/regional data changes on the enterprise model
- Can integrate the business data and process models into the enterprise model
- Recognized as a data expert in a functional area

Level 4:

- Leadership and recognized expertise in data administration and repository management
- Subject-matter expertise in the management of local, regional, and enterprise-wide information/data models
- Recognized as a data expert in major functional areas
- Can review information models for compliance, content quality, consistency, and impact on enterprise models

---

7. Improves employee morale, as more offerings are targeted to specific employees
8. Introduces the possibility that the model might become a vehicle for institutionalizing innovation (For example, BYOD [bring your own device] is currently a hot topic. Use of SPUD could force development of a competence in this area by requiring its presence in all job-competence requirements.)

It is clear that the competence-based model has much potential if it is implemented properly and is generally accepted by all employees within the company. The development of a competence-based model is necessarily time consuming, and a great deal of attention to detail is a prerequisite for its success. This requirement alone might be sufficient to railroad its success. However, there are other weaknesses:

1. The person or persons creating the competence description might create an inaccurate description. They might not be privy to all of the requirements of the job or not be familiar enough with the job to provide an adequate level of detail.
2. The same job titles within different divisions might require different competence descriptions.
3. Job descriptions do change, leading to the possibility of an out-of-sync or out-of-date situation with the competence database. Maintaining a skills-competence database is an expensive and time-consuming job.
4. It is sometimes difficult to assess and gauge implicit competencies among employees.
5. Online access to the competence database might enable managers to raid existing teams for members with desired competencies.
6. Individuals might feel that this information would be a violation of their privacy and/or limit their potential within the company.

There has been some controversy among researchers about competence mapping as well. According to Lindgren et al. (2001), descriptions of competence are fragmentary and atomistic. Competence is usually categorized beforehand in an ad hoc way with weak connections to both empirical data and theory. This serves to confirm the model of competence itself rather than a worker's competence. Finally, regardless of the number of categories, competence profiles are static, indirect, and general descriptions concerning human competence. Competence profiles do not demonstrate whether a worker actually uses the competence in accomplishing work, i.e., the competence profiles may not be rooted in actual work practice.

Six Steps for Increasing Creativity and Productivity

Harvard Essentials (2003) lists six steps for increasing creativity:

1. *Make sure your company's goals are consistent with your value system*: This is an interesting perspective in an era of few good jobs and trends toward outsourcing and offshoring. A number of studies have found that:

   - Job insecurity is a big issue.
   - More and more permanent jobs are being replaced by temporary jobs.
   - Employees are experiencing unrealistic expectations, increased workloads, and lack of support staff.

   Very few people can imagine their situation improving substantially. In fact, many believe that things will only get worse. They see the gap between rich and poor growing, and they feel that they don't know where all this change will end up.

   Managers need to realize that many, if not most, employees will harbor some or all of these feelings. Given the dire job market, they might opt to stay put rather than, as the Harvard text suggests, finding a company whose goals match their values. Therefore, it is up to the manager to somehow ameliorate the level of anxiety that accompanies these feelings such that creativity is not stifled.

2. *Pursue some self-initiated activity by choosing projects where your motivation is high*: Few employees get to choose their own task assignments. However, savvy managers need to be aware that creativity is greatly enhanced when employees are motivated to do their jobs.

   The better companies try to fit the employee to the task by creating a skills database. These permit managers to rapidly locate an employee who has the skills—and the motivation—to fulfill a particular work requirement. However, there will always be those times when the task the employee is expected to complete is simply not one he or she is especially interested in. At this point, the good CEO will use a variety of motivating techniques. Based on a study at Wichita State University, the top five motivating techniques are:

1. Manager personally congratulates employee who does a good job.
2. Manager writes personal notes about good performance.
3. Organization uses performance as basis for promotion.
4. Manager publicly recognizes employee for good performance.
5. Manager holds morale-building meetings to celebrate successes.

One doesn't have to actually give an award for recognition to happen. Giving your attention is just as effective. The Hawthorne effect says that the act of measuring (paying attention) will itself change behavior.

Nelson and Blanchard (1994) suggest the following low-cost rewards recognition techniques:

1. Make a photo collage about a successful project that shows the people who worked on it, its stages of development, and its completion and presentation.
2. Create a yearbook to be displayed in the lobby that contains each employee's photograph, along with his or her best achievement of the year.
3. Establish a place to display memos, posters, photos, and so on, recognizing progress toward goals and thanking individual employees for their help.
4. Develop a "Behind the Scenes Award" specifically for those whose actions are not usually in the limelight.
5. Say thanks to your boss, your peers, and your employees when they have performed a task well or have done something to help you.
6. Make a thank-you card by hand.
7. Cover the person's desk with balloons.
8. Bake a batch of chocolate-chip cookies for the person.
9. Make and deliver a fruit basket to the person.
10. Tape a candy bar for the typist in the middle of a long report with a note saying, "Halfway there."
11. Give a person a candle with a note saying, "No one holds a candle to you."
12. Give a person a heart sticker with a note saying, "Thanks for caring."

13. Purchase a plaque, stuffed animal—anything fun or meaningful—and give it to an employee at a staff meeting with specific praise. That employee displays it for a while, then gives it to another employee at a staff meeting in recognition of an accomplishment.
14. Call an employee into your office (or stop by his or her office) just to thank him or her; don't discuss any other issue.
15. Post a thank-you note on the employee's office door.
16. Send an e-mail thank-you card.
17. Praise people immediately. Encourage them to do more of the same.
18. Greet employees by name when you pass them in the hall.
19. Make sure you give credit to the employee or group that came up with an idea being used.
20. Acknowledge individual achievements by using employees' names when preparing status reports.

McCarthy and Allen (2000) suggest that you set up your employees for success. When you give someone a new assignment, tell the employee why you are trusting him or her with this new challenge. "I want you to handle this because I like the way you handled _____ last week." They also suggest that you never steal the stage. When an employee tells you about an accomplishment, don't steal her thunder by telling her about a similar accomplishment of yours. They also suggest that you never use sarcasm, even in a teasing way. Resist the temptation to say something like, "It's about time you gave me this report on time." Deal with the lateness problem by setting a specific time the report is due. If it's done on time, make a positive comment about timeliness.

3. *Take advantage of unofficial activity*: I know of few people who have the luxury of working on unofficial projects in larger companies. However, this is actually quite a good idea. Management should allow slack time to be used for creative purposes. Channels should be put in place such that any great idea nurtured during slack time has an equal opportunity to be presented for possible funding.

4. *Be open to serendipity*: The authors discuss how Scotchgard was invented by accident. My own company practices this technique. Several of our products were developed by accident by employees playing around with programming code. As a manager, it is very important that I be open to this sort of novel product development.

5. *Diversify your stimuli*: Employees should strive to rotate into every job they are capable of doing to induce intellectual cross-pollination. This is not a new technique, as it has been practiced for years within the high-tech industry. Rotating jobs is also a tenet of quality management systems, including ISO 9001.

   Another recommendation is to get to know people who might spark your imagination. However, this is a personal preference not shared by everyone. The challenge as a manager is, therefore, to somehow provide employees with a diversity of stimuli that might take them in new and different directions. This can be done by using some of the techniques in Step 6.

6. *Create opportunities for information communication—otherwise known as "meet and greet"*: Salespeople are natural networkers. These folks sign up for every event and learn a great deal by doing so. Other employees are somewhat less motivated to leave the office to attend industry-wide gatherings, particularly as the employee gets older and has additional familial responsibilities.

   Ideas to promote intellectual stimulation include:

   1. Fund memberships to professional organizations
   2. Fund subscriptions to trade and other magazines
   3. Invite a variety of speakers to monthly staff meetings
   4. Host industry events so that staff doesn't have to travel to get to them
   5. Promote teaming within the company
   6. Provide collaborative technologies such as a corporate intranet, video conferencing capabilities, instant chat, etc.
   7. Fund continuous training
   8. Fund higher educational opportunities

The Harvard six steps for increasing creativity are but a starting point for creating the innovative organization. All of this, however, still relies on the CEO being an advocate for innovation management.

Rewarding Employees for Innovative Ideas

There are two types of awards. Intrinsic rewards appeal to a person's desire for self-actualization, curiosity, joy, and interest in the work. Extrinsic rewards appeals to a person's desire for attainment: e.g., money, stock options, days offs, tickets to ballgames, etc. Intrinsic rewards are intangible, while extrinsic rewards are quite tangible. As one of my employees says, "Show me the money."

Many of the motivation techniques discussed in this chapter could be considered intrinsic rewards. Extrinsic reward systems are more difficult to implement, as there are usually budget considerations to deal with. In many companies, the methodology used to grant yearly raises can even be considered countermotivational. When I worked for the New York Stock Exchange, employees were rated on a scale of 1 to 5. The largest rewards (i.e., raises) were granted to the 5s. However, we were told to rate our employees using a bell-shaped curve. The result is that some 5s were cheated out of their fair share of the reward system.

This topic is so important that more than a few books have been written on the subject. Wilson (2002) talks about the use of spot bonuses, team celebrations, innovative employee benefits, and flex compensation. Pearce and Robinson (2005) discuss the subject of executive compensation in their textbook on strategic management, now in its ninth edition. Ideas that work for the senior managers should also work for the employee who greatly contributes to the profitability and/or competitive advantage of the firm:

1. Stock option grants
2. Restricted stock plan
3. Bonus income deferred, sometimes referred to as golden handcuffs
4. Cash based on accounting performance measures

Creating a workforce infused with innovation and creativity requires understanding how to work with people. You'd be surprised (or maybe not) at how differently bosses look at things than do their staff, as shown in Table 1.2. The object, clearly, is to narrow the gap.

TABLE 1.2

What Do Employees Really Want?

What Employees Want	Items	What Employers Think Employees Want
1	Interesting work	5
2	Appreciation of work	8
3	Feeling in on things	10
4	Job security	2
5	Good wages	1
6	Promotion/growth	3
7	Good working conditions	4
8	Personal loyalty	6
9	Tactful discipline	7
10	Sympathetic help with problems	9

Source: Kovach (1999).

The first step is to understand your own motivations, your strengths as a manager, and your weaknesses. Probably the best approach is to ask your peers and employees to make an anonymous appraisal of your performance as a manager. Have them rate such traits as listening and communications skills, openness, and attitude. Painful as this process may be, it will actually make you seem heroic in your employees' eyes. At the same time, it will give you some food for thought on ways to improve your own performance.

The second step—one that many managers pay only lip service to—can really make the difference between having a motivated employee and one who feels that he or she is just another number. Take the time to learn about your employees and their families. What are their dreams? Then ask yourself how you as a manager can fulfill these dreams from a business perspective.

Perhaps the best way to learn about your employees is in a nonwork atmosphere—over lunch or on a company outing. As you learn more about your employees' motives, you can help each one develop a personalized strategic plan and vision. Ultimately, you could convert those horrible yearly performance reviews into goal-setting sessions and progress reports.

Generating a positive attitude is the third step. Studies show that 87 percent of all management feedback is negative, and that traditional management theory has done little to correct the situation. Your goal should be to reverse the trend. Make 87 percent of all feedback good.

Respect for and sensitivity toward others remains essential in developing positive attitudes. Ask employees for their opinions regarding problems on the job and treat their suggestions and ideas like priceless treasures.

The partner of positive attitude in the motivational game is shared goals. A motivated workforce needs well-defined objectives that address both individual and organizational goals. This means that you should include all your employees in the strategic planning process. Getting them involved leads to increased motivation. It also acts as a quality check on whether or not you are doing the right thing. And you'll close the communication gap at the same time.

Just setting a goal is insufficient. You have to monitor progress. The goal-setting process should include preparing a detailed road map that shows the specific path each person is going to take to meet that goal. In my business, one of the things that IT professionals dislike the most is the feeling that they're left out of the business cycle. In essence, information technology is just one part of a grand strategic plan. IT staffers frequently complain that they rarely get to see the fruits of their labor. Distributing the IT function into the business unit mitigates this problem somewhat, but it is still up to the manager to put technologists into the thick of things—to make them feel like part of the entire organization.

Finally, recognizing employees or team achievement is the most powerful tool in the motivating manager's toolbox. Appreciation for a job well done consistently appears at the top of employee want lists. So hire a band, have a party, send a card, or call in a clown—but thank that person or that team.

SUMMARY

Oracle offers a plethora of tools to manage the product life cycle. Figure 1.1 provides a quick pictorial overview of what comprises this particular product set. However, as will be true with the description of all Oracle product and service offerings described in this book, tools can go only so far in delivering the competitive edge desired by the organization. It's the underlying principles and methodologies practiced that form the framework. Hence, in this first chapter, we spent quite a bit of time focusing on innovation—that which begets the services and processes that will ultimately be managed by Oracle's Agile Product Management software.

REFERENCES

Alexander, M. A. 2001. The innovation wave and secular market trends. http://www.safe-haven.com/article/71/the-innovation-wave-and-secular-market-trends (accessed March 10, 2014).

Couger, J. D., S. C. McIntyre, L. F. Higgins, and T. A. Snow. 1991. Using a bottom-up approach to creativity improvement in IS development. *Journal of Systems Management* 42 (9): 23–36.

Davenport, T. H., and L. Prusak. 2003. *What's the big idea?* Boston: Harvard Business School Press.

Davenport, T. H., and H. J. Wilson. 2003. Turning mind into matter. *CMP Optimize* 25:1–5.

Drucker, P. F. 2002. The discipline of innovation. *Harvard Business Review* 80 (8): 95–102.

Goldsmith, B. 2003. Are you an innovator or an implementer? *Office Solutions* 20 (2): 48.

Harari, O. 1993. Stop empowering your people. *Management Review* 82 (11): 26–29.

Harvard Business Essentials. 2003. *Managing creativity and innovation.* Boston: Harvard Business School Press.

Kovach, K. 1999. Employee motivation. *Addressing a crucial factor in your organization's performance: Human resource development.* Ann Arbor: University of Michigan Press.

Lindgren, R., D. Stenmark, M. Bergquist, and J. Ljungberg. 2001. Rethinking IT support for managing competence. In *Proceedings of European Conference of Information Systems* (ECIS 2001).

McCarthy, M., and J. Allen. 2000. *You made my day: Creating co-worker recognition and relationships.* New York: L-F Books.

Nelson, B., and K. Blanchard. 1994. *1001 ways to reward employees.* New York: Workman Publishing.

Olmstead, L. 2005. How Steve Lipscomb reinvented poker and built the hottest business in America. *Inc.* 27 (5): 80–92.

Palmberg, C. 2004. The sources of innovations: Looking beyond technological opportunities. *Economics of Innovation and New Technology* 13 (2): 183–97.

Pearce, J. A., and R. B. Robinson. 2005. *Strategic management: Formulation, implementation, and control.* New York: McGraw-Hill.

Pollard, D. 2005. The future of knowledge management. Executive Action Report 130. Conference Board of Canada, Ottawa, ON.

Spencer, A. 2005. The technology S-curve. http://web.njit.edu/~aspencer/slides/s-curve.ppt (accessed March 15, 2014).

Teresko, J. 2004. P&G's secret: Innovating innovation. *Industry Week* 253 (12): 26–30.

Wilson, T. B. 2002. *Innovative reward systems for the changing marketplace.* New York: McGraw-Hill.

2

Oracle Analytics: Business Intelligence and Analytic Applications

Oracle lumps together several disparate application areas into what they have designated as Oracle Business Analytics, as shown in Figure 2.1. As a purist, and for the sake of ease of understanding, I have decided that Chapter 2 will focus on just those areas that most IT folks do consider to be analytically oriented—business intelligence and analytic applications, highlighted in Figure 2.1 by using a darker gray coloring.

The focus of the Oracle Business Intelligence (BI) suite is to enable the enterprise to accelerate decision making. Oracle BI tools and technology provide a broad set of capabilities for reporting, analysis, modeling, and forecasting using a dashboard format, as shown in Figure 2.2.

Oracle BI consists of the following tools:

1. Oracle Business Intelligence Tools and Technology
2. Oracle Exalytics In-Memory Machine
3. Oracle Business Intelligence for Analyzing Big Data
4. Oracle Endeca Information Discovery
5. Oracle Real-Time Decisions

Oracle Analytic Applications cascades the BI framework, through use of the various BI tools, down to the specific industry (i.e., Education, Public Sector, Health, Financial Services, Retail, etc.) and/or business line (i.e., sales, human resources, project management, procurement, customer service, supply chain, etc.). Oracle is also neatly integrated into a variety of external tool suites (some product lines acquired by Oracle), such as JD Edwards EnterpriseOne, Siebel CRM, and SAP.

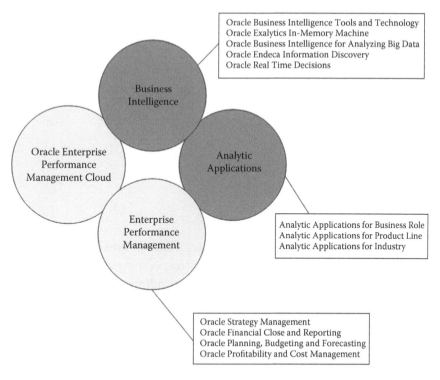

FIGURE 2.1
Oracle Business Analytics product set.

Oracle's BI offerings are all software, save for one notable exception—Oracle's Exalytics In-Memory Machine. Oracle Exalytics is a high-performance in-memory BI machine that delivers high performance for business intelligence and planning applications. With Exalytics, business decisions can be made in seconds while supporting thousands of users.

The remaining Oracle BI tools fall within the rubric of business intelligence applications that you might be familiar with—OLAP (online analytical processing), big data, real-time decisions, and information discovery. It should be noted that Oracle also has a solution that enables employees to perform BI on their mobile devices. Fully integrated with Oracle Business Intelligence Foundation Suite, Oracle BI Mobile HD provides immediate access to existing analytic content like dashboards, scorecards, and reports. Content delivered is automatically optimized for interaction on mobile devices via multitouch gestures.

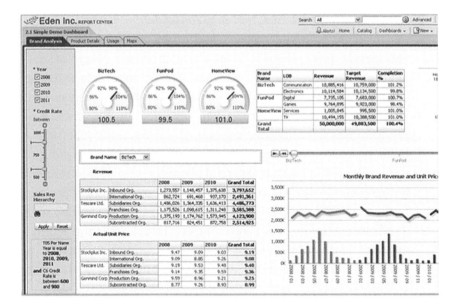

FIGURE 2.2
Oracle BI dashboard.

So, again, the key here is not the tool suite, but understanding the business context of those BI tools. Thus, the remaining sections of this chapter will focus on the discipline of BI.

BUSINESS INTELLIGENCE

Business intelligence (BI) is a set of methodologies and technologies for gathering, storing, analyzing, and providing access to data to help users make better business decisions. The goal of business intelligence is to transform data into information and, ultimately, into knowledge and wisdom. Business intelligence is usually implemented to gain sustainable competitive advantages, and it is a valuable core competence in some instances.

Brunson (2005) lists 10 trends in business intelligence:

1. *Taking data quality very seriously*: Data quality is more than just entering the data correctly. Management now realizes that data quality must be baked into the processes that stage data for analysis.

2. *Infrastructure standardization and consolidation*: Companies tend not to know how much they spend on business intelligence and data warehousing. The reason for this is that these efforts are usually undertaken in silos, where each business domain creates its own solution. Standardizing and consolidating business intelligence and warehousing is easier said than done because it involves more than just technology. It also involves political and organizational issues.

3. *Offshore sourcing*: Sending business intelligence and warehousing work offshore requires some careful planning, since it requires more business knowledge and customization than other types of projects. In spite of significant cost savings, some companies are finding some disadvantages to this trend, including quality problems and communications issues. Most recently, onshore companies are developing capabilities that broaden the issues surrounding the onsite vs. offsite vs. offshore issue.

4. *Strategic approach to information*: Very few companies have embraced the "data as asset" philosophy, although there will always be a small group of people within an organization who recognize the strategic value of information. Although companies might not be implementing business intelligence and data warehousing on an enterprise-wide basis, they are being incorporated in—and have become a critical component of—other strategic systems.

5. *Regulatory compliance as a driver for business intelligence and data warehousing*: Sarbanes-Oxley, environmental, and data-privacy legislative and regulatory directives have fundamentally shifted management's view on the need for high-quality data and the business intelligence systems to analyze this data. Regulatory compliance, therefore, has become a major impetus driving business intelligence efforts.

6. *Elevating the enterprise data-integration discussion*: Many organizations have already made the decision how to promote effective data integration. There are a variety of choices: ETL, which is an acronym for extract, transform, and load; and EAI (enterprise application integration), which involves the use of software and architectural principles to integrate two or more enterprise computer applications. EAI is related to middleware technologies, such as message-oriented middleware (MOM), and data representation technologies, such as XML (Extensible Markup Language). Newer EAI technologies

involve using web services as part of service-oriented architecture as a means of integration.

7. *Educating the end user*: Gartner suggests that it is as important to train users how to analyze the data as how to use the business intelligence tool sets.

8. *Master data management*: Master or reference data defines core entities, such as customers, products, and suppliers. Because enterprise data is frequently siloed throughout the organization, master data has become scattered across the enterprise. In addition, different domains may define *customer* in different ways. Organizational and political issues, such as who "owns" the master data, often get in the way of developing an enterprise-wide repository. It should be noted that this problem is similar to the one experienced in the 1980s, when databases were first being integrated within the organization and the debate was about centralized versus decentralized IT departments.

9. *Powerful adjuncts to the business intelligence and data warehousing market*: ERP (Enterprise Resource Planning) and CRM (Customer Relationship Management) vendors such as SAP and Oracle see a profitable opportunity in providing what was missing from their original solutions.

10. *Actionable business intelligence*: Organizations want more than strategy from their business intelligence. They want to be able to use the information for more tactical decision-making purposes. For example, if they see a problem in their supply chain, they want to know how they can fix the problem.

Using Information Technology to Gather Intelligence

The term *competitive intelligence* is very much on the tip of the tongue in today's economic maelstrom. The majority, if not all, of American companies collect some sort of information about the direction that their competitors are taking. What few realize, though, is that competitive intelligence is really only part of a larger view of the business world we live in. This view is called *business intelligence*.

Competitive intelligence is a subset of business intelligence and, as a subset, it is not the complete picture. Herbert E. Meyer (1987), noted author and consultant, as well as past vice chairman of the US National Intelligence Council, calls business intelligence the corporate equivalent of radar. As with radar, the business environment must be continually scanned to avoid danger and seize opportunities. Meyer describes business intelligence as the other half of strategic planning. Once the plan is completed, business intelligence monitors its implementation and assists in making strategic course corrections along the way.

Business intelligence is not just looking at your competition, but seeing all the changes around you, including politics, consumer affairs, and even environmental issues. All these influence the long-term future of the company. The use of competitive intelligence transcends industry boundaries and, if used correctly, provides the organization with an immediate advantage. No two companies will implement competitive intelligence systems in the same way.

Perhaps the department with the biggest need to digest huge amounts of information is corporate marketing. Aside from the product or service being marketed, it is the efforts of the marketing department that will make the biggest impact on the profitability of a company. It stands to reason that providing marketers with the appropriate tools and techniques will most certainly enhance their efforts and, in doing so, the bottom line.

Quaker Oats, acquired by PepsiCo in 2001, is a leading multibillion-dollar international food manufacturer of cereals, pancake mixes, snacks, frozen pizza, and pet foods. From a marketing perspective, this diversity of products makes it difficult to perform the necessary marketing analysis. All of these forces led Quaker Oats to build an automated decision-support tool. With its plethora of functions and ease of use, *Mikey* is a good example of that category of business intelligence systems called the Executive Information System.

Mikey gets its name from the famous Quaker Oats commercial of a bygone era where a finicky little boy tries a Quaker cereal and likes it. Mikey was developed for an ad hoc query capability of large corporate marketing bases and utilized a set of products from Information Resources, now IRi (http://www.iriworldwide.com/). Due to its distributive nature, Mikey quickly became Quaker's central coordinating facility for the creation and distribution of marketing plans, production requirements, and financial estimates.

Quaker built a robust marketing system, the components of which include business review reporting, marketing planning, ad hoc reporting, general information, and utilities. The *business review reporting* component produces standard reports based on the company's historical sales and comparisons with competitors. The standard reports can be generated for an extensive range of market, brand, time, and measure selections, or time aggregations.

The *ad hoc reporting* component allows marketing users to essentially write their own marketing analyses programs. This permits them to look at data and create their own brand or market aggregates.

The *market planning* module permits the marketing department to review the marketing performance of any particular product. The data stored, and capable of being analyzed here, include such things as package weight, cases, the cost of the product, the company, price, and advertising budget. Mikey understands the relationships among all these items. In the planning mode, if marketing staff decide to alter one of these variables, e.g., package weight, the system will automatically change the other relevant components in the mix.

Frito-Lay, another subsidiary of PepsiCo, makes corn chips, potato chips, and tortilla chips. This is an extremely competitive market, with much of the competition coming at the local and regional level. With hundreds of product lines and a thousand stores, a mountain of data is produced on a daily basis. In order to get a leg up on the competition, Frito-Lay needed to be able to collect, digest, and then act on that mound of information quickly.

Frito-Lay's solution was a combination of advanced technologies. This includes scanner data combined with sales information from field staff, all combined on a sophisticated network, encompassing handheld computers and a private satellite communications network connecting the distribution sites, ultimately accessible through a decision-support system.

The idea of electronic data entry from the sales force dates back to the late 1970s, but it wasn't until 1989 that Frito-Lay saw their vision become reality. By then, the company had equipped more than 10,000 sales representatives with handheld computers developed with Fujitsu at a cost of more than $40 million.

These handheld computers, called *bricks* by Frito-Lay, are used to track inventories at retail stores as well as to enter orders. The bricks are connected to miniprinters in all delivery trucks. At day's end, all sales data collected at stores that day are sent to the central data center at the company's headquarters by way of distributed computers at the various distribution centers.

Frito-Lay built a total intelligence system that could be customized at every level of the company. As the network developed, the company realized it could shift from a national marketing strategy to one that targeted local consumers. This is known as *micromarketing*.

Employees using the system run the gamut from the marketing support staff all the way up to the chief executive officer. On one occasion, the CEO noticed red numbers on his screen. This indicated that sales were down in the central region. Quickly calling up another screen, he located the source of the problem in Texas. Continuing on this hunt, he tracked the red numbers to a specific sales division and finally to a chain of stores. Apparently, a local company had successfully introduced a new white corn chip that was eating into Frito-Lay's market share in the location. Frito-Lay immediately put a white-corn version of Tostitos into production, which appeared on shelves a few months later.

A typical sales manager is required to pull together sales information from a variety of sources. In some cases, this took weeks to assemble and had to be obtained from telephone calls. In other cases, the data was simply not available. With Frito-Lay's info-marketing system, this information is immediately available by brand, by type of store, or even by package size. The sales manager is able to obtain results from the best or the worst of sales representatives in his or her territory as well as pricing moves by competitors. The manager can compare the results of sales reps' performance with the previous week or the previous year as well as with current targets. The sales manager can even compare products sales in different markets, such as supermarkets versus convenience stores.

The significance of these systems is that they achieve positive returns on a multitude of levels. Frito-Lay's info-marketing system has affected every level of staff and every layer of the corporate hierarchy. What originally started out as a mechanism to reduce the overhead of the sales rep in the field has turned into a bonanza of information for the marketing staff back home, has cut down on administrative overhead at the home office, has fine-tuned the production cycle by providing timely information, and has even provided an executive information system for the senior executives in the company. This system is pervasive.

Value of Executive Information Systems

Executive information systems (EIS) are hands-on tools that focus, filter, and organize information to make more effective use of that information. The principle behind these systems is that by using information more effectively and more strategically, a company can ultimately increase profitability. The goals of any EIS should be:

1. To reduce the amount of data bombarding the executive
2. To increase the relevance, timeliness, and usability of the information that reaches the executive
3. To focus a management team on critical success factors
4. To enhance executive follow-through and communication with others
5. To track the earliest of warning indicators: competitive moves, customer demands, and more

Many EIS systems are based on the paper-based briefing book, long a fixture in executive chambers. Its purpose is to advise senior executives of critical issues and the status of key projects within the organization. The problem with paper reports is that they usually arrive too late for preventive or corrective action and do not provide a format conducive to in-depth investigation. There is also no way that an executive can ask questions to get more detailed information. Thus, the briefing book is supplemented in most companies with monthly status meetings just to respond to these deficiencies.

This lack of information results in an organization's executives spending approximately 80 percent of their time in attending these status meetings. If one adds in the trickle-down requirement of rolling information down to the staff level, then these additional "one on ones" and roll-down meetings add overhead to a firm that forces it to spend more time reading about being competitive than actually being competitive.

In many companies, at least part of the problem is being addressed by automating the briefing book. There are many advantages to an automated briefing book. Each executive can receive a personalized selection of reports and charts, reducing the amount of relevant information he or she sees. In addition, each executive can set up variables responding to acceptable tolerances. For example, an automobile executive might wish to flag any line of car in which the company's market share falls below 25 percent. Because executives often like to see facts in context, automated briefing books should have the capability of comparing information on a competitive or historical basis. For example, looking at current sales data as the latest event in a continuum indicates whether sales volume is heading up or down. Similarly, executives usually want to compare information with goals, budgets, and forecasts as well as with information stored on the competition.

Perhaps the biggest obstacle to upward reporting is that the senior executive is only privy to information on a monthly basis. In an age of stiff competition but easy access to distribution channels, a fast reaction time to an event may make a major difference to the bottom line. This information float—the time it takes for information to wend its way up through the channels to senior management—can be nearly eliminated by use of this category of business intelligence software.

Once a significant variance is identified within a briefing book report, the executive must be able to investigate the variance with much more detail and from multiple perspectives. It's not enough to know that, at the consolidated level, profits have deviated from the goal by 7 percent. Some business units might be over this goal, and others might be well under the goal. The executive must have some facility to answer questions such as: What makes up the deviation? Is it a faltering distribution channel? Are there competitive problems in an established product? Is it a failure in a particular geographic area? In a particular product line? Or in one customer grouping? To do this, a multidimensional knowledge base designed to support the managerial perspective of financial performance must be made available.

Briefing-book information is a synthesis of information gathered from the far-flung corners of an organization, often referred to as the *financial value chain*. This includes processes from payroll, inventory, procurement through process management, and ultimately into the decision-making strategic-planning and forecasting-management set of processes.

Universal Studios Hollywood (USH), which is part of media and entertainment giant NBC Universal, is an example of a company that is taking advantage of software that enables automation of the financial value chain.

Universal comprises quite a few distinct businesses: operations, entertainment, ticketing, food service, merchandising, maintenance, and real estate management. They wanted to be able to easily do mission-critical activities such as category and channel management, labor scheduling optimization, and providing real-time visibility into their key performance indicators (KPI). Like many companies, Universal was suffering from fragmented data sources and practices across different business units.

Their goal was to transform their organization from one based on spreadsheets and data gathering to one that spends 80 percent of its time on analysis and 20 percent on data gathering. The company had already invested in a data-warehouse solution to track ticketing information, but wanted to add on robust budgeting functionality in order to quickly and successfully do scenario modeling for 200 venues across seven businesses. A BI system was implemented in 2002, along with an ERP solution that would feed aggregated P&L (profits and losses) performance data into the system for financial reporting. The solution was also used to build daily budgets, which are then fed back into the data-warehouse solution and to the ERP solution at the monthly level.

The BI solution sits on top of their database and talks directly to their ERP and is well integrated to their data warehouse. They use this synergy of business intelligence systems for real-time KPI reporting and a complete focus on process management. Universal is also building KPI dashboards that will link directly to monthly or quarter-to-go analysis, show top-level and detailed department P&Ls, enable dynamic month-to-date and year-to-date calculations, and provide standard reporting templates. This solution has provided the company with real-time visibility into both leading and lagging KPIs, as well as detailed category and sales-channel penetration and scenario-enabled modeling with detail on both risk management and variance analysis. The company's source systems are completely integrated with financial process controls.

The Science of Gathering Business Intelligence

Frito-Lay, Quaker Oats, and Universal Hollywood use a first-class set of BI tools and procedures to collect, collate, and reassemble internal and external data to provide enough information to perform competitive decision making. The systems, which have been refined to the point of providing these companies tailored, filtered, and usable information, required an intensive two-level effort to create. On the first level was the development of the underlying technological infrastructure, permitting the information to be distributed to and analyzed by the appropriate parties. On a higher level was the effort required to determine the depth and breadth of the information that would be required.

Sitting a hundred people in a room with access to every newspaper, journal, magazine, and book that has ever been published will produce only disconnected tidbits of information. Virtually every piece of information in these journals, magazines, books, and newspapers is available online through any of a myriad of information vendors for a fee or free via the Internet. With merely a PC, it is possible for farmers in Idaho to ascertain long-term weather conditions and for businessmen to download information on products, competitors, or trends.

Even with easy access to this wealth of information, however, you still don't have intelligence. Take the case of a major pharmaceutical company.

Over a one-year period, they spent more than $10 million in online downloads. According to the CEO, virtually all of this information was worthless. That's because they didn't have the ability, or know-how, to turn this plethora of information into intelligence. It is a capability that requires the use of tools and techniques to be able to coordinate and correlate discrete bits of information into intelligence.

Perhaps the biggest stumbling block to the process of creating BI is where it is done. Because the creation of this intelligence relies on the downloading of information, the task is often delegated to the information technology (IT) department. This was the case with the pharmaceutical company mentioned. It turned out to be an expensive mistake for them.

A profile of a department most likely to succeed in this endeavor will include the following abilities: being able to work with technology to gather the raw information; having the writing talent to present it in an understandable fashion to management; and possessing the sociopolitical skills to draw conclusions from the analyses that will be accepted by the diverse, and often conflicting, groups that make up a modern corporation.

This is the tactic that Herbert Meyer and his partner Mike Pincus take when advising their corporate clients on how to build an intelligence-gathering department. They look for people with library skills, technical skills, and familiarity with the company's business. They also look for someone who has an "in" with the CEO, so the results don't get politicized.

Part of the problem with intelligence is that when it is done well, it tends to offset bad judgment, which often comes from executive support people. These executive support management people feel threatened by intelligence, because it tends to offset their own bad opinions, according to Pincus. Where you have bad management advice, you have to bring someone into the unit who has the social/political/corporate capability to be able to move around in that environment without upsetting people and causing them to feel threatened.

The first step involved in building an intelligence unit is to develop a profile of the company. This is really a needs analysis, which will document the products and services a company manufactures or performs, its goals and priorities, as well as requirements for competitive information. Basically, this will be a comprehensive list of categories of information that the company must monitor in order to be competitive. Examples of categories include suppliers, markets, customers, and so on. The profile also uncovers irrelevant information that the company is tracking. In addition to all of this, an assessment must be made of the cultural climate of a company. How is information passed up and down the corporate hierarchy? What political machinations are in place that could possibly affect, or even impede, the information flow?

With profile in hand, the next step is to perform an intelligence audit. This is the process that determines whether the right people are getting the right information. It is really a two-step process. First, as one would expect, the information needs that are uncovered during the process of developing the profile are satisfied by locating the proper online source that contains that piece of information. As already demonstrated, virtually anything ever written can be located via the Internet. The trick is in being able to first locate it, then being able to download it, and finally being able to process it. This is where the second step of the intelligence audit comes in. The company's technological mentality should be assessed. What kind of technical expertise does the company have? What are they comfortable with? From the information collected in this process, it is possible to develop a technological solution that would best satisfy the needs and capabilities of a particular organization.

Probably the most crucial step in this entire process is in training selected personnel in how to convert the information obtained to business intelligence. This is actually done on two levels. On the technical level, one or more people must be trained to develop skills in correlating information which supports the staff that will ultimately turn this raw information into intelligence. These top-tier staff are the ones who will need to develop and hone skills to coordinate, correlate, analyze, and ultimately convert raw streams of information into useful business intelligence.

Checklist for the Information Audit

Information audits are tailored to specific companies and their individual needs. The goal of this process is to pinpoint the information requirements of a company and then proceed to recommend solutions to satisfy these requirements. Basically, the process is composed of four steps:

1. Selecting what needs to be known
2. Collecting the information
3. Transforming this collected information into finished product
4. Distributing the finished product to appropriate staff

Selecting What Needs to Be Known

Figuring out the right things to know is one of the trickiest, least understood, and most underrated jobs. To perform this feat requires not so much an expertise in one or more fields, but the ability to recognize what factors will influence the particular issue or area of concern.

The process is begun by reviewing the objectives that have been outlined by the CEO or management committee. For example: The CEO of an aluminum manufacturer wants to improve sales of the company's pop-top beverage cans. To do this requires an assessment of the prospects for growth in the beverage industry. This is the obvious information that would be required. A person experienced in performing these audits would most certainly look beyond the obvious to, say, assessing the prospects of third-world aluminum producers moving into the canning business. Even this might be obvious to some, so we need to go deeper into the assessment and evaluate producers of other materials that could replace aluminum cans (Meyer 1987). In essence, this example demonstrates the need to think about issues in a multidimensional way.

Collecting the Information

Once it has been decided what needs to be known, one can begin to collect the appropriate information. There are several categories of information. First, there is *information that is already available in-house* residing on some corporate database, on local PCs, on departmental distributed databases, or even on paper.

The next category of information can be referred to as *public information*. This is information that is on the public record, available in the form of magazines, newspapers, and from public agencies.

The next category is *private information*. This is information that is not publicly known, but is available for a fee such as LexisNexis (http://www.lexisnexis.com/) and Thomson Research's Investext (http://research.thomsonib.com/).

The final category of information is what is known as *secret information*. This is information privately held by competitor companies. Unfortunately, most of this information is impossible to obtain legally, although some of it can be gleaned from discussions with former employees of competitors, salespeople, customers, and vendors.

Transforming the Collected Information into Finished Products

Deciding upon and then collecting the information is only half the battle. For the information to be truly useful, it must be presented in analytic reports that provide the best judgments, conclusions, and projections based on this information.

Transforming this data into useful information is a multistep process. These steps require a team to study the material and then debate what the material actually means and whether it is accurate and whether it harbors any inconsistencies. It is this first step where all facts will be verified, experts consulted, and theses developed and tested.

Some approaches transform the collected information manually through the efforts of intelligence officers. These people argue over the facts and then make a decision as to the correct interpretation of the data to be delivered to the CEO or other staff member. Today's BI technology provides the ability to load all collected information into a knowledge base and then perform automatic analysis and distribution. A good example of this is the combination of the data warehouse and data mining.

Wal-Mart has the world's largest nongovernmental database as their data warehouse. Their current data warehouse has hundreds of terabytes of sales information. It is run on a massively parallel computer with thousands of processors. This machine houses all of the details from each cash register receipt for each sale at each of its many thousands of stores, supercenters, and Sam's Club stores for the past 16 months. One of Wal-Mart's tables has over two billion rows! Table scans are not a viable option for responding to a query on this table because the table is so massively large!

Wal-Mart uses its data warehouse for such things as its market basket analysis. Analyzing what is in each individual shopping cart (sales receipt), they were able to discover the correlation between cold medicine and Kleenex tissues. People who bought cold medicine usually purchased tissues. In their stores, the Kleenex tissues were with the paper products, while their cold medicine was in the pharmacy department. When they stocked the tissues next to the cold medicine as well as in the paper products area, the sales of tissues increased dramatically. Perhaps cold sufferers did not know if they had tissues at home. Seeing the tissues enticed them to go ahead and purchase them just in case they didn't have any at home.

Wal-Mart also discovered a relationship between bananas and cereal. Customers who bought cereal also were likely to purchase bananas. The cereal was often far removed from the fruit aisles. When they placed a banana display near the cereal, sales of bananas skyrocketed.

Wal-Mart also uses data mining to cluster the information of where its customers live. Using credit card information, they can determine how far its customers drove to shop at any given store. This data is utilized in the selection of locations for new stores.

The six steps of effective data mining are:

1. *Business understanding*: Understanding the specific business problem's objectives and goals
2. *Data understanding*: Initial data collection and familiarization: involves identification of data quality problems and data subsets
3. *Data preparation*: Selecting and cleaning final set of data
4. *Modeling*: Selecting and applying modeling techniques
5. *Evaluation*: Determining whether result meets business problem's specifications
6. *Deployment*: Presenting the data in a meaningful way so an end user can use it

Distributing of the Finished Product to Appropriate Staff

Information should be presented to the staff members appropriate to that staff member's level within the organization.

Robert E. Horn, while at Harvard and Columbia Universities, researched how people deal with large amounts of information. He created an approach, which he called *information mapping* (http://www.informationmapping.com/en/), that is based on learning theory, human factors engineering, and cognitive science. Horn's approach is quite similar to the Meyer and Pincus approach, and is worth discussing in a bit more detail.

Information mapping is a research-based approach to the analysis, organization, and visual presentation of information. In the *analysis* component, it is necessary to determine the purpose, audience needs, and information types. In the *organization* component, the overall structure for the information will be created based on the analysis. In the *presentation* component, the information is formatted for clarity and accessibility

TABLE 2.1

Information Map

Introduction: One of the most important procedures in an audit is preparing the data. Careful preparation ensures that the data is correct and that each step of preparation has been carried out.	

Procedure: Follow the steps below to prepare data for the audit.

Step	Action
1	For data items selected for audit, obtain the following: • Source document samples • Run data from the computer room
2	Verify the source document samples by comparing the samples to the original list
3	Record on a worksheet sufficient descriptive information to provide accurate identification for future audits.

Minimum Information Required	Examples
Attributes of the sample	• Sales territory • Effective data
Description of each data item	• Account name • Account number • Type of business

depending upon the audience. Table 2.1 demonstrates an information map that explains how to prepare data for an audit.

Information mapping has been used with success for the optimization of everything from content-management systems to work-flow analyses to ISO 9000 documentation.

Lincoln National Corporation

Lincoln National Corporation (www.lfg.com), now Lincoln Financial Group, is a 100-year-old company with $119 billion in consolidated assets under management. As is the case in any company of Lincoln's size, the process of collecting, interpreting, and disseminating information was time-consuming at best, and hit or miss at its worst.

One of the most demanding business problems Lincoln National was experiencing was a need to digest large amounts of information. In the past, this had been done by issuing a daily news digest. This paper report formed the baseline of information around which Lincoln executives and managers made their strategic decisions.

Understanding that the method of creating this daily reports left large gaps of business intelligence unaccounted for, the company began development of a corporate-wide information retrieval system using information auditing techniques.

Lincoln discovered that most executive needs were not for information on the corporate database. In general, the executives of Lincoln got their business intelligence from the various news sources. The technology group was able to create an automated morning report that retrieved, searched, and correlated textual external data to assist staff. The morning report's intelligence comes from a variety of external sources, including the *New York Times* and *Business Week*. It has given Lincoln the ability the analyze information from a wide variety of other sources as well.

The morning report is viewed by Lincoln as a BI gathering tool that feeds information into their executive support systems. Lincoln has seen some significant productivity improvements. Prior to attending meetings, staff members can review the pertinent information, negating the need to brief meeting attendees so that meetings can move forward more quickly. Perhaps the greatest benefit of all is improved communications within the company, permitting key executives to make better decisions and facilitating the company's avoidance of the inevitable filtering effect that so often happens as information makes its way through the corporate hierarchy.

Lincoln uses their executive support system for strategic planning and competitive analyses. Along with external information, Lincoln management can analyze internal sales data, competitor activities, field reports from sales staff, as well as competitor's financial data to determine the best way to compete.

Competitive analysis is a major component of Lincoln's planning process. Using the information entered by the salespeople in the field, Lincoln builds a profile of each competitor's strengths and weaknesses. This is done by identifying the factors that are considered critical for each line of business, and then ranking each competitor's capabilities in the same area. At the same time, the same criteria are used to rank Lincoln's own capabilities in those same areas. Using a side-by-side comparison of competitor versus itself, Lincoln can evaluate whether or not they are weak in the critical factors needed for success in any particular product line. If a perceived weakness is noted, Lincoln formulates a plan to strengthen the company in that particular area. At the same time, the marketing plan is modified to focus on the key strengths while minimizing the weaknesses. One of

Lincoln's greatest strengths is the ability to track and process competitor's data and then relate it to their own data, further strengthening their own product and marketing plans. Being able to monitor what a competitor is up to requires a combination of smart technology and techniques.

Competitor Analysis

Competitive analysis serves a useful purpose. It helps organizations devise their strategic plans and gives them insight into how to craft their performance indicators. The philosophy behind Combustion Engineering's technique (Conference Board 1988) is that information coupled with the experience of a seasoned industry manager is more than adequate to take the place of expensive experts in the field of competitive analysis.

The goal behind Combustion Engineering's technique is to analyze one competitor at a time to identify strategies and predict future moves. The key difference between this technique and others is the level of involvement of senior managers of the firm. In most companies, research is delegated to staff that prepare a report on all competitors at once. Combustion Engineering's method is to gather the information on one competitor, and then use senior managers to logically deduce the strategy of the competitor in question.

Combustion Engineering uses a five-step approach to performing competitive analyses:

Step 1. *Preliminary meeting*: Once the competitor is chosen, a preliminary meeting is scheduled. It should be attended by all senior managers who might have information or insight to contribute concerning this competitor. This includes the CEO as well as the general manager and managers from sales, marketing, finance, and manufacturing. A broader array of staff attending is important to this technique, because it serves to provide access to many diverse sources of information. This permits the merger of external information sources as well as internal sources collected by the organization, such as documents, observations, and personal experiences.

At this meeting, it is agreed that all attendees spend a specified amount of time collecting more recent information about a competitor. At this time, a second meeting is scheduled in which to review this more recent information.

Step 2. *Information meeting*: At this meeting, each attendee will receive an allotment of time to present his or her information to the group.

The group will then perform a relative strengths/weaknesses analysis. This will be done for all areas of interest uncovered by the information obtained by the group. The analysis will seek to draw conclusions about two criteria. First, is a competitor stronger or weaker than your company? Second, does the area of interest have the potential to affect customer behavior?

Combustion Engineering rules dictate that unless the area of interest meets both of these criteria, it should not be pursued further either in analysis or discussion. Since managers do not always agree on what areas to include or exclude, it is frequently necessary to appoint a moderator who is not part of the group.

Step 3. *Cost analysis*: At this point, with areas of concern isolated, it is necessary to do a comparative cost analysis. The first step here is to prepare a breakdown of costs for each product. This includes labor, manufacturing, cost of goods, distribution, sales, administrative as well as other relevant items of interest.

At this point, compare the competitor's cost for each of these factors according to the following scale:

- Significantly higher
- Slightly higher
- Slightly lower
- Significantly lower

Now, translate these subjective ratings to something a bit more tangible, such as slightly higher is equivalent to 15 percent By weighting each of these factors by its relative contribution to the total product cost, it is now possible to calculate the competitor's total costs.

Step 4. *Competitor motivation*: This is perhaps the most intangible of the steps. The group must now attempt to analyze their competitor's motivation by determining how the competitor measures success as well as what its objectives and strategies are.

During the research phase, the senior manager and/or his or her staff gathered considerable information on this topic. By using online databases and websites, it is possible to collect information about self-promotions, annual reports, press releases, and the like. In addition, information from former employees, the sales force, investment analysts, suppliers, and mutual clients is extremely useful and serves to broaden the picture.

Based on the senior managers' understanding of the business, it is feasible to be able to deduce the competitor's motivation. Motivation can often be deduced by observing the way the competitor measures itself. Annual reports are good sources for this information. For example, a competitor that wants to reap the benefits of investment in a particular industry will most likely measure success in terms of return on investment.

Step 5.   *Total picture*: By reviewing information on the competitor's strengths and weaknesses, relative cost structure, goals, and strategies, the total picture of the firm can be created.

Using this information, the group should be able to use individual insights into the process of running a business in a similar industry to determine the competitor's next likely moves. For example, analysis shows that a competitor is stronger in direct sales, has a cost advantage in labor, and is focused on growing from a regional to a national firm. The group would draw the conclusion that the competitor will attempt to assemble a direct sales effort nationwide, while positioning itself on the basis of low price.

Combustion Engineering also devised an approach to dealing with the situation in which an outsider enters the marketplace. In this case, the strategy outlined here obviously would not work.

Using the same group of people gathered to analyze competitor strategy, this exercise requests that the group look at the market as an objective third party would. The task is to design a fictitious company that would be able to successfully penetrate the market. Then compare this fictitious company with the competitor firms in the industry to see if any of the traditional competitors can easily adopt this approach.

When Combustion Engineering's phantom analysis uncovers a strategy that traditional competitors might easily adopt, they adopt this strategy as a preemptive move. When this same analysis reveals that an outsider could penetrate the industry by following this strategy, Combustion Engineering attempts to create additional barriers to entry. This includes forming an alliance with an outside company to pursue the phantom strategy itself.

Hruby's "missing-piece analysis" (1989) also attempts to anticipate competitor moves, but it does this by identifying key weaknesses in the competitor. By concentrating on the competitor's weaknesses, the great wealth of information on that competitor can be turned into usable, action-oriented intelligence.

The methodology for performing Hruby's missing-piece analysis is to analyze the strengths and weaknesses of the competitor in six areas. In each of these areas, the competitor is compared to the company doing the analysis:

1. *Product*: Compare the strength of the competitor's product from a consumer point of view.
2. *Manufacturing*: Compare capabilities, cost, and capacity.
3. *Sales and marketing*: How well does the competitor sell a product? Compare positioning, advertising, sales force, and so on.
4. *Finance*: Compare financial resources and performance. How strong are these relative to requirements for launching a strong competitive thrust?
5. *Management*: How effective, aggressive, and qualified are the competitor's managers?
6. *Corporate culture*: Examine values and history to determine whether the competitor is likely to enter or to attempt to dominate a market.

The goal of this exercise is to identify weaknesses in each of these areas, as well as to see whether any one of these weaknesses stands out as a major vulnerability. According to Hruby, most companies have a key weakness—or missing piece—that can be exploited.

To perform this technique requires that the competitor be rated in each of the six areas listed. Ratings are done on a scale of 1 to 5, with 1 being very weak, 2 being weak/uncompetitive, 3 being adequate/average, 4 being very strong/competitive, and 5 being excellent/superior.

Hruby recommends summarizing the scores in a competitive-strengths matrix, as shown in Table 2.2. This matrix lists the names of the competitors down the left-hand side and the competitive areas of interest across the top. Scores are entered into the appropriate

TABLE 2.2

Competitive-Strengths Matrix

			Competitive Areas			
Competitor	Product	Manufacturing	Sales & Marketing	Finance	Management	Corporate Culture
Company A	5	3	4	2	4	3
Company B	4	4	3	2	3	4
Company C	1	3	3	5	2	3
Company D	4	4	4	4	5	4

Note: 1 = Weak to 5 = Excellent.

cells. The worst score for each competitor should be highlighted. This is their weakest point and should be monitored accordingly.

In our example, Company A and Company B are both weak in the finance area. This means that they do not have enough strength to launch a major advertising campaign to bolster a new product. What this means is that if the company doing this analysis is ready, willing, and able to spend a lot of money, a new product launch would most probably be successful.

Company C scored a 1 in the product category. This means that its product is not as good as the company doing the analysis. In this case, an advertising campaign emphasizing product differences would serve to grab some market share from Company C.

Company D, on the other hand, scored strongly in all matrix areas. Given a strong product and an aggressive management team, this company is likely to make an aggressive move—perhaps a new product launch or major advertising on an existing product. It might even reduce costs. Company D certainly bears watching.

Company C, on the other hand, has a weak product but a good financial position. It just might launch a new product. However, its weak management structure might defer any product launch.

In summary, upon analysis of the competitive-strengths matrix, one would deduce that a combination of strong financial position and competent management are a mix that indicates a strong likelihood of aggressive action on the part of the competitor. By using this analysis on information obtained from various sources, it is quite possible to keep tabs on what the competition is up to as well as provide a wealth of performance indicators and measures that could be useful for performance management.

Automatic Discovery Programs—a.k.a. Data Mining

The number and size of operational databases are increasing at a progressively quickened rate. Because of the number of these databases as well as their size and complexity, there is a tremendous amount of valuable knowledge locked up that remains undiscovered. Because the tendency of most modern organizations is to cut back on staff, it follows that there will never be enough analysts to interpret the data in all the databases.

Over two decades ago, Kamran Parsaye (1990) coined the term *intelligent databases*. The goal of intelligent databases is to be able to manage information in a natural way, making the information stored within these databases easy to store, access, and use. The prototypical intelligent database would have some robust requirements. It would need to provide some high-level tools for data analysis, discovery, and integrity control. These tools would be used to allow users not only to extract knowledge from databases, but also to apply knowledge to data. So far, it is not possible to scan through the pages of a database as easily as it is to flip through the pages of a book. In order for the label *intelligent database* to be valid, this feature is necessary. Users should be able to retrieve information from a computerized database as easily as they can get from a helpful human expert. Finally, an intelligent database must be able to retrieve knowledge as opposed to data. To do this, it needs to use inferencing capabilities to determine what a user needs to know.

In developing the theory behind intelligent databases, Parsaye et al. (1990) enumerated three basic levels in dealing with the database:

1. We collect data, e.g., we maintain records on clients, products, sales, etc.
2. We query data, e.g., "Which products had increasing sales last month?"
3. We try to understand data, e.g., "What makes a product successful?"

In general, most current database systems passively permit these functions. A database is a static repository of information that will provide answers when a human initiates a session and asks pertinent questions. Parsaye came up with the idea of automatic discovery software, the purpose of which was to analyze large databases and discovered patterns, rules, and often unexpected relationships. Automatic discovery software uses statistics and machine learning to generate easy-to-read rules that characterize data, providing insight and understanding. The advent of auto discovery software changed the view of databases from a static repository of information, which only provides answers when someone asks a specific question, to a more active repository, which automatically poses queries to the database, thereby uncovering useful and sometimes unexpected information.

This was the case for a well-known computer manufacturer who suffered sporadic defect problems in their disk drive manufacturing process that they just couldn't locate. Using automatic discovery software against a database that consisted of audit logs of the manufacturing process, this company was able to pinpoint a particular operator who was causing the problem. The defect was then traced back to lack of proper training.

An even more interesting case study deals with lead-poisoning data from the University of Southern California's Cancer Registry. Analysis of this data uncovered a relationship between gender and the level of lead in the blood leading to kidney damage. Before analysis, this relationship was unknown and potentially deadly.

Oracle Endeca Information Discovery is an enterprise data-discovery platform that combines information of any type, from any source, empowering business-user independence in balance with IT governance, as shown in Figure 2.3.

FIGURE 2.3
Oracle Endeca Information Discovery.

Data Mining

Automatic discovery is considered a close adjunct to data mining. Data mining software amplifies our ability to navigate and analyze information so that it can be rapidly turned from discrete and disconnected pieces of data into real intelligence.

Data mining can not only help us in knowledge discovery, i.e., the identification of new phenomena, but it is also useful in enhancing our understanding of known phenomena. One of the key steps in data mining is pattern recognition, namely, the discovery and characterization of patterns in image and other high-dimensional data. A pattern is defined as an arrangement or an ordering in which some organization of underlying structure can be said to exist. Patterns in data are identified using measurable features or attributes that have been extracted from the data, as shown in Figure 2.4.

Data mining is an interactive and iterative process involving data preprocessing, search for patterns, knowledge evaluation, and possible refinement of the process based on input from domain experts or feedback from one of the steps. Wal-Mart is one company that champions data mining, and it has profited handsomely from its use.

The preprocessing of the data is a time-consuming, but critical, first step in the data-mining process. It is often domain and application dependent; however, several techniques developed in the context of one application or domain can be applied to other applications and

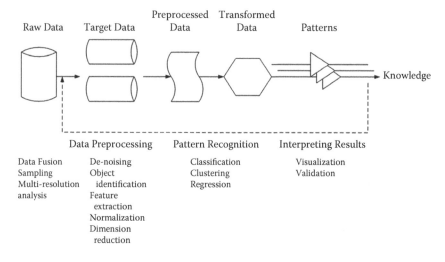

FIGURE 2.4
The process of data mining.

domains as well. The pattern-recognition step is usually independent of the domain or application.

Data mining starts with the raw data, which usually takes the form of simulation data, observed signals, or images. These data are preprocessed using various techniques such as sampling, multiresolution analysis, denoising, feature extraction, and normalization.

Sampling is a widely accepted technique to reduce the size of the data set and make it easier to handle. However, in some cases, such as when looking for something that appears infrequently in the set, sampling may not be viable. Multiresolution analysis is another technique to reduce the size of the data set. With multiresolution analysis, data at a fine resolution can be coarsened, which shrinks the data set by removing some of the detail and extracts relevant features from the raw data set. In credit card fraud, for instance, an important feature might be the location where a card is used: If a credit card is suddenly used in a country where it's never been used before, fraudulent use seems likely. Thus the key to effective data mining is reducing the number of features used to mine data, retaining only those features that provide the best discrimination among the relevant data items.

Once the data is preprocessed or transformed, pattern-recognition software is used to look for patterns. Patterns are defined as an ordering that contains some underlying structure. The results are processed back into a format familiar to the experts, who then can examine and interpret the results.

To be truly useful, data-mining techniques must be scalable. In other words, when the problem increases in size, we don't want the mining time to increase proportionally. Making the end-to-end process scalable can be very challenging, because it's not just a matter of scaling each step, but of scaling the process as a whole.

Large-scale data mining is a field very much in its infancy, making it a source of several open research problems. In order to extend data-mining techniques to large-scale data, several barriers must be overcome. The extraction of key features from large, multidimensional, complex data is a critical issue that must be addressed first, prior to the application of the pattern-recognition algorithms. The features extracted must be relevant to the problem, insensitive to small changes in the data, and invariant to scaling, rotation, and translation. In addition, we need to select discriminating features through appropriate dimension-reduction techniques. The pattern-recognition step poses several challenges as well. For example, is it possible to modify existing algorithms, or design new ones, that are scalable, robust, accurate, and interpretable? Further, can these algorithms be applied effectively and efficiently to complex, multidimensional data? And, is it possible to implement these algorithms efficiently on large-scale multiprocessor systems so that a scientist can interactively explore and analyze the data?

Data Visualization

Data visualization is the attempt to display mined information in new ways. For instance, a map was once a flat (2-D) piece of paper/parchment. As time went on, the map was overlaid onto a sphere, and we had our first globe. Data visualization hopes to take those concepts into the twenty-first century.

From a BI perspective, data visualization (called *information visualization* in this context) uses the computer to convert data into picture form. The most basic visualization is that of turning transaction data and summary information into charts and graphs. Visualization is used in computer-aided design (CAD) to render screen images into 3-D models that can be viewed from all angles and can also be animated.

OLAP (online analytical processing) places data into a cube structure that can be rotated by the user, which is particularly suited for financial summaries, as shown in Figure 2.5.

OLAP takes a snapshot of a relational database and restructures it into dimensional data. An OLAP structure created from the operational data is called an OLAP cube. The cube is created from a star schema of tables. At the center is the fact table, which lists the core facts that make up the query. Numerous dimension tables are linked to the fact tables. These tables indicate how the aggregations of relational data can be analyzed. The number of possible aggregations is determined by every possible manner in which the original data can be hierarchically linked.

For example, a set of customers can be grouped by city, by district, or by country; so with 50 cities, 8 districts, and 2 countries, there are three hierarchical levels with 60 members. These customers can be considered in relation to products; if there are 250 products with 20 categories, three families and three departments then there are 276 product members. With just these two dimensions, there are 16,560 possible aggregations. As the data considered increases, the number of aggregations can quickly total tens of millions or more.

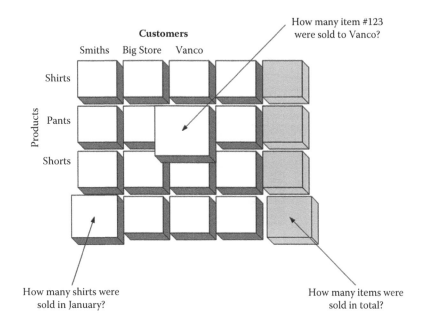

FIGURE 2.5
OLAP display information in the form of a cube so that analysts can visualize the information.

Oracle's Essbase is a multidimensional online analytical processing (OLAP) server, designed to help business users forecast likely business performance levels and deliver what-if analyses for varying conditions.

Data is categorized in Essbase in the form of dimensions. Examples of dimensions could be a time period or a product or a customer. Thus, a query might be to compare actual sales for a product in a specified state during the month of March 2014 with the corresponding budgeted value for that month. There are often relationships between members of a dimension, and these relationships are represented by a hierarchy. A hierarchy enables mathematical calculations to be executed against the data. For example, all the sales for individual states can be aggregated to create a value for the entire United States. Essbase allows multiple hierarchies to be displayed along with the dimensions in the outline, which can be seen on the left in Figure 2.6.

Big Data

Oracle has positioned their BI platform, Exalytics In-Memory Machine, and Endeca Information Discovery software to ride the crest of the big

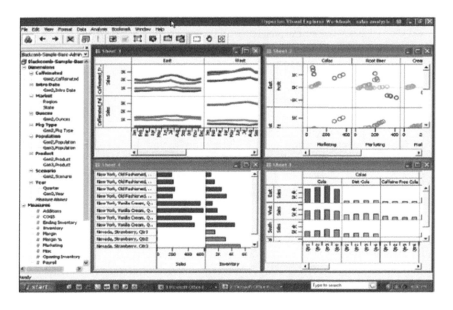

FIGURE 2.6
Oracle Essbase.

data trend. The Oracle Big Data Appliance consists of hardware and software from Oracle Corporation designed to integrate enterprise data, both structured and unstructured. It includes the Oracle Exadata Database Machine and the Oracle Exalytics Business Intelligence Machine (Oracle Exalogic), used for obtaining, consolidating, and loading unstructured data into the Oracle Database. The product also includes an open-source distribution of Apache Hadoop, Oracle NoSQL Database, Oracle Data Integrator with Application Adapter for Hadoop, Oracle Loader for Hadoop, an open-source distribution of R, Oracle Linux, and Oracle Java Hotspot Virtual Machine.

Oracle describes their "big data" product suite as follows:

- **Oracle NoSQL Database** is a distributed, scalable, key-value database based on Oracle's Berkeley DB Java Edition High Availability storage engine. It is reputed to have predictable levels of throughput and latency and requires minimal administrative interaction. NoSQL database is available in both open-source and commercial versions.
- **Apache Hadoop** is a framework that allows for the dispersed processing of large data sets across groups of computers using a simple programming model.

- **Oracle Data Integrator with Application Adapter for Hadoop**
- **Oracle Loader for Hadoop (OLH)** enables users to use Hadoop MapReduce processing to create enhanced data sets for efficient loading and analysis in the Oracle Database. The difference between this loader and others is that it generates Oracle internal formats to load data faster and use less database system resources.
- **Oracle R Enterprise** tool is the combining of the open-source distribution of R, a programming language and software environment for statistical computing and publication-quality graphics with the Oracle Database. Oracle R Enterprise uses the approach that the models will run in-database and process large data sets, using the Oracle Database and Exadata.
- **Oracle Linux** is an enterprise-class Linux distribution supported by Oracle.
- **Oracle Java Hotspot Virtual Machine** is a core component of the Java SE platform. It implements the Java Virtual Machine Specification, and is delivered as a shared library in the Java Runtime Environment.

A simplistic view is an organization would use the Oracle Big Data Appliance (Hadoop and NSQL) to capture the data, then use Big Data Connectors to a data warehouse where they can use Oracle Enterprise R or any other data-mining techniques to analyze the data further.

A visualization created by IBM of Wikipedia edits can be seen in Figure 2.7. At multiple terabytes in size, the text and images of Wikipedia are a classic example of big data.

There are some subtle differences between big data and BI:

- BI uses descriptive statistics with data with high information density to measure things, detect trends, etc.
- Big data uses inductive statistics and concepts from nonlinear system identification to infer laws (regressions, nonlinear relationships, and causal effects) from large data sets to reveal relationships and dependencies and to perform predictions of outcomes and behaviors. Most industries are now using big data software and hardware for various purposes, most interestingly scientists searching for extraterrestrial life.

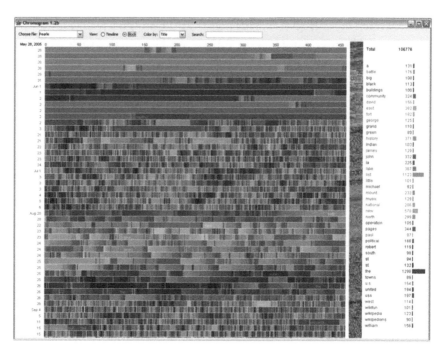

FIGURE 2.7
A visualization of Wikipedia edits, created by IBM. (*Source*: Wikimedia Commons.)

SUMMARY

Oracle Business Intelligence Foundation Suite (OBIEE+ and Essbase) is a complete, open, and architecturally unified business intelligence system for the enterprise that delivers abilities for reporting, ad hoc query and analysis, online analytical processing (OLAP), dashboards, and score-cards. All enterprise data sources as well as metrics, calculations, definitions, and hierarchies are managed in a Common Enterprise Information Model, providing users with accurate and consistent insight, regardless of where the information is consumed. Users can access and interact with information in multiple ways, including web-based interactive dashboards, collaboration workspaces, search bars, enterprise resource planning (ERP) and customer relationship management (CRM) applications, mobile devices, and Microsoft Office applications.

Sometimes OBIEE is used interchangeably with Oracle Business Intelligence Applications (OBIA), which is a prebuilt BI and data-ware-housing system built on the OBIEE technology stack. However, OBIEE is the platform, whereas OBIA is an application that uses the platform. The OBIEE+ integrates the components of the tool set to include a service-oriented architecture, data access services, an analytic and calculation infrastructure, metadata management services, a semantic business model, a security model and user preferences, and administration tools.

REFERENCES

Brunson, D. 2005. Top 10 trends in business intelligence and data warehousing for 2005 revisited. *BeyeNETWORK.* http://www.b-eye-network.com/print/969 (accessed March 15, 2014).

Conference Board. 1988. Calculating competitor action: Combustion Engineering's strategy. *Management Briefing: Marketing* October–November.

Hruby, F. M. 1989. Missing piece analysis targets the competitor's weakness. *Marketing News* 23 (1): 10.

Meyer, H. E. 1987. *Real-world intelligence.* New York: Grove and Weidenfeld.

Parsaye, K., M. Chignell, S. Khoshafian, and H. Wong. 1989. *Intelligent databases: Object-oriented, deductive hypermedia technologies.* Hoboken, NJ: Wiley.

3

Oracle Enterprise Performance Management

As mentioned in Chapter 2, Oracle lumps together several disparate application areas into what they have designated as Oracle Business Analytics, as shown in Figure 3.1. With Business Intelligence (BI) and Analytic apps already discussed, we will focus on performance management in Chapter 3.

Oracle offers a wide variety of enterprise performance management tools, residing both on in-house servers as well as on the cloud, as shown in Figure 3.2. The goal of these offerings is to help organizations of all sizes thrive by enabling them to discover new ways to strategize, plan, optimize business operations, and capture new market opportunities.

Oracle's Strategy Management enables senior management to develop realistic strategic plans, define a methodology-based strategy, align objectives with execution, monitor progress, and then communicate this information across the entire enterprise. They provide a flexible approach to strategic financial modeling and the development of KPI (key performance indicator) dashboards and scorecards, as shown in Figure 3.3.

The various tools in this category permit the organization to perform strategic financial planning, i.e., integrate long-term planning, treasury strategies, and corporate development analysis with the entire enterprise planning process. Most importantly, and something we will focus on later on in this chapter, it helps to leverage leading performance management frameworks to improve organizational alignment, including key performance indicators, historical trend analytics, and user-driven workflows, as shown in Figure 3.4.

As can be expected, this suite of tools integrates seamlessly with Oracle Essbase and other Oracle BI solutions in portal-style dashboards with scorecard and analytic content along with comprehensive multicontent search.

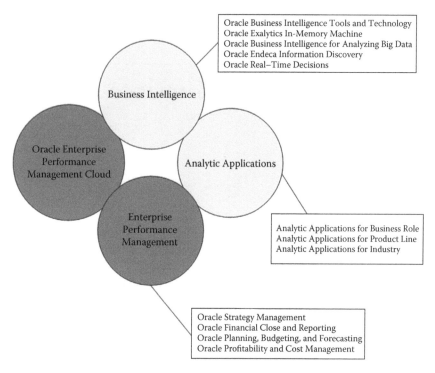

FIGURE 3.1
Oracle Business Analytics.

As you might have noticed, Figure 3.2 has quite a few products with the word *Hyperion* in its name. Hyperion Solutions Corporation was an enterprise performance management software company, located in Santa Clara, California, that was acquired by Oracle Corporation in 2007. Many of its products were targeted at the BI and business performance management markets, and as of 2013 are still actively developed and sold by Oracle as Oracle Hyperion products.

Hyperion software products include:

- Essbase
- Hyperion Intelligence and SQR Production Reporting (products acquired in 2003 takeover of Brio Technology)
- Hyperion Enterprise
- Hyperion Planning
- Hyperion Strategic Finance
- Hyperion Performance Scorecard
- Hyperion Business Modeling
- Hyperion Financial Management

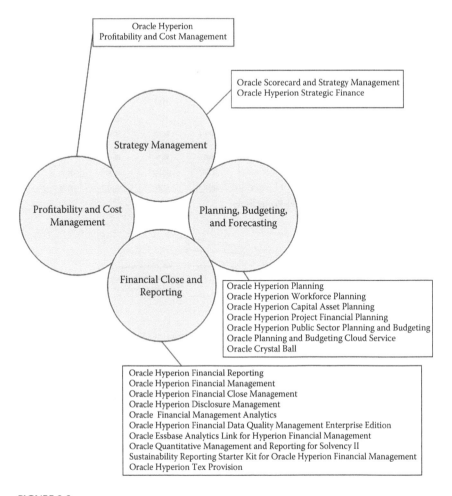

FIGURE 3.2

Oracle Enterprise Performance Management tool suites.

- Hyperion Master Data Management
- Hyperion Financial Reporting
- Hyperion Web Analysis
- Hyperion SmartView
- Hyperion EPM Workspace
- Hyperion System 9 BI+ (a combination of Interactive Reporting, SQR, Web Analysis, Financial Reporting, EPM Workspace, and SmartView)
- Hyperion Financial Data Quality Management (also referred to as FDM)

Table 3.1 presents the many tools offered within the Oracle Enterprise Performance Management (in-house server and cloud) in a tabular format.

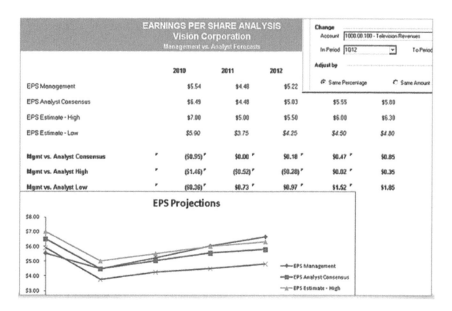

FIGURE 3.3

Oracle Strategy Management dashboards and scorecards.

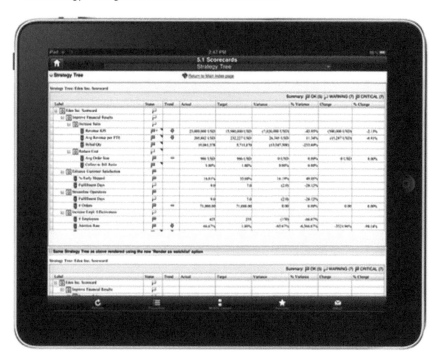

FIGURE 3.4

Oracle strategic scorecard.

TABLE 3.1

Oracle Enterprise Performance Management Suite of Tools

Product	Purpose	Features
Oracle Hyperion Strategic Finance	Oracle Hyperion Strategic Finance is a feature-rich financial forecasting and modeling solution with on-the-fly scenario analysis and modeling capabilities. It helps users quickly model and evaluate financial scenarios, and offers out-of-the-box treasury capabilities for sophisticated debt and capital structure management. Oracle Hyperion Strategic Finance integrates closely with Oracle Hyperion Planning to provide a complete integrated closed-loop planning process.	Integrate financial modeling for strategic planning, treasury, and corporate development Model with integrity and transparency to minimize risk and create efficiencies Minimize model-building efforts with packaged financial modeling tools Deploy and implement quickly with minimal IT support
Oracle Hyperion Planning	Oracle Hyperion Planning is a centralized, Microsoft Office and web-based planning, budgeting, and forecasting solution that integrates financial and operational planning processes and improves business predictability.	Reduce planning, budgeting, and forecasting cycles by weeks or months Improve accuracy of plans and forecasts Shrink the user learning curve by leveraging Microsoft Office products as an interface into Oracle Hyperion Planning Eliminate time lag between when plans are updated and reports are refreshed Reduce cost of ownership through superior application deployment, management tools, and packaged data integration Choose to deploy in the Oracle Cloud, on premises, in a third-party data center, or any combination concurrently Lay the foundation for the transition to Enterprise Business Planning *(Continued)*

TABLE 3.1 (CONTINUED)

Oracle Enterprise Performance Management Suite of Tools

Product	Purpose	Features
Oracle Hyperion Workforce Planning	Oracle Hyperion Workforce Planning makes headcount, salary, and compensation planning fast and efficient across the enterprise. Designed with prebuilt functionality and best practices, it simplifies the planning of workforce and workforce-related expenses such as bonuses, fringe benefits, overtime, and merit increases. Link your workforce expense plans into Oracle Hyperion Planning to quickly understand the business impact of workforce decisions on overall expense plans.	Simplify implementation and reduce maintenance requirements with prebuilt functionality Address all workforce planning requirements with a fully flexible and open architecture Achieve greater accuracy, predictability, and accountability Assess real-time impact of salaries and associated workforce expenses Reduce workforce planning cycle time
Oracle Hyperion Capital Asset Planning	Oracle Hyperion Capital Asset Planning automates the planning of capital assets and capital asset-related expenses such as depreciation, maintenance, and insurance. Prebuilt functionality and best practices enable you to easily plan for all capital expenses. Immediately assess the impact of capital expenses on overall expenses and financial statements by directly linking it to Oracle Hyperion Planning.	Simplify implementation processes and reduce maintenance requirements Manage all capital expenses easily Assess the immediate impact of capital asset decisions on financial statements Achieve greater accuracy, predictability, and accountability by involving operational-level planners Eliminate manual steps by using a comprehensive planning solution Gain security over data, calculations, and global settings

Oracle Hyperion Project Financial Planning	Oracle Hyperion Project Financial Planning supports financial planning and forecasting for contract, capital, and indirect projects. It bridges the gap between project-management systems and financial-planning processes, supporting the complete project financial management life cycle.	Reduce reliance on spreadsheets and manual processes Improve insights into the financial impacts of proposed initiatives Accurately report and forecast financial results of ongoing projects Integrate project planning with financial planning and forecasting Leverage investments in existing project management and ERP systems Improve management of initiatives and projects
Oracle Hyperion Public Sector Planning and Budgeting	Designed for public sector, health care, and higher education, Oracle Hyperion Public Sector Planning and Budgeting integrates and simplifies budget preparation, review and approval, publication, and disclosure processes. Prebuilt position and employee planning models, and sophisticated planning and budgeting process management features, help you project and evaluate the impact of employee compensation and benefits on overall budgets while supporting accurate forecasting.	Reduce cost of implementation and ownership by leveraging packaged public sector functionality Create workforce plans and position budgets quickly and accurately Reduce budgeting and planning cycles by weeks or months Improve forecast accuracy by gaining visibility into plan/actuals/budget/forecast comparisons Reduce the time spent on creating reports and budget books
Oracle Planning and Budgeting Cloud Service	Oracle's market-leading Enterprise Performance Management applications enable organizations to achieve business excellence by integrating strategy, planning, and execution across management and operational systems. Oracle's performance management applications are a modular suite of integrated applications that integrate with both Oracle and non-Oracle transactional systems and feature common web and Microsoft Office interfaces, common reporting tools, mobile information delivery, and common administration.	Subscription-based (SaaS) deployment model with easy, predictable pricing EPM Services initially includes enterprise planning, budgeting, and forecasting with extensive collaboration and reporting functionality Engineered for the global enterprise with market-leading functionality but through SaaS deployment, affordable and manageable for all organizations Highly scalable—capable of supporting thousands of users and deep, complex planning models Modern user experience optimized for today's collaborative, hyperconnected, and mobile workforce

(Continued)

TABLE 3.1 (CONTINUED)

Oracle Enterprise Performance Management Suite of Tools

Product	Purpose	Features
Oracle Financial Services Balance Sheet Planning	Oracle Financial Services Balance Sheet Planning is designed to help financial services institutions budget for a full balance sheet and the associated profit and loss statement. Banks have a number of very unique needs when looking ahead. They must be sensitive to economic conditions, and create plans that not only forecast future performance, but also the forward risks they are assuming. Most importantly, they require tools that accurately forecast net interest margin. By accurately modeling the detailed and complex events on a bank's balance sheet, for both the current book of business and forecasted new volumes, Oracle Financial Services Balance Sheet Planning enables the delivery of accurate margin forecast and comprehensive, meaningful budgets.	Eliminate disparate and incompatible systems with an end-to-end solution that encompasses all aspects of the planning process, including profit planning, budgeting and forecasting, strategy formulation, human resource planning, and capital expenditure budgeting Maximize productivity and performance by effectively communicating corporate goals to every level of each business unit; promptly initiate feedback up the line while achieving unit-by-unit budgeting and forecasting that is consistent with bank-wide reality Establish the vital connection between the budget and day-to-day performance of your financial organization; develop financial targets and measures of accountability with a single, consistent framework Maintain consistency with your asset/liability management process by modeling financial instrument behavior with standard or custom cash flows; incorporate matched maturity transfer pricing into forecasts; evaluate an unlimited number of what-if scenarios; consolidate both results and assumptions to higher levels Access user-friendly dashboards, interactive analytics, and richly formatted financial reports through a single interface; key banking metrics, ratios, and KPIs come predelivered

Oracle Crystal Ball	Oracle Crystal Ball is the leading spreadsheet-based application for predictive modeling, forecasting, simulation, and optimization. It gives you unparalleled insight into the critical factors affecting risk. With Crystal Ball, you can make the right tactical decisions to reach your objectives and gain a competitive edge under even the most uncertain market conditions.	Builds on existing Monte Carlo and predictive modeling tools Provides advanced optimization and calculation capabilities Combines Oracle Crystal Ball and Oracle Crystal Ball Decision Optimizer
Oracle Hyperion Financial Reporting	One of the greatest challenges confronting businesses today is the need to increase operational efficiencies when creating and distributing GAAP-compliant financial reports and other highly formatted management reports. Oracle Hyperion Financial Reporting Enterprise Edition meets this challenge head-on by generating highly formatted, book-quality financial and management reports.	Generally accepted accounting principles-compliant automatic report production Multiple output options (including Web, PDF, and Microsoft Office and mobile devices) Flexible scheduling and scalable architecture Alerts Report annotations Multiformat publishing Financial close process integration Disclosure management process integration

(Continued)

TABLE 3.1 (CONTINUED)

Oracle Enterprise Performance Management Suite of Tools

Product	Purpose	Features
Oracle Hyperion Financial Management	Oracle Hyperion Financial Management is a financial consolidation and reporting application built with advanced web technology. It provides financial managers the ability to rapidly consolidate and report financial results, meet global regulatory requirements, reduce the cost of compliance, and deliver confidence in the numbers.	Reduce consolidation, close, and reporting cycles by days or weeks Deliver timely results, internally and externally Reduce compliance costs and deliver a single version of the truth to improve internal and external transparency Maintain a regulatory filing to general ledger audit trail, providing confidence in the financial results Conduct in-depth analysis of key performance and operational metrics easily Realize new benefits quickly with packaged regulatory reporting functionality
Oracle Hyperion Financial Close Management	Oracle Hyperion Financial Close Management is built for centralized, web-based management of period-end close activities across the extended financial close cycle. The first application of its kind, it helps manage all financial close cycle tasks, including ledger and sub-ledger close, data loading and mapping, financial consolidation, account reconciliation, tax/treasury and internal and external reporting processes—any task associated with the extended financial close.	Reduce consolidation, close, and reporting cycles by days or weeks and deliver timely results internally and externally Reduce compliance costs and deliver a single version of the truth to improve internal and external transparency Maintain a regulatory filing to general ledger audit trail, providing confidence in the financial results Conduct in-depth analysis of key performance and operational metrics easily Realize new benefits quickly with packaged regulatory reporting functionality

Oracle Hyperion Disclosure Management	Oracle Hyperion Disclosure Management enables you to effectively manage the creation of XBRL and inline XBRL (iXBRL) documents. Featuring deep integration with existing Oracle Hyperion financial reporting tools, it is the easiest and most straightforward approach to XBRL reporting. It is the first application of its kind—a full featured XBRL solution that leverages best-in-class Oracle Hyperion reporting technologies.	Microsoft Office–based approach for ease of use Full XBRL and iXBRL generation capabilities with SEC, HMRC, IFRS, and XBRL formula validation support Centralized XBRL metadata storage and direct mapping to Oracle Hyperion data sources XBRL tag override and suppression capabilities Rollover report management to streamline the tagging process XBRL taxonomy management and extension development Oracle WebCenter Content Management for best-in-class document routing, approval, security, and revision control
Oracle Financial Management Analytics	Oracle Financial Management Analytics provides finance executives with visibility and insight into the status of their financial close process and financial results. Leveraging Oracle's world-class Hyperion Financial Close Suite applications and Business Intelligence technology, it provides a unified solution that can be very quickly deployed with out-of-the-box integration as well as packaged dashboards and analytics.	Reduce complexity and TCO with prebuilt dashboards and analytics Prebuilt integration with Hyperion applications using best-in-class BI technology Reporting on real-time data Common security and single sign-on with other Oracle EPM Applications Provides unified insights into financial results and close process status Leverages existing investments in Oracle EPM and BI technology Fast deployment

(Continued)

TABLE 3.1 (CONTINUED)

Oracle Enterprise Performance Management Suite of Tools

Product	Purpose	Features
Oracle Hyperion Financial Data Quality Management Enterprise Edition	Finance organizations need to enhance the quality of internal controls and reporting processes. To meet these goals, you need a source-to-report view of financial data. Oracle Hyperion Financial Data Quality Management, Enterprise Edition allows business analysts to develop standardized financial data management processes and validate data from any source system—all while reducing costs and complexity.	Achieve timeliness of data with a web-guided workflow process and standardized repeatable financial processes Increase your confidence in the numbers with complete data validations and error checking Simplify financial data collection and transformation through automated data mapping and loading Use prepackaged system adapters Deliver process transparency through audit trails, detailed audit reviews, and reconciliations Lower the cost of compliance with support for multi-GAAP reporting Support for standard file formats as well as direct connections to transaction systems
Oracle Essbase Analytics Link for Hyperion Financial Management	Oracle Essbase Analytics Link for Hyperion Financial Management enables the delivery of effective management and financial analytic reporting to a broad user community. It integrates and merges multiple operational data sources into a single data model, providing detailed information for analytical measurements (KPIs) and the application of advanced analytics. Merging financial and operational information in a single platform makes it easy to deliver a comprehensive management reporting environment.	Automatically create an Oracle Essbase application based on an Oracle Hyperion Financial Management application Reduce IT costs through fast implementation and limited hardware requirements Improve business insight through real-time management reporting with real-time or on-demand data synchronization Enhance reporting scalability with no impact on Oracle Hyperion Financial Management Deliver continuous, always available management reporting Improve efficiencies through real-time data synchronization Reduce risk by ensuring data integrity and reliability between source and target systems

Oracle Quantitative Management and Reporting for Solvency II	Solvency II imposes a whole new risk- and capital-management regime on European insurers and prescribes a number of statutory reporting requirements. One of the most important of these is to produce the Quantitative Reporting Template (QRT)—successor to the Quantitative Impact Study 5 (QIS5) process.	Reduce barriers to sharing financial data more broadly Automate the quantitative quarterly and annual reporting requirements, as prescribed by EIOPA for both solo and group entities, eliminating errors and inconsistencies in the QRT process Include key solvency calculations such as SCR, MCR, and others Consolidate data from multiple systems, subsidiaries, and lines of business (including currency translation, intercompany elimination, and equity elimination) Full QRT template and reporting support based on EIOPA requirements Predefined QRT task integration activities for Oracle Hyperion Financial Close Management Prebuilt QRT asset validations and reporting leveraging Oracle Hyperion Financial Data Quality Management A complete Oracle Hyperion Financial Management application including metadata, rules, forms, and reports
Sustainability Reporting Starter Kit for Oracle Hyperion Financial Management	Sustainability Reporting Starter Kit for Oracle Hyperion Financial Management enables financial and sustainability reporting within a single system.	Consolidate corporate sustainability reporting data using GRI-based chart of accounts Improve communication and relations with key stakeholders such as customers, employees, partners, and suppliers Improve brand image through increased sustainability reporting transparency

(Continued)

TABLE 3.1 (CONTINUED)

Oracle Enterprise Performance Management Suite of Tools

Product	Purpose	Features
		Improve compliance with sustainability reporting requirements with full audit trails, process management, and security
		Deploy quickly with prebuilt web data-entry forms, conversion rules, and report templates
		Leverage existing investments in Oracle Hyperion Financial Management
Hyperion Tax Provision	Oracle Hyperion Tax Provision is a first-of-its-kind tax-reporting solution that integrates directly with the broader financial reporting process. With access to financial data and processes, you can build an effective, efficient, and transparent tax function.	Easily address US GAAP, IFRS, and statutory tax reporting with a powerful tax provision calculation engine
		Improve efficiency through integration of data/metadata with source ERP and financial consolidation systems
		Leverage a tax-provision solution based on the same technology trusted by thousands of corporate finance organizations
		Automate tax differences with an easy-to-use wizard
		Leverage a comprehensive suite of tax reports for the consolidated tax provision, including tax disclosure
		Leverage powerful reporting tools to support analysis and tax planning in a single solution
		Integrate the tax compliance process
		Handle unique data collection and calculation requirements with configurable supplemental schedules

Oracle Hyperion Profitability and Cost Management	Oracle Hyperion Profitability and Cost Management provides actionable insights into costs and profitability. It drives business performance by discovering the drivers of cost and profitability and empowering users to improve resource alignment. Oracle Hyperion Profitability and Cost Management leverages Oracle Essbase for faster, more powerful, multidimensional analysis.	Perform faster, easier, multidimensional analysis and scenario modeling leveraging Oracle Essbase, the industry's leading online analytical processing (OLAP) server
		Leverage a user-driven profitability modeling environment to create, maintain, and deploy cost and profitability models
		Deliver a flexible allocation platform that supports multiple cost and revenue modeling approaches, and can be combined to form custom allocation methodologies
		Drive rapid application design and iterations with a flexible business rules engine and intuitive interface, making it easy to build dimensions, hierarchies, metrics, and scenarios
		Reveal a new level of transparency into cost and revenue allocations via traceability maps that can verify that business rules have been correctly applied

Scanning through these offerings, the reader will get a sense that a thorough background in performance management is a requirement. The remainder of this chapter will cover the required bases in this arena.

PERFORMANCE MANAGEMENT FUNDAMENTALS

There are certain attributes that set apart successful performance measurement and management systems, including:

1. *A conceptual framework is needed for the performance measurement and management system.* Every organization, regardless of type, needs a clear and cohesive performance measurement framework that is understood by all levels of the organization and that supports objectives and the collection of results.
2. *Effective internal and external communications are the keys to successful performance measurement.* Effective communication with employees, process owners, customers, and stakeholders is vital to the successful development and deployment of performance measurement and management systems.
3. *Accountability for results must be clearly assigned and well understood.* High-performance organizations clearly identify what it takes to determine success and make sure that all managers and employees understand what they are responsible for in achieving organizational goals.
4. *Performance measurement systems must provide intelligence for decision makers, not just compile data.* Performance measures should be limited to those that relate to strategic organizational goals and objectives, and that provide timely, relevant, and concise information for use by decision makers—at all levels—to assess progress toward achieving predetermined goals. These measures should produce information on the efficiency with which resources are transformed into goods and services, on how well results compare to a program's intended purpose, and on the effectiveness of organizational activities and operations in terms of their specific contribution to program objectives.
5. *Compensation, rewards, and recognition should be linked to performance measurements.* Performance evaluations and rewards need to be tied to specific measures of success by linking financial and

nonfinancial incentives directly to performance. Such a linkage sends a clear and unambiguous message to the organization as to what's important.

6. *Performance measurement systems should be positive, not punitive.* The most successful performance measurement systems are not *gotcha* systems, but *learning* systems that help the organization identify what works—and what does not—so as to continue with and improve on what is working and repair or replace what is not working. Performance measurement systems run in tandem with modern workforce management systems. Many of these systems were indeed quite punitive, leading companies to understaff offices and stores, resulting in unhappy employees and customers. More modern workforce management software utilizes the theories set forth by MIT's Zeynep Ton (http://sloan.mit.edu/faculty/detail.php?in_spseqno=51388), who champions the complete opposite—that increasing the workforce, and paying and treating them better, will often yield happier customers, more engaged workers, and larger corporate profits.

7. *Results and progress toward program commitments should be openly shared with employees, customers, and stakeholders.* Performance measurement system information should be openly and widely shared with an organization's employees, customers, stakeholders, vendors, and suppliers.

Mention FedEx to anybody, and the first image conjured up is overnight delivery. Most laypersons are quite astounded by FedEx's ability to pick up a package today and deliver it by 10:30 a.m. tomorrow—even if the package needs to travel thousands of miles. They are even more impressed when they find that all FedEx planes converge on a single airport in Tennessee in the middle of the night to redistribute their loads and fly to all points north, south, east, and west. Few realize how large a role technology plays in this somewhat superlogistical feat.

It all started when Fred Smith, founder and still head of the multibillion dollar company, conceived the idea for express delivery as a project in business school. No matter how or why he came up with the idea, Smith was certainly a visionary by understanding, as far back as the '70s, the importance of technology and quality measurements to the success of his scheme.

Smith's reliance on technology to build the foundation of his business is more uncommon than first meets the eye. Smith was not, and is not, a technologist. However, he does understand the relationship between information technology (IT) and business strategy, and actively embarks on policies and projects that reflect this commitment. Understanding and commitment are quite different.

Smith represents this most perfect combination. He's a businessman with a keen interest in what technology can do for FedEx. In fact, his interest is so pronounced that it is said he personally reads voluminous computer trades to keep abreast of any new development that can be leveraged by his company.

FedEx tech centers, which process millions of transactions on a daily basis, are scattered across the globe. The main unit is located at FedEx's headquarters in Memphis, with others in Los Angeles and London. The most interesting unit is located in Colorado Springs. When FedEx began their quest for the perfect system, they had trouble hiring the technical people that they needed. Many balked at making a move to Memphis, mostly famous as the home of Elvis Presley.

In the '70s, in an effort to attract the best talent, FedEx did a study to identify the most ideal place to relocate. This turned out to be Colorado Springs. To this day, FedEx senior management believe that this concession to staff morale was instrumental in their ultimate success.

Even in the early 1970s, Smith clearly understood the growing closeness of the world, now called *globalization* but referred to by Smith then as *worldwide logistics*. At the same time, FedEx's strategic planning sessions were questioning where the business was going and what the competitors were doing. They asked themselves what FedEx would have to do to stay competitive over the next decade or two. You'll note some interesting things about FedEx that set it apart from most of their contemporaries in the 1970s (and even today). First, it understood the coming push toward globalization, even though this trend is one that they didn't begin to pursue until at least 10 years later. Second, FedEx's planning horizon stretched out over two decades, which was more Japanese-oriented than its American counterparts, which usually worked in a window of two to five years. Third, technology was considered the key part of their strategy. Finally, and most importantly, it understood the concept of *balanced scorecard* long before the term was invented by Kaplan and Norton in the early 1990s. FedEx has certainly been a strategy-focused organization since the day Smith conceived it three decades ago.

There are three key measurement indicators applied at FedEx. The goal of the *customer-value creation indicator* is to define a customer value that is not currently being met and then use technology to meet that need. Ultimately, the information produced by the system should be stored for analysis.

A hallmark of the FedEx way is that they really listen to their customers and create services and technology to fulfill core needs. When FedEx initiated its overnight services in the 1970s, customers told them that their peace of mind required access to more extensive delivery information. The original tracking service was a tedious, manual process requiring numerous telephone calls to a centralized customer service center. In turn, customer service had to call one or more of 1,400 operations centers to track a single package. This process was expensive and slow. Today's rapid online tracking capability was conceived to meet this need.

FedEx's tracking system also fulfills another important company requirement. The system automatically calculates whether the commitment to the customer was met by comparing ship date and service type to delivery date and time. This information forms the basis of FedEx's money-back guarantee, and appears on customer invoices. More importantly, this statistic is aggregated for the internal index on service quality that Threat (1999) describes as the focal point for corporate improvement activities.

Another key FedEx indicator is *performance support*. The goal here is to create appropriate tools that enable frontline employees to improve their personal performance using the information in FedEx's vast databases. Individual performance is then aggregated to location, geographic unit, and ultimately makes its way into the corporate-wide statistics. These stats are available on every desktop in the company.

An example of performance-support indicators, from the perspective of a courier, include:

1. Does the count of packages delivered equal the Enhanced Tracker's count of deliverables?
2. Does the count of revenue forms equal the Enhanced Tracker's count of shipments picked up?

As the courier is closing out his day's activities, he uses his handheld device, the Enhanced Tracker, to guide him through this series of performance measurements. During the day, the Tracker records activity information and timer per activity as the courier does his job. Information from the handheld Tracker gets ported to the corporate database with the aggregated historical information ultimately used for manpower tracking, or comparison of actual achievements to performance standards.

Perhaps the most important indicator is *business goal alignment*. This is used to align the incentives of employees and management with corporate and customer objectives.

These indicators, then, form the basis for FedEx's balanced scorecard. The FedEx corporate philosophy—called People, Service, Profit—guides all decisions.

Balanced Scorecard

The technique that many companies have selected is indeed the balanced scorecard, as shown in Figure 3.5. Heralded by the *Harvard Business Review* as one of the most significant management ideas of the past 75 years, balanced scorecard has been implemented in companies to both measure as well as manage the IT effort.

Robert S. Kaplan and David P. Norton developed the balanced-score-card approach in the early 1990s to compensate for their perceived short-comings of using only financial metrics to judge corporate performance. They recognized that in this New Economy, it was also necessary to value intangible assets. Because of this, they urged companies to measure such esoteric factors as quality and customer satisfaction. By the mid-1990s,

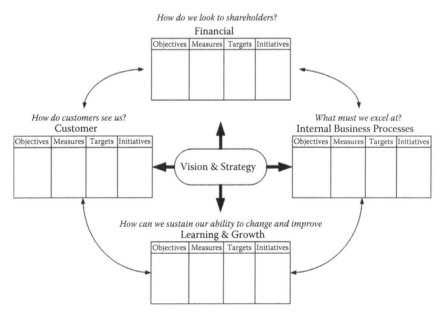

FIGURE 3.5
The balanced scorecard and its four perspectives.

balanced scorecard became the hallmark of a well-run company. Kaplan and Norton often compare their approach for managing a company to that of pilots viewing assorted instrument panels in an airplane cockpit—both have a need to monitor multiple aspects of their working environment.

In the scorecard scenario, a company organizes its business goals into discrete, all-encompassing perspectives: Financial, Customer, Internal Process, and Learning/Growth. The company then determines cause–effect relationships, e.g., satisfied customers buy more goods, which increases revenue. Next, the company lists measures for each goal, pinpoints targets, and identifies projects and other initiatives to help reach those targets.

Departments create scorecards tied to the company's targets, and employees and projects have scorecards tied to their department's targets. This cascading nature provides a line of sight between each individual, what they're working on, the unit they support, and how that impacts the strategy of the whole enterprise. A vast majority of organizations are now using a balanced-scorecard approach. General Electric, Home Depot, Wal-Mart, and Mobil are among the many well-publicized companies using this approach.

Kaplan and Norton (2001) both emphasize that the approach is more than just a way to identify and monitor metrics. It's also a way to manage change and increase a company's effectiveness, productivity, and competitive advantage. Essentially, as Kaplan and Norton put it, a company that uses the scorecard to identify and then realize strategic goals is a *strategy-focused organization*. Cigna is a good example of this. According to Norton, when Cigna started its balanced-scorecard process, the company had negative shareholder value. The parent company was trying to sell it but had no takers. Five years and a few balanced scorecards later, Cigna was sold for $3 billion.

For IT managers, the balanced scorecard is an invaluable tool that will finally permit IT to link to the business side of the organization using a cause-and-effect approach. Some have likened balanced scorecard to a new language, which enables IT and business line managers to think together about what IT can do to support business performance. A beneficial side effect of the use of the balanced scorecard is that, when all measures are reported, one can calculate the strength of relations between the various value drivers. For example, if the relation between high development costs and high profits levels is weak for a long time, it can be inferred that the developed software does not sufficiently contribute to results as expressed by the other (e.g., financial) performance measures.

So, how does a company adopt a successful scorecard approach? According to Kaplan (2001 pp. 72–78):

> Each organization we studied did it a different way, but you could see that, first, they all had strong leadership from the top. Second, they translated their strategy into a balanced scorecard. Third, they cascaded the high-level strategy down to the operating business units and the support departments. Fourth, they were able to make strategy everybody's everyday job, and to reinforce that by setting up personal goals and objectives and then linking variable compensation to the achievement of those target objectives. Finally, they integrated the balanced scorecard into the organization's processes, built it into the planning and budgeting process, and developed new reporting frameworks as well as a new structure for the management meeting.

The key, then, is to develop a scorecard that naturally builds in cause-and-effect relationships, includes sufficient performance drives and, finally, provides a linkage to appropriate financial measures. At the very lowest level, a discrete software system can be evaluated using balanced scorecard. The key, here, is the connectivity between the system and the objectives of the organization as a whole.

Developing Benchmarks

The central component of any scorecard is benchmarking. *Merriam Webster's* online dictionary definition of benchmark is: "A point of reference from which measurements may be made." It is something that serves as a standard by which others may be measured.

The purpose of benchmarking is to assist in the performance improvement process. Specifically, benchmarking can:

1. Identify opportunities
2. Set realistic but aggressive goals
3. Challenge internal paradigms on what is possible
4. Understand methods for improved processes
5. Uncover strengths within your organization
6. Learn from the leaders' experiences
7. Better prioritize and allocate resources

TABLE 3.2

Benchmarking vs. Not Benchmarking

	Without Benchmarking	**With Benchmarking**
Defining customer requirements	Based on history/gut feel Acting on perception	Based on market reality Acting on objective evaluation
Establishing effective goals	Lack external focus Reactive Lagging industry	Credible, customer-focused Proactive Industry leadership
Developing true measures of productivity	Pursuing pet projects Strengths and weaknesses not understood	Solving real problems Performance outputs known, based on best in class
Becoming competitive	Internally focused Evolutionary change Low commitment	Understand the competition Revolutionary ideas with proven performance High commitment
Industry practices	Not invented here Few solutions	Proactive search for change Many options Breakthroughs

Table 3.2 describes the ramifications of not using benchmarking (Kendall 1999):

Obviously, benchmarking is critical to your organization. However, benchmarking needs to be done with great care. There are actually times when you shouldn't benchmark:

1. You are targeting a process that is not critical to the organization.
2. You don't know what your customers require from your process.
3. Key stakeholders aren't involved in the benchmarking process.
4. Inadequate resources, including budgetary, have been committed.
5. You're benchmarking an organization rather than a process.
6. There is strong resistance to change.
7. You are expecting results instantaneously.

Most organizations use a four-phase model to implement benchmarking:

1. Plan
2. Collect
3. Analyze
4. Adapt

Plan

When planning a benchmarking effort, considerable thought should be given to who is on the benchmarking team. In some cases, team members will need to be trained in the different tools and techniques of the benchmarking process.

The creation of a benchmarking plan is similar to the creation of a project plan for a traditional systems development effort, with a few twists:

1. The scope of the benchmarking study needs to be established. All projects must have boundaries. In this case, you will need to determine which departmental units and/or processes will be studied.
2. A purpose statement should be developed. This should state the mission and goals of the plan.
3. If benchmarking partners (i.e., other companies in your peer grouping who agree to be part of your effort) are to be used, specific criteria for their involvement should be noted. In addition, a list of any benchmarking partners should be provided. Characteristics of benchmarking partners important to note include: policies and procedures, organizational structure, financials, locations, quality, productivity, competitive environment, products/services.
4. Define a data collection plan and determine how the data will be used, managed, and ultimately distributed.
5. Finally, your plan should discuss how implementation of any improvements resulting from the benchmarking effort will be accomplished.

Collect

The collection phase of a benchmarking effort is very similar to the requirements-elicitation phase of software engineering. The goal is to collect data and turn it into knowledge.

During the collection phase, the focus is on developing data collection instruments. The most widely used is the questionnaire, with follow-up telephone interviews and site visits. Other methods include interviewing, observation, participation, documentation, and research.

Analyze

Once the data has been collected, it should be analyzed. Hopefully, you've managed to secure the cooperation of one or more benchmarking partners so that your analysis will be comparative rather than introspective.

The goal of data analysis is to identify any gaps in performance. Once you find these, you will need to:

1. Identify the operational best practices and enables. In other words, what are your partners doing right that you're not? Then you need to find out exactly how they're doing it.
2. Formulate a strategy to close these gaps by identifying opportunities for improvement.
3. Develop an implementation plan for these improvements.

The analysis phase uses the outputs of the data collection phase, i.e., the questionnaires, interviews, observations, etc. It is during this phase that process mapping and the development of requisite process performance measurements is performed.

Process performance measurements should be:

1. Tied to customer expectations
2. Aligned with strategic objectives
3. Clearly reflective of the process and not influenced by other factors
4. Monitored over time

Stewart and Mohamed (2001) suggest a metric template that enables the organization to clearly define a measurement and then track its performance. Table 3.3 details a measurement description card format for a typical process metric, while Table 3.4 shows the reported results.

Adapt

Once the plan has been formulated and receives approval from management, it will be implemented in this phase. Traditional project management techniques should be used to control, monitor, and report on the project. It is also during this phase that the continuous improvement plan is developed. In this plan, new benchmarking opportunities should be identified and pursued.

TABLE 3.3

Measurement Description Card for Measure OP1-M1

Field	Description
Decision-making tier:	Project
Performance perspective (criteria):	Operational (OP)
Performance indicator (subcriteria):	Facilitate document transfer and handling (OP1)
Indicator objectives:	IT assists in the efficient transfer and handling of project documents. Project staff are proficient with the use of IT-based procedures
Performance measure:	OP1-M1
Measure weight:	50% of performance indicator
Measure description:	% of users proficient with IT-based procedures employed on the project
Performance metric:	%
Measure outcome:	Ensure that 90% of users are proficient with IT-based project procedures
Performance baseline:	50% of users are proficient with IT-based project procedures
Performance targets:	**Degree of Performance Improvement** / **Degree of Improvement Proficiency**
	None — 50%
	Minor — 60%
	Moderate — 70%
	High — 80%
	Excellent — 90%
Data source:	Staff will undertake computer proficiency exams
Responsible component:	Project IT manager
Data collector:	Project IT professional
Collection frequency:	Tests will be taken monthly
Report frequency:	Measure is reported on completion of project
Remarks:	None

TABLE 3.4

Monthly Measurement Results for Measure OP1-M1

Month	1	2	3	4	5	6	7
Result (%)	52	55	57	60	61	65	68

The American Productivity and Quality Center (APQC 2001) recommends the Benchmarking Maturity Matrix for a periodic review of the benchmarking initiative. They stress that to understand an initiative's current state and find opportunities for improvement, the organization must examine its approach, focus, culture, and results. The Benchmarking Maturity Matrix demonstrates the maturity of 11 key elements derived from five core focus areas: management culture (e.g., expectation of long-term improvement), benchmarking focal point (e.g., team), processes (e.g., coaching), tools (e.g., Intranet), and results.

The 11 key elements within the matrix are:

1. Knowledge management/sharing
2. Benchmarking
3. Focal point
4. Benchmarking process
5. Improvement enablers
6. Capture storage
7. Sharing dissemination
8. Incentives
9. Analysis
10. Documentation
11. Financial impact

The five maturity levels are, from lowest to highest:

1. Internal financial focus, with short-term focus that reacts to problems
2. Recognition of the need for external focus to learn
3. Setting of goals for knowledge sharing
4. Adoption of learning as a corporate value
5. Recognition of knowledge sharing as a corporate value

Based on these two grids, a series of questions are asked and a score calculated:

Key 1: Which of the following descriptions best defines your organization's orientation toward learning?

Key 2: Which of the following descriptions best defines your organization's orientation toward improving?

Key 3: How are benchmarking activities and/or inquiries handled within your organization?

Key 4: Which of the following best describes the benchmarking process in your organization?

Key 5: Which of the following best describes the improvement enablers in place in your organization?

Key 6: Which of the following best describes your organization's approach for capturing and storing best-practices information?

Key 7: Which of the following best describes your organization's approach for sharing and disseminating best-practices information?

Key 8: Which of the following best describes your organization's approach for encouraging the sharing of best-practices information?

Key 9: Which of the following best describes the level of analysis done by your organization to identify actionable best practices?

Key 10: How are business impacts that result from benchmarking projects documented within your organization?

Key 11: How would you describe the financial impact resulting from benchmarking projects?

The maturity matrix is a good tool for internal assessment and as well as for comparisons to other companies.

Analytic Hierarchy Process

The analytic hierarchy process (AHP) is a framework of logic and problem solving that organizes data into a hierarchy of forces that influence decision results. It is a simple, adaptable methodology in use by government as well as many commercial organizations. One of the chief selling points of this methodology is that it is participative, promotes consensus, and does not require the use of any specialized skill sets.

AHP is based on a series of paired comparisons in which users provide judgments about the relative dominance of the two items. Dominance can be expressed in terms of preference, quality, importance, or any other criterion.

Four sets of metrics need to be determined, one for each of the four balanced-scorecard perspectives. Metric selection usually begins by gathering participants together for a brainstorming session. The number of participants selected should be large enough to ensure that a sufficient number of metrics are initially identified.

TABLE 3.5

AHP Pairwise Comparisons

Comparative Importance	Definition	Explanation
1	Equally important	Two decision elements (e.g., indicators) equally influence the parent decision element.
3	Moderately more important	One decision element is moderately more influential than the other.
5	Strongly more important	One decision element has stronger influence than the other.
7	Very strongly more important	One decision element has significantly more influence over the other.
9	Extremely more important	The difference between influences of the two decision elements is extremely significant.
2, 4, 6, 8	Intermediate judgment values	Judgment values between equally, moderately, strongly, very strongly, and extremely.
Reciprocals		If v is the judgment value when i is compared to j, then $1/v$ is the judgment value when j is compared to i.

Participants, moderated by a facilitator, brainstorm a set of possible metrics, and the most important metrics are selected. Using a written survey, each participant is asked to compare all possible pairs of metrics in each of the four errors as to their relative importance using a scale as shown in Table 3.5.

From the survey responses, the facilitator computes the decision model for each participant that reflects the relative importance of each metric. Each participant is then supplied with the decision models of all other participants and asked to rethink their original metric choices. The group meets again to determine the final set of metrics for the scorecard. The beauty of this process is that it makes readily apparent any inconsistencies in making paired comparisons and prevents metrics from being discarded prematurely.

Clinton, Weber, and Hassell (2002) provide an example of using AHP to determine how to weight the relative importance of the categories and metrics. A group of participants meet to compare the relative importance of the four balanced-scorecard categories in the first level of the AHP hierarchy. They may want to consider the current product life-cycle stage when doing their comparisons. For example, while in the product intro-duction stage, formalizing business processes may be of considerable rela-tive importance. When dealing with a mature or declining product, on the other hand, the desire to minimize variable cost per unit may dictate that the financial category be of greater importance than the other three scorecard categories. They provide the following illustrative sample sur-vey question that might deal with this issue:

> Survey question: In measuring success in pursuing a differentiation strategy, for each pair, indicate which of the two balanced-scorecard categories is more important. If you believe that the categories being compared are equally important in the scorecard process, you should mark a 1. Otherwise, mark the box with the number that corresponds to the intensity on the side that you consider more important described in Table 3.5.

Consider the following examples:

Customer	9	8	7	6	5	4	3	2	1	2	3	4	5	6	7	8	9	Financial
					X													

In this example, the customer category is judged to be strongly more important than the financial category.

Customer	9	8	7	6	5	4	3	2	1	2	3	4	5	6	7	8	9	Internal
									X									Business
																		Processes

In this example, the customer category is judged to be equally important to the internal business processes category.

The values can then be entered into AHP software, such as Expert Choice (http://www.expertchoice.com/), which will compute local and global weights, with each set of weights always equal to 1. Local weights are the relative importance of each metric within a category, and global weights are the relative importance of each metric to the overall goal. The software will show the relative importance of all metrics and scorecard categories. For example, in our prior example, the results might have been:

Category	Relative Weight
Innovation and learning	0.32
Internal business processes	0.25
Customer	0.21
Financial	0.22
Total	1.00

The results show that the participants believe that the most important category is innovation and learning. If, within the innovation and learning category, it is determined that the market-share metric is the most important, with a local weight of 0.40, then we can calculate the global outcome by multiplying the local decision weights from level 1 (categories) by the local decision weight for level 2 (metrics).

Clinton, Webber, and Hassell (2002) provide a good example of the final calculation, as shown in Table 3.6.

These results indicate that the least important metric is revenue from the customer category and the most important metric is market share, from the innovation and learning category.

A study by Utunen (2003) determined the following priorities for financially based technology measurement: commercialization of technology, customer focus, technology stock, technology protection, technology acquisition, competence of personnel, and management focus. For each indicator, one or more metrics were established, as shown in Table 3.7.

Phillips (1997) contends that ROI (return on investment) calculation is not complete until the results are converted to dollars. This includes looking at combinations of hard and soft data. Hard data include such traditional measures as output, time, quality, and costs. In general, hard data are readily available and relatively easy to calculate. Soft data are hard to calculate and include morale, turnover rate, absenteeism, loyalty, conflicts avoided, new skills learned, new ideas, successful completion of projects, etc., as shown in Table 3.8.

TABLE 3.6

AHP Global Outcome Worksheet

Balanced Scorecard

Strategic Objective: Success in pursuing a differentiation strategy

Categories and Metrics	Level One × Level Two	Global Outcome
Innovation and Learning		
Market share	(.40 × .32)	.128
# of new products	(.35 × .32)	.112
Revenue from new products	(.25 × .32)	.080
Total: Innovation and Learning		.320
Internal Business Processes		
# of product units produced	(.33 × .25)	.08333
Minimizing variable cost per unit	(.33 × .25)	.08333
# of on-time deliveries	(.33 × .25)	.08333
Total: Internal Business Processes		.250
Customer		
Revenue	(.20 × .21)	.042
Market share	(.38 × .21)	.080
QFD (Quality Function Deployment) score	(.42 × .21)	.088
Total: Customer		.210
Financial		
Cash value-added	(.28 × .22)	.062
Residual income	(.32 × .22)	.070
Cash flow ROI	(.40 × .22)	.088
Total: Financial		.220
Sum of the Global Weights		1.00

SUMMARY

The Oracle Enterprise Performance Management tool suites run the gamut: from strategy management to planning budgeting to forecasting, from financial reporting to profitability to cost management. While these Oracle tools provide powerful functionality, the organization still needs to develop the expertise to develop the methodologies and metrics that provide the framework surrounding these tool sets.

TABLE 3.7

Financially Based Financial Measurement

Indicator	Metric
Commercialization of Technology	
Product cost savings	Total product costs
	Costs of acquired technology
	Total R&D expenditure
Sales of new or improved product	Total sales
Customer Focus	
Customer complaints	Number of technical problems solved
Customer intelligence expenditure	Amount of R&D invested in researching R&D ideas among customers
Number of projects aligned with customers	Number of technology projects performed in cooperation with customer
Technology Stock	
Stock amount	Number of technologies owned or possessed by the company
Stock competitiveness	Qualitative evaluation of technology compared to competitors
Technology Protection	
Patenting activity	Number of new patents generated by R&D
Patentable innovations	Number of patentable innovations that are not yet patented
Importance of patents	Number of patents protecting the core of a specific technology or business area
Technology Acquisition	
Allocation of R&D	Total R&D expenditure
R&D efficiency and effectiveness	Amount of R&D expenditure spent on successfully commercialized technologies
New projects	Total number of new R&D projects started
Merger and acquisition	Amount of new technology acquired through mergers and acquisitions
Personnel Competence	
Personnel competence level	Qualitative evaluation of the level of personnel competencies
Management Focus	
Top management focus	Total number of working hours
Top management reaction time	Top management reaction time to strategic or environmental changes
R&D link to strategy	% of R&D directly in line with business strategy

TABLE 3.8

Hard Data vs. Soft Data

Hard Data	
Output	Units produced
	Items assembled or sold
	Forms processed
	Tasks completed
Quality	Scrap
	Waste
	Rework
	Product defects or rejects
Time	Equipment downtime
	Employee overtime
	Time to complete projects
	Training time
Cost	Overhead
	Variable costs
	Accident costs
	Sales expenses
Soft Data	
Work habits	Employee absenteeism
	Tardiness
	Visits to nurse
	Safety-rule violations
Work climate	Employee grievances
	Employee turnover
	Discrimination charges
	Job satisfaction
Attitudes	Employee loyalty
	Employee self-confidence
	Employee's perception of job responsibility
	Perceived changes in performance
New skills	Decisions made
	Problems solved
	Conflicts avoided
	Frequency of use of new skills
Development and advancement	Number of promotions or pay increases
	Number of training programs attended
	Requests for transfer
	Performance-appraisal ratings

(Continued)

TABLE 3.8 (CONTINUED)

Hard Data vs. Soft Data

Initiative	Implementation of new ideas
	Successful completion of projects
	Number of employee suggestions

REFERENCES

APQC. 2001. *A new approach to assessing benchmarking progress.* Houston, TX: American Productivity and Quality Center.

Clinton, B., S. A Webber, and J. M. Hassell. 2002. Implementing the balanced scorecard using the analytic hierarchy process. *Management Accounting Quarterly* 3 (3): 1–11.

Kaplan, R. S., and D. P. Norton. 2001. On balance (Interview). *CFO, Magazine for Senior Financial Executives* 17 (2): 72–78.

Kendall, K. (1999, November). Benchmarking from A to Z. http://www.orau.gov/pbm/presentation/kendall.pdf. Accessed May 23, 2014.

Merriam-Webster online dictionary. (n.d.) http://www.merriam-webster.com/dictionary/benchmark. Accessed May 23, 2014.

Phillips, J. J. 1997. *Handbook of training evaluation and measurement methods.* 3rd ed. Houston, TX: Gulf Publishing.

Stewart, R. A., and S. Mohamed. 2001. Utilizing the balanced scorecard for IT/IS performance evaluation in construction. *Journal of Construction Innovation* 1 (3): 147–63.

Threat, H. 1999. Measurement is free. *Strategy & Leadership* 27 (3): 16–19.

Utunen, P. 2003. Identify, measure, visualize your technology assets. *Research Technology Management* 46 (3): 31–39.

4

Social Business

The world is a changed place. The collaborative web has caught our collective imagination, and there is no turning back, particularly in the business world. Some have taken to calling this use of collaborative technologies in business Enterprise 2 (E 2.0). Wikipedia may have been the first company to popularize the phenomenon of user-generated knowledge, but this encyclopedia is just the tip of the iceberg. Companies far and wide are wiki-izing. Nokia hosts a number of wikis, some of which are used internally to coordinate technology research. Dresdner Kleinwort, an investment bank, operates the largest corporate wiki. About 50 percent of Dresdner staff use this wiki to make sure that all team members are on the same project-management page.

E 2.0 is more than just wikis, of course. It constitutes the entirety of social networking applications, which includes blogs, discussion boards, workspaces, and anything else that is sharable or even combinable (e.g., mash-ups). IBM uses E 2.0 for everything from collaborative document production to internal project collaboration. Nokia uses it for all-purpose teamware. A whole host of companies use it for knowledge management. Honeywell was one of the first to use E 2.0 to perform knowledge discovery, research, and sharing across miles, regardless of whether users even know each other. It would appear, then, that E 2.0 using social networking technologies has wide applicability to all things business—including software engineering.

Given this hot trend, it's reasonable to expect Oracle to have quickly jumped on the social networking bandwagon, so much so that one of the five major categories listed under CIO Solutions in Oracle's C-Central CIO forum is "social business."

ORACLE'S OFFERINGS

Oracle Social Cloud is a cloud service that helps manage and scale the relationship with customers on social media channels. Oracle has integrated the best-in-class social relationship management (SRM) components—social listening, social engagement, social publishing, social content and apps, and social analytics—into one unified cloud service to give you the most complete SRM solution on the market.

Oracle Social Relationship Management (SRM) enables organizations to socially enable the way they do business, but without the cost and complexity of social silos. It's a strategy to be more engaging and responsive at scale, listen, and respond at the speed of social media with a consistency and transparency customers will value. Oracle SRM includes three social solutions:

- Oracle Social Engagement & Monitoring Cloud Service, as seen in Figure 4.1
- Oracle Social Marketing Cloud Service, as seen in Figure 4.2
- Oracle Social Network, as seen in Figure 4.3

FIGURE 4.1
Oracle's Social Engagement & Monitoring Cloud Service.

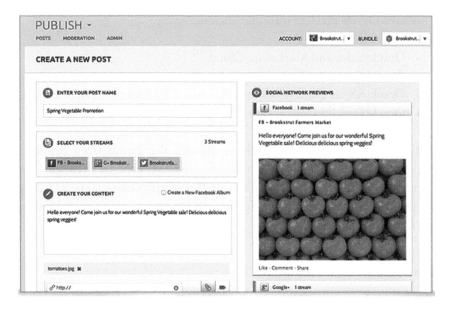

FIGURE 4.2
Oracle Social Marketing Cloud Service.

FIGURE 4.3
Oracle Social Network.

Related Oracle product offerings include:

- Oracle Sales and Marketing Cloud
- Oracle Customer Experience Solutions
- Oracle Social CRM (Customer Resource Management) Applications
- Oracle Beehive Collaboration Server

As you can see, Oracle's applications run the gamut from support-ing customers to supporting employees, and everyone in between. The remainder of this chapter will delve into the specifics of social networking for the IT enterprise so that the reader can get a sense of the usefulness of the Oracle social product set.

Why Social Networking

The Standish Group's (2009) 2009 CHAOS Report painted a dismal pic-ture of the state of software development. The Boston, Massachusetts, research firm surveyed 400 organizations and found a decrease in IT proj-ect success rates and an increase in IT project failure rates in a short two-year period. Only 32 percent of surveyed projects were considered to be successful (i.e., on time, on budget, and with the required functionality and feature set). Nearly one-quarter of IT projects were considered to be failures. The rest were considered to be challenged, a euphemism for late, over budget, or implemented without the full set of promised functions and features. It should be noted, however, that there are many who dispute the CHAOS report findings. What is undisputed is that a large number of projects do fail.

Quite a few things can, and do, go wrong with software development efforts. McConnell (1996) neatly categorized these, as shown in Table 4.1.

Hyvari (2006) provides an updated view of this, as shown in Table 4.2. The names may have changed, but the problems remain more or less the same.

As you can see, there are a host of reasons that can negatively impact project success, but high up on the list is the human element. Ewusi-Mensah (2003) states simply that "the software development enterprise is a purely abstract and conceptual endeavor, and as such places an undue burden on all the stakeholders to collaborate with a clear vision of what is to be achieved, how it is to be achieved, and at what cost and in what time frame."

TABLE 4.1

Classic Software Development Project Problems

People-Related Mistakes	Process-Related Mistakes	Product-Related Mistakes	Technology-Related Mistakes
Undermined motivation	Overly optimistic schedules	Requirements gold-plating, i.e., too many product features	Silver-bullet syndrome, i.e., latching onto a new technology or methodology that is unproven for the particular project
Weak personnel	Insufficient risk management	Feature creep	Overestimated savings from tools or methods
Uncontrolled problem employees	Contractor failure	Developer gold-plating, i.e., developers using technology just for the sake of using that technology	Switching tools in the middle of a project
Heroics	Insufficient planning	Push-me, pull-me negotiation, i.e., constantly changing schedule	Lack of automated source code control
Adding people to a late project	Abandonment of planning under pressure	Research-oriented development, i.e., stretching the limits of technology	
Noisy crowded offices	Wasted time before project actually starts, i.e., the approval and budgeting process		
Friction between developers and customers	Shortchanged upstream activities, e.g., requirements analysis, etc.		
Unrealistic expectations	Inadequate design		

(Continued)

TABLE 4.1 (CONTINUED)

Classic Software Development Project Problems

People-Related Mistakes	Process-Related Mistakes	Product-Related Mistakes	Technology-Related Mistakes
Lack of effective project sponsorship	Shortchanged quality assurance		
Lack of stakeholder buy-in	Insufficient management controls		
Lack of user input	Premature or too frequent convergence, i.e., release of the product too early		
Politics over substance	Omitting necessary tasks from estimates		
Wishful thinking	Planning to catch up later		
	Code-like-hell programming		

Having the right people on a project team is certainly key to the success of a project. In a large pharmaceutical company, the lead designer walked off a very important project. Obviously, that set the team back quite a bit, as no one else had enough experience to do what he did. Even if the IT staff says put, there is still the possibility that a people issue will negatively affect the project. For example, a change in senior management might mean that the project you are working on gets canned or moved to a lower priority. A project manager working for AOL Time Warner had just started an important new project when a new president was installed. He did what all new presidents do: He engaged in a little housecleaning. Projects got swept away, and so did some people. When the dust settled, the project manager personally had a whole new set of priorities—as well as a bunch of new team members to work with.

As you can see, today's dynamically changing and very volatile business landscape can play havoc with software engineering efforts, and going global adds an entirely new dimension to the mix. What we need, then, is a whole new paradigm of software development that places the human aspect at the center of software engineering.

TABLE 4.2

Success/Failure Factors

Factors related to project	Size and value
	Having a clear boundary
	Urgency
	Uniqueness of project activities
	Density of the project network (in dependencies between activities)
	Project life cycle
	End-user commitment
	Adequate funds/resources
	Realistic schedule
	Clear goals/objectives
Factors related to the project manager/ leadership	Ability to delegate authority
	Ability to trade off
	Ability to coordinate
	Perception of his or her role and responsibilities
	Effective leadership
	Effective conflict resolution
	Having relevant past experience
	Management of changes
	Contract management
	Situational management
	Competence
	Commitment
	Trust
	Other communication
Factors related to project team members	Technical background
	Communication
	Troubleshooting
	Effective monitoring and feedback
	Commitment
Factors related to the organization	Steering committee
	Clear organization/job descriptions
	Top management's support
	Project organization structure
	Functional manager's support
	Project champion

(Continued)

TABLE 4.2 (CONTINUED)

Success/Failure Factors

Factors related to the environment	Competitors
	Political environment
	Economic environment
	Social environment
	Technological environment
	Nature
	Client
	Subcontractors

Social Network

Social networking is a hot topic. More than 30 billion pieces of content are shared on Facebook each month, and Nielsen researchers say that consumers spend more than five and a half hours on social networking sites per day. So I am sure it doesn't come as a surprise that social networking has made its way into the workplace.

An AT&T study—based on 2,500 people surveyed in five countries—found that the use of social networking tools has led to an increase in efficiency. According to the study, 65 percent said that use of these tools has made them or their colleagues more efficient, and 46 percent insisted that it has sparked ideas and creativity.

Deep Nishar is vice president of products and user experience at LinkedIn. He is in charge of a group of data researchers that look at everything from data center behavior to trends in search and mobile communications. His eclectic staff have experience in such fields as brain surgery, computer science, meteorology, and poetry. According to Nishar, machine-based systems like Google can't keep up with organizing the data they are capturing. Interesting and important problems will be solved by looking at social networks (Hardy 2010).

In 1976, sci-fi author Richard Dawkins coined the term *meme*, which is an idea that moves from person to person and onward. With social networking tools, staff can check to see what ideas people are discussing within the organization. Some refer to these sorts of tools as a "meme broadcast tool." Where marketers have Twitter to communicate with people outside the company, businesspeople can use services such as Yammer (yammer.com) to share information within the company, discuss relevant

TABLE 4.3

Non-Oracle Social Networking Tools

Social networking	Facebook, Friendster, LinkedIn, Ning, Orkut, Bebo, KickApps, OpenACircle, Vyew, MOLI, Fast Pitch!, Plaxo, Yammer, EurekaStreams.org, ResearchGate.net
Publishing	TypePad, Blogger, Wikipedia, Joomla
Photo sharing	Radar.net, SmugMug, Zooomr, Flickr, Picasa, Photobucket, Twitxr
Audio	iTunes, Rhapsody, Podbean, Podcast.com
Video	YouTube, Metacafe, Hulu, Viddler, Google Video, Brightcove
Microblogging	Twitxr, Twitter, Plurk
Livecasting	SHOUTcast, BlogTalkRadio, TalkShoe, Justin.tv, Live365
Virtual worlds	There, Second Life, ViOS, ActiveWorlds
Productivity	ReadNotify, Zoho, Zoomerang, Google Docs
Aggregators	Digg, Yelp, iGoogle, Reddit, FriendFeed, TiddlyWiki
Rich site summary (RSS)	RSS 2.0, Atom, PingShot
Search	Technorati, Redlasso, EveryZing, MetaTube, IceRocket, Google Search
Mobile	Jumbuck, CallWave, airG, Jott, Brightkite
Interpersonal	WebEx, iChat, Meebo, Acrobat Connect, GoToMeeting, Skype

issues, and more. Table 4.3 lists some of the more popular non-Oracle social networking tools in use today.

Bleeding-edge organizations have already figured out how to make social networking profitable for them. SolarWinds, a network management company, built a 25,000-member user community of network administrators who help each other with various problems. This allows the company to support a customer base of over 88,000 companies with just two customer support people. Cisco created employee councils and shifted decision making down to these levels. The councils are supported using collaborative technologies. Indeed, Cisco's CEO, John Chambers, insists that most of the progress made during the past two years has been because of collaborative and social technologies.

When IBM transformed an intranet into a social network, it provided each of IBM's 365,000 employees a voice and identity that not only helped increase effectiveness and productivity, but also helped workers transcend national cultures (Hathi 2009). IBM uses a variety of social networking tools. Long before Facebook graduated from college, IBM had created its own internal social networking site, which they called BluePages. It lists basic information about an employee as well as views of that individual, such as who reports to them, who they report to, what organization they're in, and what communities they are a part of. Employees can self-edit their listing and even add a picture. Clicking on an entry allows someone to send an instant message.

Perhaps the most powerful feature is social tagging, also called *social bookmarking*. Clicking on an employee not only brings up identifying data; it also brings up the employees tags, i.e., blog feeds, RSS feeds, communities joined, social networks joined, recent forum entries, and wiki participation. Ethan McCarty, who is former editor-in-chief of IBM's intranet. describes it like this: "If you think of the phases of the intranet and even Internet communication: First it's about access to information; then it's about transacting with it—like e-business; and now it's more about people" (personal communication).

The people we refer to as the millennials come into the workplace with cell phone glued to their ear and fingers firmly glued to the keyboard, tweeting and facebooking to friends and strangers alike. These folks think that talking on the phone is passé. Some don't even have landlines. These folks are communicating via social networks, instant message, Twitter, and smartphones. However, it's their older brothers and sisters, Gen-Y, who are working to convince tech management of the value of these new technologies, according to a Forrester Research (2009) survey of 2000 IT professionals. This isn't all that surprising, as a 2010 Pew report found that Internet users from all age groups increased their usage between 2008 and 2010. While 83 percent of those between 18 and 33 use social networking, those 45 and older more than doubled their participation (Pew Research 2010).

Software Engineering Social Network

The development of software systems has long been considered to be a social activity. Software is developed using a team model, where the work is divided among the various team members. Various studies suggest that on large projects, developers spend between 70 and 85 percent of their time working with others. Thus, it is important that the team collaborate effectively to achieve their common goal.

One of the earliest to research the psychology and sociology behind software engineering was Gerald M. Weinberg in 1971. His seminal book on the psychology of programming was radical for its time. Aside from coining the term *egoless programming*, Weinberg's book on microorganizational behavior delves deeply into the concept of programming as a social construct and offers advice on dealing with team dysfunction.

Much of the literature on the psychology of software development concludes that most of the social problems inherent in development teams can be solved by a critical analysis of the dynamics between the people involved. This sort of introspective analysis (Ahmadi et al. 2008) can be helpful to explain:

- Why certain people are excluded from group decision making
- Why there is always someone who resists the decisions of project leadership
- Why certain kinds of people should never be grouped together to avoid group fragmentation
- Why groups often divide themselves into subgroups
- What is the difference between the real chain of command and the formal one

Fischer (2005) has discussed the individual and social perspectives that affect design. Individuals often worry about whether they are interested enough to be effective during the span of the project. They also worry about whether they have something relevant to add to the group, and whether they can express it clearly so that others might understand them. On the other hand, the group is interested in hearing from a wide variety of stakeholders. Thus, the group is concerned with encouraging individuals to contribute; preventing voices from being lost because there might be too much information; avoiding illegitimate voices; preventing getting stuck in groupthink; and eliminating sources of exclusion.

There have been a multitude of studies that discuss the vast amount of time spent on communication and collaboration with others. Because software development is an inherently collaborative and distributed process, with teams of developers working intra- and inter-organizationally and globally, it is logical that these teams would require tool sets designed specifically for the collaborative, distributed nature of their work.

Collaborative Applications

The computer-supported cooperative work (CSCW) community has been studying computer-assisted collaboration for quite some time. CSCW researchers have developed a number of frameworks that seek to categorize

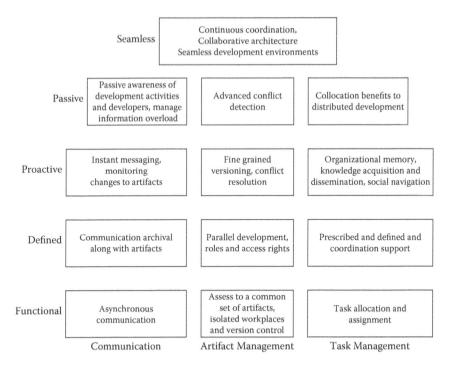

FIGURE 4.4
Collaboration framework.

the requirements of the collaborative tool set. Whitehead (2007) categorizes collaborative software engineering tools into four groups:

1. Model-based collaboration tools
2. Process support tools
3. Collaboration awareness tools
4. Collaboration infrastructure tools

On the other hand, Sarma's (2005) framework classifies tools based on the required effort to collaborate effectively. The framework consists of five layers and three strands, as shown in Figure 4.4. The layers are tools, and strands are critical needs that permeate all aspects of collaboration.

As is often the case, many of the tool sets discussed in the literature are experimental and are not offered for use by those in the field. In 2003, Booch and Brown surveyed both experimental and commercial collaborative development environments (CDE). Their definition of a CDE is a virtual space wherein all the stakeholders of a project, even if distributed

TABLE 4.4

Recommended Feature Set of a Collaborative Development Environment

Coordination

Centralized information management
Configuration control of shared artifacts
Online event notification
Calendaring and scheduling
Project resource profiling
Project dashboards and metrics (Booch and Brown 2003)
Searching and indexing of resources and artifacts
Electronic document routing and workflow
Virtual agents and scripting of tasks (Booch and Brown 2003)

Collaboration

Threaded discussion forums (Booch and Brown 2003)
Virtual meeting rooms
Instant messaging
Online voting and polling
Shared whiteboards
Cobrowsing of documents
Multiple levels of information visibility (Booch and Brown 2003)

Community Building

Personalization capabilities (Booch and Brown 2003)
Established protocols and rituals
Well-defined scope and leadership
Self-publication of content (Booch and Brown 2003)
Self-administration of projects (Booch and Brown 2003)

by time or distance, may negotiate, brainstorm, discuss, share knowledge, and generally labor together to carry out some task, most often to create an executable deliverable and its supporting artifacts. As encompassing as this definition is, it does not necessarily distinguish between private and public (open source) projects and does not necessarily stress software development. Still, it is worthwhile discussing their analysis of the requirements of a CDE. They base their requirements list on Fournier (2001). Table 4.4 shows the combined Fournier, Booch, and Brown requirements list for this sort of environment.

Web 2 technologies have finally given a voice to the collaborative needs of software developers and can lend a hand toward building the type of CDE envisioned in Table 4.2. Web 2 engages users to build collective intelligence. One of the most common examples of this is the wiki (*wiki* is a variant of the Hawaiian word *wicki*, which means "fast"), which we've already mentioned. Wikis are so ubiquitous that the learning curve is minimal. Quite a few organizations use this tool, specifically IT departments within the organization. There have been many articles written about the use of wikis to promote software reuse within the IT department. However, wikis have their own attendant problems. Insufficient usage and decaying structure all need to be addressed if wikis are to be successful.

The advent of social networking services such as LinkedIn, Facebook, and MySpace demonstrate the power of social networks and give us an insight into what could be created specifically for software engineering. Of course, the current state-of-the-art social networks do have some limitations, as Ahmadi et al. (2008) thoroughly describe. Chief among the described problems is the lack of interoperability between social networks. The authors suggest leveraging Semantic Web technologies, one of which is ontologies, as a solution to this problem. An ontology is a formal representation of specific domain concepts and the relationship between those concepts. Several ontologies (e.g., www.foaf-project.org, www.sioc-project.org, www.semanticdesktop.org/ontologies/2007/11/01/pimo/#) have become universally recognized, and it is expected that at some point, interoperability between social networks using ontologies will become standard practice.

Indeed, some researchers have advocated for the use of ontologies to improve the discipline of software development itself. Mavetera and Kroeze (2010) have discussed the different ontology types that can be used. A domain ontology describes the knowledge to be captured during the requirements-analysis phase of software development. Method ontologies capture the knowledge and reasoning needed to perform a task. Status ontologies, either dynamic or static, capture the status characteristics of a system. Intentional ontologies model the softer aspects of living things, such as beliefs, desires, and intentions. Process ontologies capture the three aspects of enterprise knowledge, i.e., enterprise knowledge (i.e., processes, organizational structure, IT structure, products, customers), domain knowledge (i.e., terms, concepts, relationships), and information knowledge (i.e., document types and structures). Finally, social ontologies describe the organizational structure and the interdependencies that exist among the social actors (i.e., analyst, tester, developer, etc.).

SOCIAL NETWORKING TOOLS AT WORK

Most professionals, when they think of social networking at all, think in terms of Facebook and Twitter. CIOs see great potential in these sorts of tools. IBM conducted a worldwide study of 2,500 CIOs in late 2010. The collective take on collaboration tools is that they need to be institutionalized to meet the demands of the business. Surprisingly, as we will shortly show, and with some effort, all of these can be "institutionalized" in some way to enhance the productivity of the software engineering discipline.

Given the popularity of these sorts of tools among consumers, it is no wonder that a variety of these sorts of tools have cropped up that are geared to specific business disciplines.

Tools That Provide Networking Capabilities

Salesforce.com, the enterprise CRM giant, has begun to involve itself in providing social networking capabilities. Its new Chatter service is available on Salesforce's real-time collaboration cloud. Users establish profiles and generate status updates. These might be questions, bits of information and/or knowledge, or relevant hyperlinks. All of this is then aggregated and broadcast to coworkers in their personal network. Essentially, a running feed of comments and updates flow to those within that particular network.

Employees can also follow colleagues from around the company, not just in their own personal network, enabling cross-organizational knowledge sharing. Toward that end, Chatter also provides a profile database that users can tap into to find needed skills for a particular project. Chatter is accessible via desktop or mobile.

Like Salesforce.com, more than a handful of well-known software companies have developed collaboration tools, all for a fee. Oracle's Beehive provides a spate of tools such as instant messaging, e-mail, calendaring, and team workspaces, as shown in Figure 4.5.

There are also a wide variety of free tools available that can be adapted for our purposes, although keep in mind that much of what I am going to talk about can be done via the Beehive or other Oracle social platforms. LinkedIn has been widely used to provide networking capabilities for businesspeople. A relevant feature is LinkedIn groups. A group can be created for any purpose, with permission granted to join. Thus, project teams can make use of the already developed facilities LinkedIn provides. For

FIGURE 4.5
Oracle Beehive.

example, the Tata Research Development and Design Centre (TRDDC) was established in 1981 as a division of Tata Consultancy Services Limited, India's largest IT consulting organization. TRDDC is today one of India's largest research and development centers in software engineering and process engineering. TRDDC has its own membership-by-request LinkedIn group. It is quite easy to create a members-only LinkedIn group for a particular project, and limited to specific members, as shown in Figure 4.6.

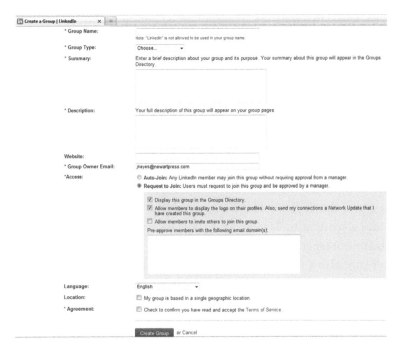

FIGURE 4.6
Creating a members-only LinkedIn group.

FIGURE 4.7
Project artifact wiki.

Of all of the collaborative tools available, particularly those that are free, wikis are the most prominently used. Zoho.com provides a wide range of tools, including chat, discussions, meetings, and projects, but it is their wiki tool that I'd like to focus on here.

In Figure 4.7, I created a wiki to store all of the artifacts for a typical project, i.e., project plan, systems requirement specifications, analysis docs, etc. In Figure 4.8 you can see the project plan artifact in wiki form. Note the ability to post comments.

Twitter, a social networking app made famous by celebrities who tweet hourly updates on what they are doing (e.g., eating lunch, shopping, etc.), has morphed into an enterprise social networking application called Yammer. With the ability to integrate with tools such as SharePoint, Yammer provides a suite of tools, including enterprise microblogging, communities, company directory, direct messaging, groups, and knowledge base. SunGard employees actually started using Yammer on their own to share information about projects they were working on. Now it has been rolled out to all 20,000+ employees.

Much of what Yammer offers is free with their basic service. Their Gold subscription provides such corporate niceties as security controls, admin controls, broadcast messages, enhanced support, SharePoint integration,

FIGURE 4.8
Project plan wiki, demonstrating ability to include comments.

keyword monitoring, and virtual firewall solution. Yammer can be used by the software development team to interactively discuss any aspect of a project, as shown in Figure 4.9.

Project groups have used wikis in some creative ways: writing up personal research and making comments on others' research; asking questions; posting links to resources that might be of interest to others in the group; adding details for upcoming events and meetings; letting each other know what they're up to; adding comments to other team members' information and pages; and recording minutes of meetings in real time. One might think that the use of these sorts of ad hoc discussion tools would degenerate into chaos. In truth, this rarely happens—even in a social network of anonymous users. Anderson (2006) talks about the fact that the largest wiki of all, Wikipedia, is fairly resistant to vandalism and ideological battles. He stresses that the reason for this is "the emergent behavior of a Pro-Am [professional and amateur] swarm of self-appointed curators." This group of curators has self-organized what Anderson terms the most comprehensive encyclopedia in history—creating order from chaos. Welcome to the world of peer production.

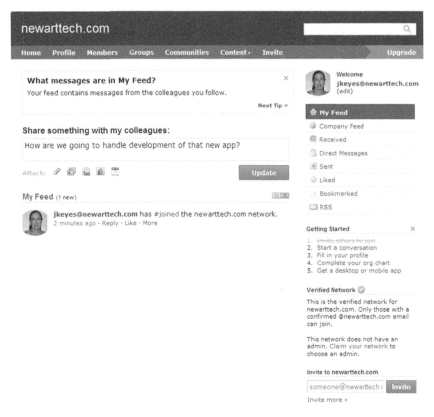

FIGURE 4.9
Dynamic discussion using Yammer.

Wikis in Action

Intellipedia (www.intelink.gov/wiki) is an online system for collaborative data sharing used by the US intelligence community (IC). It consists of three different wikis with different levels of classification: Top Secret, Secret, and Sensitive but Unclassified. They are used by individuals with appropriate clearances from the 16 agencies of the IC and other national security–related organizations, including Combatant Commands and other federal departments. The wikis are not open to the public. Intellipedia includes information on the regions, people, and issues of interest to the communities using its host networks. Intellipedia uses MediaWiki, the same software used by the Wikipedia free-content encyclopedia project. Officials say that the project will change the culture of the US intelligence community, widely blamed for failing to connect the dots before the September 11 attacks.

The Secret version predominantly serves Department of Defense and Department of State personnel, many of whom do not use the Top Secret network on a day-to-day basis. Users on unclassified networks can access Intellipedia from remote terminals outside their workspaces via a VPN (virtual private network), in addition to their normal workstations. Open Source Intelligence (OSINT) users share information on the unclassified network.

Intellipedia was created to share information on some of the most difficult subjects facing US intelligence and to bring cutting-edge technology into its ever-more-youthful workforce. It also allows information to be assembled and reviewed by a wide variety of sources and agencies to address concerns that pre–Iraq War intelligence did not, including robust dissenting opinions on Iraq's alleged weapons programs.

Some view Intellipedia as risky because it allows more information to be viewed and shared, but most agree that it is worth the risk. The project was greeted initially with a lot of resistance because it runs counter to past practice, which sought to limit the pooling of information. Some encouragement has been necessary to spur contributions from the traditional intelligence community. However, the system appeals to the new generation of intelligence analysts because this is how they like to work, and it's a new way of thinking.

The wiki provides so much flexibility that several offices throughout the community are using it to maintain and transfer knowledge on daily operations and events. Anyone with access to read it has permission to create and edit articles. Because Intellipedia is intended to be a platform for harmonizing the various points of view of the agencies and analysts of the intelligence community, Intellipedia does not enforce a neutral point-of-view policy. Instead, viewpoints are attributed to the agencies, offices, and individuals participating, with the hope that a consensus view will emerge.

During 2006–2007, Intellipedia editors awarded shovels to users to reward exemplary wiki "gardening" and to encourage others in the community to contribute. A template with a picture of the limited-edition shovel (actually a trowel) was created to place on user pages for Intellipedians to show their gardening status. The handle bears the imprint: "I dig Intellipedia! It's wiki wiki, Baby." The shovels have since been replaced with a mug bearing the tag line "Intellipedia: It's what we know." Different agencies have experimented with other ways of encouraging participation. For example, at the CIA, managers have held contests for best pages, with prizes such as free dinners.

Chris Rasmussen, knowledge management officer at the Defense Department's National Geospatial-Intelligence Agency (NGA), argues that gimmicks like the Intellipedia shovel, posters, and handbills encourage people to use web 2.0 tools like Intellipedia and are effective low-tech solutions to promote their use. Also, Rasmussen argues that social software-based contributions should also be written in an employee's performance plan (Walker 2007).

Semantic Web

Tim Berners-Lee, who invented the World Wide Web as well as HTML, also came up with the idea of the *Semantic Web*, as shown in Figure 4.10. The Semantic Web is a synthesis of all corporate and external data—including results from data mining activities, hypermedia, knowledge systems, etc.—that use a common interface to make data easily accessible by all (e.g., suppliers, customers, employees).

The Semantic Web is sometimes called the *Defined Web* and is the ultimate repository of all content and knowledge on the web. It uses XML (extensible markup language, a formalized version of HTML) to tag information on intranets, extranets, and the Internet.

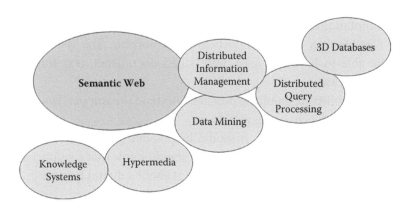

FIGURE 4.10
The Semantic Web.

Tim Berners-Lee et al. (2001) explained the Semantic Web as follows:

> At the doctor's office, Lucy instructed her Semantic Web agent through her handheld web browser. The agent promptly retrieved information about Mom's *prescribed treatment* from the doctor's agent, looked up several lists of *providers*, and checked for the ones *in-plan* for Mom's insurance within a *20-mile* radius of her *home* and with a *rating* of *excellent* or *very good* on trusted rating services. It then began trying to find a match between available *appointment times* (supplied by the agents of individual providers through their web sites) and Pete's and Lucy's busy schedules.

Hewlett-Packard's Semantic Web Research Group frequently circulates items of interest such as news articles, software tools, and links to websites. They call these snippets, or information nuggets (Cayzer 2004). Because e-mail is not the ideal medium for this type of content, they needed to find a technique for decentralized, informal knowledge management. They began a research project to create a system that was capable of aggregating, annotating, indexing, and searching a community's snippets. For this system, the required characteristics include:

1. Ease of use and capture.
2. Decentralized aggregation. Snippets will be in a variety of locations and formats. It will be necessary to integrate them and perform some global search over the result.
3. Distributed knowledge. The information consumer should be able to add value by enriching snippets at the point of use by adding ratings, annotations, etc.
4. Flexible data model. Snippets are polymorphic. The system should be able to handle e-mail, web pages, documents, text fragments, images, etc.
5. Extensibility. It should be possible to extend the snippet data schema to model the changing world.
6. Inferencing capability. It should be possible to infer new metadata from old. For example, a machine should know that a snippet about a particular HP Photosmart model is about a digital camera.

Some have suggested that blogs make the ideal tool for this type of content and knowledge management. However, today's blogging tools offer only some of the capabilities mentioned. Traditional blogging has many limitations, but the most important limitation is that metadata is used only for headline syndication in a blog. Metadata is not extensible, is not linked to a risk-flexible data model, and is not capable of supporting vocabulary mixing and inferencing.

The researchers, therefore, looked to the Semantic Web for a solution. As we've discussed, the premise of the Semantic Web is that data can be shared and reused across applications, enterprises, and community boundaries. RSS 1.0 (web.resource.org/rss/1.0) is a Semantic Web vocabulary that provides a way to express and integrate with rich information models. The Semantic Web standard Resource Description Framework (RDF) specifies a web-scale information-modeling format (www.w3.org/RDF). Using these tools, they came up with a prototype for creating what they called a Semantic Blog. The prototype has some interesting searching capabilities. For example, snippets can be searched for either through their own attributes (e.g., "I'm interested in snippets about HP") or through the attributes of their attached blog entry (e.g., "I'm interested in snippets captured by Bob").

Virtual Worlds

Perhaps the most interesting of all social-based community software is Linden Labs Second Life (www.secondlife.com). Though primarily used for such fun activities as fantasy role-playing (pirates, Goths, sci-fi, and all that), Second Life does have a serious side.

In 2008, IBM's Academy of Technology held a virtual world conference and annual meeting in Second Life, as shown in Figure 4.11. The virtual meeting conference space had room for breakout sessions, a library, and various areas for community gathering. IBM estimates that the ROI for the virtual world conference was about $320,000 and that the annual meeting cost one-fifth that of a real-world event.

Just think of the possibilities. Project team members near and far can use Second Life to hold virtual, but tactile, team meetings and even work with end users.

Knowledge Management Tools

Knowledge management (KM) has been defined as the identification and analysis of available and required knowledge—and the subsequent

FIGURE 4.11
Using Second Life to host a conference.

planning and control of actions—to develop these into knowledge assets that will enable a business to generate profits and/or increase its competitive position. The major focus of knowledge management is to identify and gather content from documents, reports, and other sources and to be able to search that content for meaningful relationships. A variety of business-intelligence, artificial-intelligence, and content-management methodologies and tools are the framework under which knowledge management operates.

Groups of individuals who share knowledge about a common work practice over a period of time, even though they are not part of a formally constituted work team, are considered to be "communities of practice." Communities of practice (CoPs) generally cut across traditional organizational boundaries. They enable individuals to acquire new knowledge faster. They may also be called "communities of interest" if the people share an interest in something but do not necessarily perform the work on a daily basis. For example, in one government agency, a group of employees who were actively involved in multiparty, multi-issue settlement negotiations began a monthly discussion group during which they explored process issues, discussed lessons learned, and shared tools and techniques. CoPs can be more or less structured, depending on the needs of the membership.

CoPs provide a mechanism for sharing knowledge throughout one organization or across several organizations. They lead to an improved network of organizational contacts, provide opportunities for peer-group recognition, and support continuous learning, all of which reinforce knowledge transfer and contribute to better results. They are valuable for sharing tacit (implicit) knowledge.

To be successful, CoPs require support from the organization(s). However, if management closely controls their agendas and methods of operation, they are seldom successful. This is more of an issue for communities of practice within organizations.

Communities of practice can be used virtually anywhere within an organization: within one organizational unit or across organizational boundaries, with a small or large group of people, in one geographical location or multiple locations, etc. They can also be used to bring together people from multiple companies, organized around a profession, shared roles, or common issues.

CoPs create value when there is tacit information that, if shared, leads to better results for individuals and the organization. They are also valuable in situations where knowledge is being constantly gained and where sharing this knowledge is beneficial to the accomplishment of the organization's goals.

There are different kinds of CoPs. Some develop best practices; some create guidelines; and others meet to share common concerns, problems, and solutions. They can connect in different ways: face to face, in small or large meetings, or electronically. These virtual communities of practice are simply called VCoPs.

VCoPs (as well as face-to-face CoPs) need a way to capture their collective experiences for online examination. Daimler AG does this using something they call the EBOK (engineering book of knowledge) system. It provides best-practice information on pretty much everything related to the manufacture of cars. Tech CoPs share knowledge related across car processes and then consolidate this knowledge within the EBOK system.

CoPs provide a great degree of what academics refer to as *social capital*. It is social capital that provides the motivation and commitment required to populate knowledge stores such as EBOK. One of the more recent advances in CoP methodology is to take it from small-team interaction to large-group intervention, although some dispute whether this can be effectively done at all. There have been some experiments where up to 300 people were brought together within a CoP to work through organizational issues. While it would be unusual for a software engineering effort to be of such proportions, it would not be out of the question to have to develop a system where team members and stakeholders together came close to this number.

There are a variety of CoP-based designs for groups of this size. The World Café is perhaps the most well known and popular of these designs, which also includes Open Space Technology, Participative Design, and Wisdom Circles.

The World Café (www.theworldcafe.com) describes its process this way: It is an innovative yet simple methodology for hosting conversations. These conversations link and build on each other as people move between groups, cross-pollinate ideas, and discover new insights into the questions and issues raised. As a process, the World Café can evoke and make visible the collective intelligence of any group, thus increasing people's capacity for effective action in pursuit of a common aim.

In a face-to-face environment, the way to do this is quite simple. Tables are provided where a series of conversational rounds, lasting from 20 to 45 minutes, are held to tackle a specific question. Participants are encouraged to write, doodle, or draw key ideas and themes on the tablecloths, as shown in Figure 4.12. At the end of each round, one person remains at the table as the host, while the others travel to new tables. The hosts welcome the newcomers and share the table's conversation so far. The newcomers share what they discussed from the tables they've already visited. And so on. After the last round, participants return to their individual tables to integrate all of this information. At the end of the session, everyone shares and explores emerging themes, insights, and learning. This serves to capture the collective intelligence of the whole (Raelin 2008).

A visit to the World Café's website demonstrates how they have modified this construct to suit the online environment. One of the outputs of this sort of brainstorming session might be a tag cloud, which is a visual depiction of user-generated tags based on discussions. Tags are usually single words and are normally listed alphabetically, and the importance of a tag is shown with font size or colors, as shown in Figure 4.13.

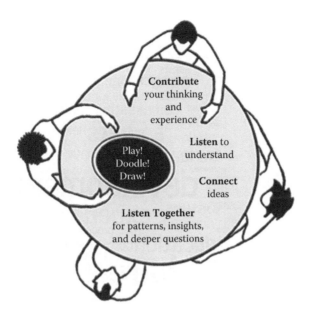

FIGURE 4.12
The World Café methodology.

Tag clouds were popularized by websites such as Flickr and Technorati. They serve a very useful purpose for software engineers by providing a way to classify, organize, and prioritize the results of any meetings. Because individual tags can serve as hyperlinks, it is possible to use this as a way to store increasingly granular levels of information. Perhaps the most well known of cloud tag generators is Wordle (www.wordle.net/create).

SUMMARY

This chapter has explored the possibilities that social networking presents to various types of organizations, particularly to IT. While tools other than Oracle have been presented (as they are the most familiar to us), the Oracle platform does provide the wherewithal to design and build a social platform for customers and IT folks alike.

FIGURE 4.13
Tag cloud.

REFERENCES

Ahmadi, N., M. Jazayeri, F. Lelli, and S. Nesic. 2008. A survey of social software engineering. Paper presented at 23rd IEEE/ACM International Conference on Automated Software Engineering. Accessed March 20, 2014. doi: 10.1109/ASEW.2008.4686304.

Anderson, C. 2006. *The long tail.* New York: Hyperion.

Berners-Lee, T., J. Hendler, and O. Lassila. 2001. The Semantic Web. *Scientific American* 284 (5): 34–43. http://student.bus.olemiss.edu/files/conlon/others/others/Bus669_CompInfo/SemanticWeb/SemanticWeb_SciAmerican.htm (accessed March 19, 2014).

Booch, G., and A. W. Brown. 2003. Collaborative development environments. *Advances in Computers* 59: 2–29.

Cayzer, S. 2004. Semantic blogging and decentralized knowledge management. *Communications of the ACM* 47 (12): 47–52.

Ewusi-Mensah, K. 2003. *Software development failures.* Cambridge, MA: MIT Press.

Fischer, G. 2005. Social creativity: Making all voices heard. *Proceedings of the HCI International Conference (HCII)*, Las Vegas, July 2005. http://l3d.cs.colorado.edu/~gerhard/papers/social-creativity-hcii-2005.pdf (accessed March 20, 2014).

Forrester Research. 2009. *Gen Y and the Future of the Workplace.* Webinar presented by T.J. Keitt, Heidi Shey, Claire Schooley. September 2, 2009.

Fournier, R. 2001. Teamwork is the key to remote development. *Infoworld.* http://www.itworld.com/IW010305tcdistdev (accessed March 20, 2014).

Hardy, Q. 2010. LinkedIn plots career success paths. *Forbes.com.* http://www.forbes.com/forbes/2010/0830/e-gang-linkedin-social-networking-deep-nishar-be-the-boss.html (accessed March 20, 2014).

Hathi, S. 2009. How social networking increases collaboration at IBM. *Strategic Communication Management* 14 (1): 32–35.

Hyvari, I. 2006. Success of projects in different organizational conditions. *Project Management Journal* 37 (4): 31–41.

Mavetera, N., and J. H. Kroeze. 2010. An ontology-driven software development framework. *Proceedings of the 14th International Business Information Management Association Conference* (14th IBIMA), 1713–24. http://dspace.nwu.ac.za/bitstream/handle/10394/3135/Mavetera_Kroeze_Ontology-DrivenSoftware.pdf?sequence=1 (accessed March 20, 2014).

McConnell, S. 1996. *Rapid development: Taming wild software schedules.* Redmond, WA: Microsoft Press.

Pew Research. 2010. Major trends in online activities. *Pew Internet.* http://pewinternet.org/Reports/2010/Generations-2010/Trends/Social-network-sites.aspx (accessed March 20, 2014).

Raelin, J. A. 2008. *Work-based learning: Bridging knowledge and action in the workplace.* San Francisco: Jossey-Bass.

Sarma, A. 2005. A survey of collaborative tools in software development. Institute for Software Research. ISR Technical Report UCI-ISR-05-3. Donald Bren School of Information and Computer Science, University of California, Irvine. http://isr.uci.edu/tech_reports/UCI-ISR-05-3.pdf (accessed March 20, 2014).

Standish Group. 2009. *2009 CHAOS report: Worst failure rate in a decade.* Boston: Standish Group.

Walker, R. W. 2007. Government taps the power of us: Officials turn to blogs and wikis to share information and achieve goals. *Federal Computer Week*, May 21.

Whitehead, J. 2007. Collaboration in software engineering: A roadmap. In *2007 Future of Software Engineering* (FOSE '07), 214–25. Piscataway, NJ: IEEE Computer Society.

5

Oracle Cloud

It should come as no surprise that Oracle is deep into all things "cloud." As shown in Figure 5.1, Oracle delivers a very broad selection of enterprise-grade cloud solutions, including software as a service (SaaS), platform as a service (PaaS), and infrastructure as a service (IaaS). Table 5.1 shows the scale of Oracle's public cloud offerings. Virtually, all of their software is available for use on their public cloud.

As shown in Table 5.2, Oracle also delivers end-to-end managed cloud services across its broad portfolio of business applications, middleware, database, and hardware technologies.

Finally, as shown in Table 5.3, Oracle provides an integrated set of products and services to support private cloud applications, platforms, and infrastructure. The product and service set includes applications, life-cycle management, and security.

From a technical perspective, much of Oracle's cloud offerings are based on the Oracle Cloud File System. CloudFS, a storage management suite developed by Oracle Corporation, consists of a cluster file system called ASM Cluster File System (ACFS) and a cluster volume manager called ASM Dynamic Volume Manager (ADVM).

ACFS is a standard-based POSIX (Linux, UNIX) and Windows cluster file system with full cluster-wide file and memory-mapped I/O cache coherency and file locking. ACFS provides direct I/O for Oracle database I/O workloads. However, for better response time, ACFS implements indirect I/O for general purpose files that typically perform small I/O. CloudFS is designed to scale to billions of files and supports very large file and file systems sizes (up to exabytes of storage).

CloudFS is built on top of Oracle Automatic Storage Management (ASM) and Oracle clustering technologies to provide cluster volume and file services to clients. ADVM and ACFS leverage ASM striping, mirroring, and

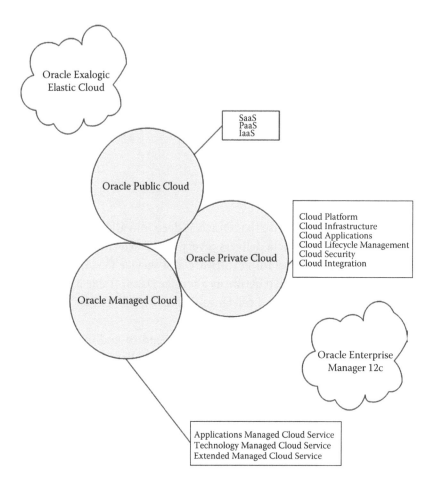

FIGURE 5.1
Oracle's cloud offerings.

automatic I/O rebalancing features to manage volumes that are dynamically resizable. ACFS supports Oracle database files as well as general purpose files.

Database as a Service (DBaaS) offers organizations accelerated deployment, elastic capacity, greater consolidation efficiency, higher availability, and lower overall operational cost and complexity. Oracle database 12c provides an innovative multitenant architecture featuring pluggable databases that makes it easy to offer DBaaS and consolidate databases on clouds. To support customers' move to this model, Oracle Enterprise Manager 12c adds new automation capabilities to enable quick provisioning of database clouds through self-service, saving administrators

TABLE 5.1

Oracle Public Cloud Offerings

Business Area	Product
Marketing	Oracle Eloqua
Sales	Oracle Sales Cloud:
	• Oracle Sales Cloud for Outlook
	• Oracle Sales Cloud Mobile
	• CX Integrations to Oracle Sales Cloud
	• Oracle Sales Cloud Customer Data Management
Service	Oracle Service:
	• Oracle RightNow Virtual Assistant Cloud Service
	• Oracle RightNow Analytics Cloud Service
	• Oracle RightNow CX Cloud Service May 2012 Release— Capabilities and Benefits
	• Oracle RightNow Chat Cloud Service
	• Oracle RightNow Cobrowse Cloud Service
	• Oracle RightNow Dynamic Agent Desktop Cloud Service
	• Oracle RightNow Dynamic Agent Desktop Cloud Service: Contact Center Experience Designer Feature
	• Oracle RightNow Dynamic Agent Desktop Cloud Service for Case Management
	• Oracle RightNow Email Management Cloud Service
	• Oracle RightNow Feedback Cloud Service
	• Oracle RightNow Government Cloud Platform Cloud Service
	• Oracle RightNow Guided Assistance Cloud Service
	• Oracle RightNow Innovation Community Cloud Service
	• Oracle RightNow Intent Guide Cloud Service
	• Oracle RightNow Outreach Cloud Service
	• Oracle Policy Automation for Mobile Devices
	• Oracle RightNow PCI Certified Cloud Platform Cloud Service
	• Oracle RightNow Platform
	• Oracle RightNow Social Experience
	• Oracle RightNow Self Service for Facebook Cloud Service
	• Oracle RightNow Social Monitor Cloud Service
	• Oracle RightNow Support Community Cloud Service
	• Oracle RightNow Virtual CIO Cloud Service
	• Oracle RightNow Web Self Service Cloud Service
	• Oracle Knowledge Release 8.5—Capabilities and Benefits
	• Oracle Knowledge Analytics

(Continued)

TABLE 5.1 (CONTINUED)

Oracle Public Cloud Offerings

Business Area	Product
	• Oracle Knowledge for Contact Center
	• Oracle Knowledge Solutions
	• Oracle Knowledge for Web Self Service
	• Oracle Knowledge Products and Oracle CRM On Demand
	• Oracle Policy Automation for Insurance
	• Oracle Policy Automation for Financial Services
	• Oracle Policy Automation Solution for Public Sector
	• Oracle Policy Automation Solution for Social Services
	• Oracle Policy Automation for Immigration
	• Oracle Policy Automation for Mobile Devices
Global human resources	Oracle Human Capital Management:
	• Oracle Human Capital Management
	• Oracle Global Payroll and Global Payroll Interface
	• Oracle Global Benefits Management
	• Oracle Performance Management
	• Oracle Goal Management
	• Oracle Talent Review and Succession Management
	• Oracle Workforce Compensation
	• Oracle Workforce Predictions
	• Oracle Transactional Business Intelligence
Talent management	Oracle Talent Management:
	• Oracle Talent Management Base
	• Oracle Taleo Recruiting Cloud Service
	• Oracle Taleo Onboarding Cloud Service
	• Oracle Performance Management
	• Oracle Goal Management
	• Oracle Talent Review and Succession Management
	• Oracle Workforce Compensation
	• Oracle Transactional Business Intelligence
Talent management for SMB	Oracle Taleo Business Edition
ERP	Oracle ERP:
	• Oracle Financials Cloud Service
	• Oracle Project Portfolio Management Cloud Service
	• Oracle Project Management Cloud Service
	• Oracle Project Resource Management Cloud Service
	• Oracle Task Management Cloud Service
	• Oracle Procurement Contracts

(Continued)

TABLE 5.1 (CONTINUED)

Oracle Public Cloud Offerings

Business Area	Product
	• Oracle Purchasing
	• Oracle Sourcing
	• Oracle Product Hub Cloud Service
	• Oracle Inventory and Cost Management
Enterprise planning	Oracle Planning and Budgeting Cloud Service
Financial reporting	Oracle Financial Reporting Cloud Service
Social networking	Oracle Social Network
Social marketing	Oracle Social Marketing:
	• Oracle Social Marketing Cloud Service
	• Oracle Social Engagement and Monitoring
	• Oracle Social Data and Insight
Build apps	Oracle Build Apps:
	• Database
	• Java
	• Developer
	• Documents
	• Business Intelligence
	• Mobile
Cloud marketplace	Apps from third-party vendors

time and effort. These new capabilities can help customers adopt Oracle Database 12c faster and pave the way to a DBaaS delivery model.

Oracle has also thrown a hardware solution into the mix. Oracle Exalogic Elastic Cloud is a computer appliance available since 2010. It is a cluster of x86-64 servers running Oracle Linux or Oracle Solaris preinstalled. Two 64-bit operating systems run on the server nodes of the appliance: Oracle Linux version 5.5 or Solaris 11. All servers have an installed cluster configuration of Oracle WebLogic Server and distributed memory cache Oracle Coherence. To run Java applications on a machine, there is a choice of HotSpot or JRockit. Management of the appliance is available in the Oracle Enterprise Manager toolset, which is also preinstalled in the appliance. A transaction monitor Tuxedo is optionally supplied.

Exalogic is being used by a wide variety of organizations, including the University of Melbourne, Food and Drug Administration (FDA), Amway, the Hyundai Motor Group, and the Bank of Chile.

TABLE 5.2

Oracle Managed Cloud Services

	Purpose	Features
Applications managed cloud service	With Oracle Applications Managed Cloud Service, the organization is able to choose the best deployment model for its business needs without lock-in. Oracle can manage applications onsite, through Oracle's partners, or at one of their data centers.	• Complete cloud-management services for any Oracle application • Ensures best practices across functional pillars in the cloud • Lets you manage your cloud applications any way you want • Offers choice of hosting @ Oracle, @ customer, @ partner, and hybrid options • Ensures enterprise-grade cloud security and performance
Technology managed cloud service	Oracle Technology Managed Cloud Service provides end-to-end management services delivered in the cloud and managed by Oracle.	• Delivers and manages Oracle technology and applications in the cloud • Uses standard configurations, including ITL-based compliant processes • Includes architecture design, monitoring, change management, security, and more • Provides hosting and management for the Oracle Technology Platform • Offers hosting and management for Oracle Engineered Systems
Extended managed cloud service	Oracle Extended Managed Cloud Service goes beyond core infrastructure and application management services to provide services that span the entire software life cycle, from migration, testing, and deployment to compliance and disaster recovery.	• Security services • Testing services • Transition services • Disaster recovery services

TABLE 5.3

Oracle Private Cloud

	Purpose	**Features**
Cloud platform	The Oracle Cloud Platform (also known as Platform as a Service [PaaS]) provides a shared and elastically scalable platform for consolidation of existing applications and new application development and deployment.	• Delivers greater agility through faster application development • Leveraging standards-based shared services and elastic scalability on demand • Includes database functionality based on Oracle Database and Oracle Exadata Database Machine • Features middleware technology based on Oracle Fusion Middleware and Oracle Exalogic Elastic Cloud • Engineered systems such as Exadata and Exalogic provide extreme performance and efficiency for mixed workloads
Cloud infrastructure	Oracle Cloud Infrastructure provides a complete selection of servers, storage, networking fabric, virtualization software, operating systems, and management software to support diverse public and private cloud applications.	• Flexible cloud infrastructure supports dynamic resource pooling, elastic scalability, and rapid application deployment • Includes Oracle Enterprise Manager, a complete cloud life-cycle management solution that allows you to quickly set up, manage, and support enterprise clouds and traditional Oracle IT environments from applications to disk • Built-in security and high availability • Application-aware virtualization and management capabilities

(Continued)

TABLE 5.3 (CONTINUED)

Oracle Private Cloud

	Purpose	**Features**
Cloud applications	Oracle's Cloud Applications are a complete and modular set of enterprise applications	• Complete and best-practice business processes across functional pillars in the cloud • Cloud applications any way you want them: in a public, private, or hybrid cloud • Global and enterprise-grade cloud security and performance to meet even the most-demanding requirements
Cloud life-cycle management	Oracle Enterprise Manager is Oracle's complete cloud life-cycle management solution. It provides self-service provisioning balanced against centralized, policy-based resource management, integrated chargeback and capacity planning, and complete visibility of the physical and virtual environment from applications to disk.	• Plan and set up the cloud with capacity and optimization planning, analysis, and recommendations, including definition of policies and rules needed to automate self-service provisioning • Build, test, and deploy applications on the cloud with an out-of-the-box, self-service portal • Track, report, and manage resource utilization and performance, including policy-driven scale-up and scale-down of resources; includes monitoring for cloud resource usage and request management • Meter, charge, and optimize your cloud with application-to-disk resource metering that tracks resource utilization and cost, ties back to internal billing and management reporting systems as needed, and automatically optimizes resources • Consolidate underutilized servers for migration to the cloud

(Continued)

TABLE 5.3 (CONTINUED)

Oracle Private Cloud

	Purpose	Features
Cloud security	Oracle Cloud Security leverages Oracle expertise in data security, identity management, and governance, risk, and compliance to provide a comprehensive, reliable solution for deployment in any cloud environment.	• Provides a comprehensive set of solutions to mitigate threats across your databases and applications • Deployed by thousands of leading organizations to address compliance for multiple government and industry regulations
Cloud integration	Oracle simplifies cloud integration by providing a unified and comprehensive solution to integrate disparate cloud and on-premise applications. Oracle cloud integration leverages Oracle Cloud Services as well as components from Oracle's SOA, BPM, and data-integration technologies.	• Comprehensive and unified set of components seamlessly integrating on-premises and cloud applications and services • Proven integration technologies deployed by thousands of leading organizations to ensure high reliability, real-time performance, and trusted integration • Leverages existing investments in Oracle database, middleware, applications, and hardware systems while working with third-party cloud applications

MANAGING THE CLOUD

Oracle's cloud products and services make it possible to run the entirety of an organization's business applications, and host all of its information assets, in the cloud. While many opt for a private cloud, more than a few organizations have moved to public or managed clouds. Thus, it is worthwhile to consider the cloud dynamic, including selection, legal issues, and security. The federal government's CIO Council carefully considered these issues (2012). This chapter aligns with their findings and recommendations.

The adoption of cloud computing represents a dramatic shift in the way organizations buy IT—a shift from periodic capital expenditures to lower cost and predictable operating expenditures. With this shift comes a learning curve regarding the effective procurement of cloud-based services.

Cloud computing presents a paradigm shift that is larger than IT, and while there are technology changes with cloud services, the more substantive issues that need to be addressed lie in the business and contracting models applicable to cloud services. This new paradigm requires organizations to rethink not only the way they acquire IT services in the context of deployment, but also how the IT services they consume provide mission and support functions on a shared basis. Organizations should begin to design and/or select solutions that allow for purchasing based on consumption in the shared model that cloud-based architectures provide.

Cloud computing allows consumers to buy IT in a new, consumption-based model. Given the dynamic nature of end-user needs, the traditional method of acquiring IT has become less effective in ensuring the organization effectively covers all of its requirements. By moving from purchasing IT in a way that requires capital expenditures and overhead, and instead purchasing IT on-demand as an organization consumes services, unique requirements have arisen that organizations need to address when contracting with cloud service providers (CSPs).

Selecting a Cloud Service

The primary driver behind purchasing any new IT service is to effectively meet a commodity, support, or mission requirement that the organization has. Part of the analysis of that need or problem is determining the appropriate solution. Choosing the cloud is only the first step in this analysis. It is also critical for organizations to decide which cloud service and deployment model best meets their needs.

The National Institute of Standards and Technology (NIST) has defined three cloud computing service models: Infrastructure as a Service, Platform as a Service, and Software as a Service.

These service models can be summarized as:

1. *Infrastructure*: The provision of processing, storage, networking, and other fundamental computing resources
2. *Platform*: The deployment of applications created using programming languages, libraries, services, and tools supported by a cloud provider

3. *Software*: The use of applications running on a cloud infrastructure environment

Each service model offers unique functionality depending on the class of user, with control of the environment decreasing as you move from infrastructure to platform to software. Infrastructure is most suitable for users like network administrators, as organizations can place unique platforms and software on the infrastructure being consumed. Platform is most suitable for users like server or system administrators in development and deployment activities. Software is most appropriate for end users, since all functionalities are usually offered out of the box. Understanding the degree of functionality and what users will consume the services is critical for organizations in determining the appropriate cloud service to procure.

NIST has also defined four deployment models for cloud services: Private, Public, Community, and Hybrid. These service deployments can be summarized as:

1. *Private*: For use by a single organization
2. *Public*: For use by general public
3. *Community*: For use by a specific community of organizations with a shared purpose
4. *Hybrid*: A composition of two or more cloud infrastructures (public, private, community)

These deployment models determine the number of consumers (multi-tenancy) and the nature of other consumers' data that may be present in a cloud environment. A public cloud does not allow a consumer to know or control who the other consumers of a cloud service provider's environment are. However, a private cloud can allow for ultimate control in selecting who has access to a cloud environment. Community clouds and hybrid clouds allow for a mixed degree of control and knowledge of other consumers. Additionally, the cost for cloud services typically increases as the control over other consumers and knowledge of these consumers increases. When consuming cloud services, it is important for organizations to understand what type of data they will be placing in the environment and to select the deployment type that corresponds to the appropriate level of control and data sensitivity.

To choose a cloud service that will properly meet a unique need, it is vital to first determine the proper level of service and deployment.

Organizations should endeavor to understand not only what functionality they will receive when using a cloud service, but also how the deployment model a cloud service utilizes will affect the environment in which data is placed.

CSP and End-User Agreements

CSPs enforce common acceptable-use standards across all users to effectively maintain how a consumer uses a CSP environment. Thus, use of a CSP environment usually requires end users to sign terms-of-service (TOS) agreements. Additionally, organizations can also require CSPs to sign nondisclosure agreements (NDAs) to enforce acceptable CSP personnel behavior when dealing with data. TOS and NDAs need to be fully contemplated and agreed upon by both CSPs and organizations to ensure that all parties fully understand the breadth and scope of their duties when using cloud services. These agreements are new to many IT contracts because of the nature of the interaction of end users with CSP environments.

Terms of Service Agreements

Organizations need to know if a CSP requires an end user to agree to TOS in order to use the CSP's services prior to signing a contract. TOS restrict the ways consumers can use CSP environments. They include provisions that detail how end users may use the services, the responsibilities of the CSP, and how the CSP will deal with customer data. Provisions within a TOS may contradict organizational policies. Given that, organizations are advised to work with CSPs to understand what they require in order for end users to access a CSP environment and at the same time ensure that any TOS document incorporated into the contract is acceptable to the organization. If the TOS are not directly within the contract but only referenced within the contract, the TOS should be negotiated and agreed upon prior to contract award.

Additionally, TOS sometimes include provisions relating to CSP responsibilities, controlling law, indemnification, and other issues that are more appropriate for the terms and conditions of the contract. If these provisions are included within service agreements, they should be clearly defined. Furthermore, any agreements must address time requirements that a CSP will need to follow to comply with rules and regulations.

Nondisclosure Agreements

Some organizations require CSP personnel to sign NDAs when dealing with data. These are usually requested by organizations in order to ensure that CSP personnel protect nonpublic information that is procurement sensitive or affects predecisional policy, physical security, etc. Organizations will need to consider the requirements and enforceability of NDAs with CSP personnel. The acceptable behavior prescribed by NDAs requires oversight, including examining the NDAs' requirements in the rules of behavior and monitoring of end-user activities in the cloud environment. CSP and end-user agreements such as TOS and NDAs are important to both organizations and CSPs in order to clearly define the acceptable behavior by end users and CSP personnel when using cloud services. These agreements should be fully contemplated by both CSPs and organizations prior to cloud services being procured. All such agreements should be incorporated, either by full text or by reference, into the CSP contract in order to avoid the usually costly and time-consuming process of negotiating these agreements after the enactment of a cloud computing contract.

Service-Level Agreements

Service-level agreements (SLAs) are agreements under the umbrella of the overall cloud computing contract between a CSP and an organization. SLAs define acceptable service levels to be provided by the CSP to its customers in measurable terms. The ability of a CSP to perform at acceptable levels is consistent among SLAs, but the definition, measurement, and enforcement of this performance varies widely among CSPs. Organizations should ensure that CSP performance is clearly specified in all SLAs and that all such agreements are fully incorporated, either by full text or by reference, into the CSP contract.

Terms and Definitions

SLAs are necessary between a CSP and customer to contractually agree upon the acceptable service levels expected from a CSP. SLAs across CSPs have many common terms, but definitions and performance metrics can vary widely among vendors. For instance, CSPs can differ in their definition of uptime (one measure of reliability) by stating that uptime is not met only when services are unavailable for periods exceeding one hour. To further complicate this, many CSPs define availability (another measure of reliability sometimes used within the definition of uptime) in a way that may exclude CSP planned service outages. Organizations need to fully understand any ambiguities in the definitions of cloud computing terms in order to know what levels of service they can expect from a CSP.

Measuring SLA Performance

When organizations place data in a CSP environment, they are inherently giving up control over certain aspects of the services that they consume. As a best practice, SLAs should clearly define how performance is guaranteed (such as response time, resolution/mitigation time, availability, etc.) and require CSPs to monitor their service levels, provide timely notification of a failure to meet the SLAs, and evidence that problems have been resolved or mitigated. SLA performance clauses should be consistent with the performance clauses within the contract. Organizations should enforce this by requiring in the reporting clauses of the SLA and the contract that CSPs submit reports or provide a dashboard so that organizations can continuously verify that service levels are being met. Without this provision, an organization may not be able to measure CSP performance.

SLA Enforcement Mechanisms

Most standard SLAs provided by CSPs do not include provisions for penalties if an SLA is not met. The consequence to a customer if an SLA is not met can be catastrophic (unavailability during peak demand, for example). However, without a penalty for CSPs in the SLA, CSPs may not have sufficient incentives to meet the agreed-upon service levels. In order to incentivize CSPs to meet the contract terms, there should be a credible consequence (for example, a monetary or service credit) so that a failure to meet the agreed-upon terms creates an undesired business outcome for the CSP in addition to the customer.

With many of the high-profile cases of cloud service provider failures relating to provisions covered by SLAs, as a best practice, organizations need SLAs that provide value and can be enforced when a service level is not met. SLAs with clearly defined terms and definitions, performance metrics measured and guaranteed by CSPs, and enforcement mechanisms for meeting service levels will provide value to organizations and incentives for CSPs to meet the agreed-upon terms.

CSP, Organization, and Integrator Roles and Responsibilities

Many organizations procure cloud services through integrators. In these cases, integrators can provide a level of expertise within CSP environments that organizations may not have, thus making an organization's transition to cloud services easier. Integrators may also provide a full range of services from technical support to help-desk support that CSPs might not provide. When deciding to use an integrator, the organization may procure services directly from a CSP and separately with an integrator, or it may procure cloud services through an integrator as the prime contractor and the CSP as subcontractor. Whichever method the organization decides to use, the addition of an integrator to a cloud computing implementation creates contractual relationships with at least three unique parties, and the roles and responsibilities for all parties need to be clearly defined.

Contracting with Integrators

Integrators can be contracted independently of CSPs or can act as an intermediary with CSPs. This flexibility allows organizations to choose the most effective method for contracting with integrators to help implement their cloud computing solutions. As a best practice, organizations need to consider the technical abilities and overall service offerings of integrators and how these elements impact the overall pricing of an integrator's proposed services. Additionally, if an organization contracts with an integrator acting as an intermediary, the organization must consider how this affects the organization's continued use of a CSP environment when the contract with an integrator ends.

Clearly Defined Roles and Responsibilities

Whether an organization contracts with an integrator independently or uses one as an intermediary, roles and responsibilities need to be clearly defined. Scenarios that need to be clearly defined within a cloud computing solution that incorporate an integrator include:

- How an organization interacts with a CSP to manage the CSP environment
- What access an integrator has to data within a CSP environment
- What actions an integrator may take on behalf of an organization

Failure to address the roles and responsibilities of each party can hinder the end user's ability to fully realize the benefits of cloud computing. For instance, if initiating a new instance of a virtual machine requires an organization to interact with an integrator, then this interaction breaks the on-demand essential characteristic of cloud computing.

The introduction of integrators to cloud computing solutions can be a critical element of success for many organizations. However, the introduction of an additional party to a cloud computing contract requires organizations to fully consider the most effective method of contracting with an integrator and clearly define the roles and responsibilities among CSPs, organizations, and integrators.

Standards

Standards are available in support of many of the functions and requirements for cloud computing. While many of these standards were developed in support of pre-cloud computing technologies, such as those designed for web services and the Internet, they also support the functions and requirements of cloud computing. Other standards are now being developed in specific support of cloud computing functions and requirements, such as virtualization.

Security

Placing data on an information system involves risk, so it is critical for organizations to ensure that the IT environment in which they are storing and accessing data is secure.

Because of the variability in risk postures among different CSP environments and differing missions and needs, the determination of the appropriate levels of security vary across organizations and across CSP environments.

Organizations must evaluate the type of data they will be placing into a CSP environment and categorize their security needs accordingly.

Based on the level of security that an organization determines a CSP environment must meet, the organization then must determine which security controls a CSP will implement within the cloud environment. Within this framework, organizations need to explicitly state not only the security impact level of the system (i.e., the CSP environment must meet high, moderate, or low impact level), but organizations must also specify the security controls associated with the impact level the CSP must meet.

Continuous Monitoring

After organizations complete a security authorization of a system based on clear and defined security authorization requirements detailing the security controls a CSP must implement on their system, organizations must continue to ensure that a CSP environment maintains an acceptable level of risk. In order to do this, organizations should work with CSPs to implement a continuous monitoring program. Continuous monitoring programs are designed to ensure that the level of security through a CSP's initial security authorization is maintained while organizational data resides within a CSP's environment.

Incident Response

Incident response refers to activities addressing breaches of systems, leaks/ spillage of data, and unauthorized access to data. Organizations need to work with CSPs to ensure that CSPs employ satisfactory incident response plans and have clear procedures regarding how the CSP responds to incidents as specified in the organization's computer security incident-handling guidelines.

Organizations must ensure that contracts with CSPs include CSP liability for data security. An organization's ability to effectively monitor for incidents and threats requires working with CSPs to ensure compliance with all data security standards, laws, initiatives, and policies.

Generally, CSPs take ownership of their environment but not the data placed in their environment. As a best practice, cloud contracts should not permit a CSP to deny responsibility if there is a data breach within its environment. Organizations should make explicit in cloud computing contracts that CSPs indemnify organizations if a breach should occur, and the CSP should be required to provide adequate capital and/or insurance to support their indemnity. In instances where expected standards are not met, then the CSP must be required to assume the liability if an incident occurs directly related to the lack of compliance. In all instances, it is vital for organizations to practice vigilant oversight.

When incidents do occur, CSPs should be held accountable for incident responsiveness to security breaches and for maintaining the level of security required by the organization. Organizations should work with CSPs to define an acceptable time period for the CSP to mitigate and resecure the system.

At a minimum, when implementing an incident response policy, organizations should ensure that:

1. CSPs are contractually complying with organizational security guidelines.
2. CSPs are accountable for incident responsiveness, including providing specific time frames for restoration of secure services in the event of an incident.

Key Escrow

Key escrow (also known as a fair cryptosystem or key management) is an arrangement in which the keys needed to decrypt encrypted data are held in escrow so that, under certain circumstances, an authorized third party may gain access to those keys. Procedural and regulatory regimes in environments where the organizations own the systems storing and transporting encrypted data are fairly well settled. These regimes, however, become increasingly complex when inserted into a cloud environment.

Organizations should carefully evaluate CSP solutions to understand completely how a CSP fully does key management, including how the key's encrypted data are escrowed and what terms and conditions of escrow apply to accessing encrypted data.

Forensics

When an organization uses a CSP environment, it should ensure that a CSP only makes changes to the environment on pre-agreed-upon terms and conditions or as required by organization to defend against an actual or potential incident. Organizations should require CSPs to allow forensic investigations for regulatory, criminal, and noncriminal purposes, and these investigations should be able to be conducted without affecting data integrity and without interference from the CSP. In addition, CSPs should only be allowed to make changes to the cloud environment under specific standard operating procedures agreed to by the CSP and organization in the contract.

Audit Logs

Organizations must work with CSPs to ensure that audit logs of a CSP environment are preserved with the same standards as are required by organizations. Organizations must outline which CSP personnel have access to audit logs prior to placing data in the CSP environment. All CSP personnel who have access to the audit logs must have the proper clearances as required by the organization. Essentially:

1. All audit/transaction files should be made available to authorized personnel in read-only mode.
2. Audit transaction records should never be modified or deleted.
3. Access to online audit logs should be strictly controlled. Only authorized users may be allowed to access audit transaction files.
4. Audit/transaction records should be backed up and stored safely off site.

Privacy Impact Assessments (PIA)

The PIA process helps ensure that organizations evaluate and consider how they will mitigate privacy risks while complying with applicable privacy laws and regulations governing an individual's privacy in order to ensure confidentiality, integrity, and availability of an individual's personal information at every stage of development and operation. Typically, organizations conduct a PIA during the security authorization process for IT systems before operating a new system and update.

Some of the normal PIA considerations to include are:

1. What information will be collected and put into the CSP environment
2. Why the information is being collected
3. Intended use of the information
4. With whom the information might be shared

5. Whether individuals will be notified that their information will be maintained in a CSP environment and what opportunities individuals have to decline to provide information that will be maintained in a CSP environment

6. What ability individuals have to consent to particular uses of the information, and how individuals can grant consent

7. How the organization and CSP will secure information in the cloud

In addition, a cloud computing PIA should focus specific attention on:

1. The physical location of the data maintained by the CSP
2. The retention policies that apply to the data maintained in a CSP environment
3. The mechanism by which an organization maintains control over data (e.g., by contractual provisions, nondisclosure agreements, etc.) that is maintained by CSPs
4. The means by which the CSP will terminate storage and delete data at the end of the contract or project life cycle

Data Location

Many CSP environments involve the storage of data across multiple facilities, often across the globe. Where data resides changes an organization's applicable legal rights, expectations, and privileges based on the laws of the country where the data is located. To fully understand who may have access to this data, organizations need to first consider the type of data they plan to place in a cloud environment and then review the laws and policies of the country where the cloud providers' servers are located.

Almost every country has different standards and laws for handling personal information that CSPs must meet if they maintain facilities within their borders. Some countries allow persons with rights of access to personal information that may not directly align with the legal framework in the United States. Other countries may permit law enforcement to request more data from cloud providers than within the United States. It may not be clear how the privacy laws and protections apply in these situations. In any situation where a CSP environment goes outside of US territories, there is a potential for conflict of law, and organizations must take sufficient time to proactively consult with legal counsel about the possible ramifications.

Breach Response

When placing data that contains personally identifiable information (PII) in a CSP environment, organizations need to be aware of issues related to data loss incidents or breaches that are specific to the CSP environment. Organizations need to ensure that they can expand their breach policies and plans as required to ensure compliance with existing requirements for response. These policies must specify which parties are responsible for the cost and containment or mitigation of harm and for notifying affected individuals where required, as well as provide for instruction and requirements on terminating storage and deleting data upon expiration of the agreement or the agreement term and extension options.

It is important to ensure that an organization's breach policies and plans adequately address the new relationship between the organization and CSP, including the assignment of specific roles and tasks between the organization and the CSP, even before determination of ultimate responsibility in the case of a data breach. It is important to establish clear contractual duties and liability of the CSP for timely breach reporting, mitigation (i.e., administrative, technical, or physical measures to contain or remedy the breach), and costs, if any, of providing notice, credit monitoring, or other appropriate relief to affected individuals as appropriate under the circumstances. It is also important to address when the termination of services and assertion of the organization's rights of ownership, custody, transfer (return), or deletion of any data stored in a CSP environment will be invoked by the organization as a remedy for a breach. Finally, it is important to ensure that there are appropriate audit rights to permit compliance reviews.

SUMMARY

Oracle offers robust cloud services, but it is very important that the organization make a reasoned decision as to whether and which cloud services to utilize. The assessment must most importantly include level of support and security. Readers are also urged to review Cloud Procurement

TABLE 5.4

Notable 2013 Cloud Outages

Date	Cloud Provider Affected
January 2013	Dropbox
February 2013	Microsoft
March 2013	Microsoft
April 2013	Apple
August 2013	Amazon
	Google
September 2013	Amazon
October 2013	Microsoft
	Verizon
December 2013	Yahoo

Source: www.crn.com/slide-shows/cloud/240165024/
the-10-biggest-cloud-outages-of-2013.htm.

Questions, Appendix 1 (available on CRC Press website http://www.crc-press.com/product/isbn/9781482249941), which provides a comprehensive worksheet for cloud vendor selection. Readers will also be interested in reviewing Appendix 2, which provides a detailed security checklist that can be used when accessing cloud vendors and web service providers. Finally, readers are urged to carefully examine the stability of the product. As you can see from Table 5.4, there have been quite a few notable cloud outages in the past year.

REFERENCE

CIO Council. 2012. *Creating effective cloud computing contracts for the federal government: Best practices for acquiring IT as a service.* Washington, DC: General Services Administration. http://www.gsa.gov/portal/mediaId/164011/fileName/cloudbest-practices.action (accessed March 21, 2014).

6

Data Management

Oracle rose to prominence on the back of its Oracle RDBMS (relational database management system). All of the products on the left side of Figure 6.1 are related in some way to Oracle's primary database product. With each release of its database, Oracle extended the database's capabilities to integrate with current technology trends at that time. In 2004, Oracle Corporation shipped release 10g (*g* standing for *grid*) as the then-latest version of Oracle Database. Oracle Application Server 10g using Java EE integrates with the server part of that version of the database, making it possible to deploy web technology applications. The application server comprises the first middle-tier software designed for grid computing. The interrelationship between Oracle 10g and Java allows developers to set up stored procedures written in the Java language as well as those written in the traditional Oracle database programming language, PL/SQL.

Oracle Database 11g Release 2 is the database version most widely available since September 2009. This version is available in four commercial editions—Enterprise Edition, Standard Edition, Standard Edition One, Personal Edition—and one free edition, the Express Edition. The licensing of these editions shows various restrictions and obligations and is complex. The Enterprise Edition (DB EE)—the most expensive of the database editions—has the least restrictions but nevertheless has a complex licensing. The Standard Edition (DB SE) and Standard Edition One (SE1) are constrained by more licensing restrictions, which reflects their lower price. In summer 2013, Oracle released 12c (the *c* designating the *cloud*). Table 6.1 summarizes these offerings.

On the right side of Figure 6.1 you'll note that the following are additional database technologies that have been acquired and developed by Oracle:

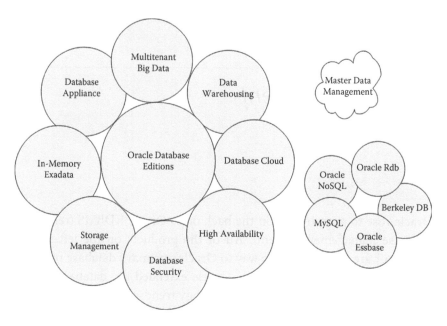

FIGURE 6.1
Oracle Database Management offerings.

- Oracle Essbase continues the Hyperion Essbase tradition of multidimensional database management.
- Berkeley DB offers embedded database processing.
- MySQL, a relational database management system licensed under the GNU Affero General Public License (GNU AGPL), was initially developed by MySQL AB.
- Oracle NoSQL Database is a scalable, distributed key-value NoSQL database.
- Oracle Rdb, a relational database system, runs on OpenVMS platforms. Oracle acquired Rdb in 1994 from Digital Equipment Corporation. Oracle has since made many enhancements to this product, and development continues today.

We talked about Essbase in Chapter 2, on analytics, so we won't delve into it here. Berkeley DB is written in C with API (application programming interface) bindings for C++, C#, PHP, Java, Perl, Python, Ruby, Tcl, Smalltalk, and many other programming languages. Berkeley DB is not a relational database.

Berkeley DB can support thousands of simultaneous threads of control or concurrent processes, manipulating databases as large as 256

TABLE 6.1

The Oracle 12c Environment

Product	Overview	Features
Database	Oracle Database 12c comes in three editions and features a wide range of enterprise-edition options to meet specific customer requirements in the areas of performance and availability, security and compliance, data warehousing and analytics, unstructured data, and manageability.	• Oracle Database Express Edition (11-GB limit on database size) • Oracle Database Standard Edition One • Oracle Database Standard Edition • Oracle Database Enterprise Edition (Multitenant, Big Data, Data Warehousing)
Multitenant	Oracle Multitenant offers a new architecture for consolidating databases on clouds, allowing you to manage many databases as one without application changes, resulting in a fast, scalable, reliable, and secure database platform.	• Simplified database consolidation at a greater density • Efficient database provisioning, patching, and upgrading • Multitenant architecture in the database tier rather than the application tier for SaaS requirements • Complements Oracle Database options such as Oracle Real Application Clusters and Oracle Active Data Guard
Big data	Oracle offers a broad portfolio of products to help you acquire and organize diverse data sources and analyze them alongside your existing data to find new insights and capitalize on hidden relationships.	• Oracle Big Data Appliance • Oracle Exadata Database Machine • Oracle Big Data Connectors • See Chapter 2

(Continued)

TABLE 6.1 (CONTINUED)

The Oracle 12c Environment

Product	Overview	Features
Data warehousing	Oracle Database 12c, complete with in-database advanced analytics, introduces new integration, performance, scalability, and analytics capabilities that support data warehouses and big data, providing a fast, cost-effective platform for data-warehousing and business-intelligence applications.	• Oracle Database Oracle Exadata • Oracle Advanced Analytics • Big Data • Industry data models
Database clouds	Oracle offers a broad portfolio of software and hardware products and services to enable public and private clouds.	• Private Database Cloud • Oracle Database Cloud Services • See Chapter 5
High availability	With Oracle Database 12c and Oracle's Maximum Availability Architecture, you can reduce downtime costs by protecting your business from all common causes of planned and unplanned downtime, including human error.	• Provides HA (high availability) features as part of Oracle's Maximum Availability Architecture • Enhances Oracle Real Application Clusters and Oracle Active Data Guard
Storage management	Oracle Database 12c provides cost-effective storage management by automating processes, minimizing costly I/O operations, compressing data, and maximizing the utilization of tiered storage resources for all your enterprise databases.	• Oracle Automatic Storage Management simplifies the relationship between database and storage to ensure the best I/O performance for database workloads while significantly reducing storage costs and complexity.

(Continued)

TABLE 6.1 (CONTINUED)

The Oracle 12c Environment

Product	Overview	Features
		• Oracle Partitioning enhances database manageability, performance, and availability for a wide variety of applications by allowing tables, indexes, and index-organized tables to be subdivided into smaller pieces and managed cost effectively on different tiers of storage to improve access performance.
		• Oracle Advanced Compression helps businesses manage data growth more cost effectively by automating data management processes that maximize resource utilization with compression rates of 2–4× across all types of data and applications to save disk space and improve query performance.
		• Oracle Hybrid Columnar Compression differentiates Oracle Exadata Database Machine and Oracle SAN and NAS storage systems by reducing the size of data warehousing tables by 10× and archive tables by 15×, improving performance and reducing storage costs for primary, standby, and backup databases.
Database security	Oracle provides a comprehensive portfolio of security solutions to ensure data privacy, protect against insider threats, and enable regulatory compliance.	• Oracle Audit Vault and Database Firewall • Oracle Advanced Security • Oracle Database Vault • Oracle Label Security Oracle Data Masking

(Continued)

TABLE 6.1 (CONTINUED)

The Oracle 12c Environment

Product	Overview	Features
In-Memory	Oracle TimesTen In-Memory Database is a full-featured relational database that's designed to run online transaction processing (OLTP) and business-intelligence applications in the middle tier, store all data in the main memory for fast performance, and provide high throughput with very low latency.	• Oracle TimesTen In-Memory Database stores data in application tier main memory, and with no network latency or disk I/O, transactions take just microseconds and complex analytic queries happen at the speed of thought. • Provides enterprise-class reliability and availability by logging data and transactions to disk to enable a full recovery and, with high-speed replication, Oracle TimesTen In-Memory Database can be configured for high availability and instant failover. • Oracle TimesTen In-Memory Database is embedded in Oracle Exalytics In-Memory Machine, enabling Oracle Business Intelligence Standard Edition users to perform complex analytic queries at real-time speeds. • Oracle TimesTen In-Memory Database supports full SQL transaction semantics and includes OCI, Pro*C, and PL/SQL for compatibility with Oracle Database. • Accelerates existing Oracle Database applications when used as a high- performance cache for Oracle Database, Enterprise Edition.
Exadata	Oracle Exadata is the only database machine that provides extreme performance for both data warehousing and OLTP applications, making it the ideal platform for consolidating mixed database workloads onto private clouds.	• The Oracle Exadata Database Machine X4-2 comes in eighth-, quarter-, half-, and full-rack configurations to meet varying application requirements and to enable you to easily scale as your requirements change. The full rack comes complete with eight two-socket database servers, 14 Oracle Exadata Storage Servers,

(Continued)

TABLE 6.1 (CONTINUED)

The Oracle 12c Environment

Product	Overview	Features
		InfiniBand switches, and more than 44 terabytes of Exadata Smart Flash Cache to support extremely fast transaction response times and high throughput.
		• The Exadata Database Machine X3-8 is designed for database deployments that require very large amounts of data, delivering extreme performance and petabyte scalability for all applications, including online transaction processing (OLTP), data warehousing (DW), and consolidation of mixed workloads. It comes complete with two eight-socket database servers, 14 Oracle Exadata storage servers, InfiniBand switches, and more than 44 terabytes of Exadata Smart Flash Cache to support extremely fast transaction response times and high throughput.
		• Oracle Exadata Storage Expansion Rack X4-2 enables you to grow the Oracle Exadata storage capacity and bandwidth of Oracle Exadata Database Machine X4-2 and X3-8 and Oracle SuperCluster. It is designed for database deployments that require very large amounts of data, including historical or archive data, backups and archives of Oracle Exadata Database Machine data, documents, images, files and XML data, LOBs, and other large unstructured data.

(Continued)

TABLE 6.1 (CONTINUED)

The Oracle 12c Environment

Product	Overview	Features
Database Appliance	The Oracle Database Appliance enables you to take advantage of the world's most popular database (Oracle Database) in a single, easy-to-deploy and -manage system now supporting virtualization. It's a complete package of software, server, storage, and networking that's engineered for simplicity, saving time and money by simplifying deployment, maintenance, and support of database and application workloads.	• A fully integrated and redundant system of software, servers, storage, and networking in a single box that delivers high-availability database services for a wide range of homegrown and packaged online transaction processing (OLTP) and data warehousing applications. • Saves up to 2,000 hours of labor over a three-year period with simple deployment, maintenance, and support of database workloads, all supported by a single vendor—Oracle. • Capacity On-Demand software licensing allows you to quickly scale from 2 processor cores to 48 processor cores without incurring the costs and downtime usually associated with hardware upgrades. • Allows businesses to consolidate OLTP and data warehousing databases up to 18 terabytes in size, making it ideal for midsize companies and departmental systems. • Virtualization support enables customers to quickly deploy complete, highly available solution appliances to remote branch-office locations.

terabytes, on a wide variety of operating systems including most Unix-like and Windows systems as well as real-time operating systems. Berkeley DB is also used as the common name for three distinct products; Oracle Berkeley DB, Berkeley DB Java Edition, and Berkeley DB XML. Starting with the 6.0/12c releases, all Berkeley DB products are licensed under the GNU AGPL. The product ships with complete source code, build script, test suite, and documentation. The code quality and general utility along with the licensing terms have led to its use in a multitude of free and open-source software. Those who do not wish to abide by the terms of the GNU

AGPL have the option of purchasing another proprietary license for redistribution from Oracle Corporation. This technique is called *dual licensing*.

Berkeley DB has an architecture notably simpler than that of other database systems like relational database management systems. For example, like SQLite, it does not provide support for network access; programs access the database using in-process API calls. A program accessing the database is free to decide how the data is to be stored in a record. Berkeley DB puts no constraints on the record's data. The record and its key can both be up to four gigabytes long. Despite having a simple architecture, Berkeley DB supports many advanced database features such as ACID (Atomicity, Consistency, Isolation, Durability) transactions, fine-grained locking, hot backups, and replication.

Each edition has separate database libraries, despite the common branding. The first is the traditional Berkeley DB, written in C. It contains several database implementations, including a B-Tree and one built around extendible hashing. It supports multiple language bindings, including C/C++, Java (via JNI), C#.NET, Perl, and Python.

Berkeley DB Java Edition (JE) is a pure Java database. Its design resembles that of Berkeley DB without replicating it exactly, and has a feature set that includes many of those found in the traditional Berkeley DB and others that are specific to the Java Edition. Because it is written in pure Java, no native code is required. It has a log-structured storage architecture, which gives it different performance and concurrency characteristics. Three APIs are available: a Direct Persistence Layer, which is Plain Old Java Objects (POJO); one that is based on the Java Collections Framework (an object persistence approach); and one based on the traditional Berkeley DB API. The Berkeley DB Java Edition High Availability option (Replication) is available. Note that traditional Berkeley DB also supports a Java API, but it does so via JNI and thus requires an installed native library.

The Berkeley DB XML database specializes in the storage of XML documents, supporting XQuery via XQilla. It is implemented as an additional layer on top of (a legacy version of) Berkeley DB and the Xerces library. DB XML is written in C++ and supports multiple language bindings, including C++, Java (via JNI), Perl, and Python.

Many well-known applications are built using BDB, including Bitcoin, MySQL, and Oracle NoSQL.

A NoSQL database provides a mechanism for storage and retrieval of data that is modeled in means other than the tabular relations used in relational databases. Motivations for this approach include simplicity of design, horizontal scaling, and finer control over availability. NoSQL databases are often highly optimized key-value stores intended primarily for simple retrieval and appending operations, whereas an RDBMS is intended as a general purpose data store. There will thus be some operations where NoSQL is faster and some where an RDBMS is faster. NoSQL databases are finding significant and growing industry use in big-data and real-time web applications. MySQL, on the other hand, is the world's most popular open-source database, enabling the cost-effective delivery of reliable, high-performance, and scalable web-based and embedded database applications.

Rdb was originally created by Digital Equipment Corporation (DEC) in 1984 as part of the VMS Information Architecture, intended to be used for data storage and retrieval by high-level languages and/or other DEC products such as DATATRIEVE, RALLY, and TEAMDATA. The original name was Rdb/VMS. In 1994, DEC sold the Rdb division to Oracle Corporation, where it was rebranded Oracle Rdb. Oracle is still offering this product, although Oracle Database products get the lion's share of Oracle's advertising budget. It currently runs on OpenVMS for VAX, Alpha, and IA-64 (Itanium). Rdb featured one of the first cost-based optimizers, and after acquisition, Oracle introduced a cost-based optimizer in its regular Oracle RDBMS product.

ORACLE AND DATA MANAGEMENT

Oracle recognizes the need for sophisticated data management capabilities. Their Oracle Hyperion Data Relationship Management helps proactively manage changes in master data across operational, analytical, and enterprise performance-management silos. Users may make changes in their departmental perspectives while ensuring conformance to enterprise standards. Oracle Enterprise Data Quality delivers a complete, best-of-breed approach to party and product data, resulting in trustworthy master data that integrates with applications to improve business insight. Both of these products are part of Oracle's Master Data Management (MDM) suite of tools, as shown in Table 6.2.

At a basic level, MDM seeks to ensure that an organization does not use multiple (potentially inconsistent) versions of the same master data in

TABLE 6.2

Oracle's Master Data Management Tool Suite

Oracle Customer Hub	Oracle Customer Hub is a customer data integration (CDI) solution that enables organizations to centralize information from heterogeneous systems, creating a single view of customer information that can be leveraged across all functional departments and analytical systems.
Oracle Data Relationship Governance	Oracle Data Relationship Governance provides essential change management and data quality remediation workflows, capturing business changes and applying them with consistency and accuracy across transactional and analytical system silos. This ensures data quality, policy compliance, repeatable business processes, cross-functional collaboration, and change awareness throughout the enterprise.
Oracle Data Relationship Management	Oracle Data Relationship Management helps proactively manage changes in master data across operational, analytical, and enterprise performance-management silos. Users may make changes in their departmental perspectives while ensuring conformance to enterprise standards. Whether processing financial or analytical information, Oracle Data Relationship Management delivers timely, accurate, and consistent master data to drive ongoing operational execution, business intelligence, and performance management.
Oracle Enterprise Data Quality	Oracle Enterprise Data Quality delivers a complete, best-of-breed approach to party and product data, resulting in trustworthy master data that integrates with applications to improve business insight.
Oracle Fusion Customer Hub	Oracle Fusion Customer Hub enables organizations to centralize business-critical information from heterogeneous systems to create a single view of customer information that can be leveraged across all functional departments and analytical systems.
Oracle Fusion Product Hub	Oracle Fusion Product Hub enables organizations to take control of their product master data across their entire portfolio of applications. With Oracle Fusion Product Hub, product information is shared across systems and users, resulting in improved data accuracy, better decisions, and accelerated time to market.

(Continued)

TABLE 6.2 (CONTINUED)

Oracle's Master Data Management Tool Suite

Oracle Product Hub	Oracle Product Hub enables organizations to centralize product information from heterogeneous systems, as well as eliminate the challenge of fragmented product data. The end result is a trusted, single view of products across the enterprise.
Oracle Site Hub	Oracle Site Hub is a mastering data solution focused on solving the problems of distributed, fragmented, incomplete, and inconsistent site data.
Oracle Supplier Hub	Oracle Supplier Hub empowers applications with the ability to unify and share critical information about an organization's supply base. Consolidated supplier information enables companies to quickly onboard, evaluate, and manage suppliers.

different parts of its operations, which is something that can occur in large organizations. A common example of poor MDM is the scenario of a bank at which a customer has taken out a mortgage and the bank begins to send mortgage solicitations to that customer, ignoring the fact that the person already has a mortgage account relationship with the bank. This happens because the customer information used by the marketing section within the bank lacks integration with the customer information used by the customer services section of the bank. Thus the two groups remain unaware that an existing customer is also considered as a sales lead. The process of record linkage is used to associate different records that correspond to the same entity, in this case the same person.

Other problems include (for example) issues with the quality of data, consistent classification and identification of data, and data-reconciliation issues. Master data management of disparate data systems requires data transformations as the data extracted from the disparate-source data system is transformed and loaded into the master data management hub. To synchronize the disparate-source master data, the managed master data extracted from the master data management hub is again transformed and loaded into the disparate-source data system as the master data is updated. As with other Extract, Transform, Load-based data movement, these processes are expensive and inefficient to develop and to maintain, which greatly reduces the return on investment for the master data management product.

The Data Management Association's (www.dama.org) definition of data management is the development and execution of architectures, policies, practices, and procedures that properly manage the full data life-cycle needs of an enterprise. Disciplines in data management include:

1. Data modeling
2. Database administration
3. Data warehousing
4. Data movement
5. Data mining
6. Data quality assurance
7. Data security
8. Metadata management (data repositories and their management)
9. Strategic data architecture

There is a difference between data and information. Data is stored in multiple applications systems on multiple platforms using multiple methods and is used to perform day-to-day operations. If this distributed data is grouped together in a meaningful format, it can provide valuable information to business organizations and their decision makers.

Data is captured using online transaction processing (OLTP) systems to perform mission-critical daily operations. Typically, many users simultaneously add, modify, delete, and view data using OLTP applications. OLTP systems are characteristically designed to perform transactions one record at a time.

Information is derived from online analytical processing (OLAP) systems used for analysis, planning, and management reporting through access to a variety of sources. An OLAP system usually references information that is stored in a data warehouse. Use of this technology enables the facility to present a comprehensive view of the enterprise.

Data and information are extremely valuable assets. Data architecture defines an infrastructure for providing high-quality, consistent data to be used as the basis for decision support and executive information services as well as traditional transaction applications statewide. Data architecture defines all the components, interfaces, and processes for implementing and managing an integrated, cohesive data policy. These components are defined in the following subsections.

Data

Text and numeric data: Data fields comprising rows of information containing discrete values related to some business entity. Most operational databases are almost completely text and numeric data fields. Because there are discrete values, these can be individually retrieved, queried, and manipulated to support some activity, reporting need, or analysis.

Images: Scanned pictures of documents, photos, and other multidimensional forms can be stored in databases. The scanned image is a single data field and is retrieved and updated as a single fact. Software outside of the DBMS is used to manipulate the image.

Geographic data: Geographic data is information about features on the surface and subsurface of the Earth, including their location, shape, description, and condition. Geographic information includes spatial and descriptive tabular information in tabular and raster (image) formats. A geographic information system (GIS) is a hardware and software environment that captures, stores, analyzes, queries, and displays geographic information. Geographic information is typically the basis for location-based decision making, land-use planning, emergency response, and mapping purposes.

Multimedia: voice, animation, and video: Multimedia applications are increasing as we employ new modalities of communicating with users. Voice can be stored in a database to capture instructional, informative messages that can then be played back rather than displayed as text. This facilitates those situations where keyboards and visual displays are difficult to utilize. Graphics, animation, and video, likewise, offer an alternative way to inform users where simple text does not communicate easily the complexity or the relationships between informational components. An example might be graphic displays of vessels and equipment allowing drill down to more detailed information related to a part or component. Video may be useful in demonstrating some complex operation as part of a training program.

Objects: Objects are composites of other data types and other objects. Unlike the relational model, objects form a hierarchy of information. Objects contain facts about themselves and exhibit certain behaviors implemented as procedural code. They also inherit the facts and behaviors of their parent objects up through the hierarchy. Relational databases store everything in rows and columns. Although they may support large binary object (LOB) fields that can hold anything, an object database can support any type of data combined with the processing to display it.

Databases

Databases organize data and information into physical structures, which are then accessed and updated through the services of a database management system. A database is an organization method that links files together as required. In nonrelational systems (e.g., hierarchical, network, etc.), records in one file contain embedded pointers to the locations of records in another, such as customers to orders and vendors to purchases. These are fixed links set up ahead of time to speed up daily processing. An RDBMS is software designed to manage a collection of data, where data is organized into related sets of tables, rows, and columns so that relationships between and among data can be established. For example, a vehicle database can contain two tables, one for customer information and one for vehicle information. An "owns" relationship is then established between the two tables.

A multidimensional database management system (MDDBMS) is specifically designed for efficient storage and retrieval of large volumes of data. Multidimensional databases are organized into fact tables and dimensions that intersect with the facts table to identify what the fact pertains to. Databases of this construction are used for online analytical processing, also known as OLAP.

Data Warehouse: Data Marts

A data warehouse is a database designed to support decision making in an organization or enterprise. It is refreshed, or batch updated, and can contain massive amounts of data. When the database is organized for one department or function, it is often called a *data mart* rather than a data warehouse, as shown in Figure 6.2.

The data in a data warehouse is typically historical and static in nature. Data marts also contain numerous summary levels. They are structured to support a variety of elaborate analytical queries on large amounts of data that can require extensive searching.

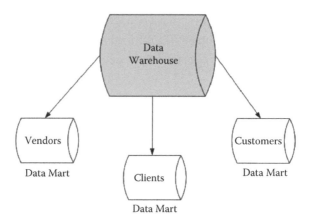

FIGURE 6.2
Data warehouse and its associated data marts.

A data warehouse is a record of an enterprise's past transactional and operational information, stored in a database designed for efficient data analysis and reporting (especially OLAP). Two basic ideas guide the creation of a data warehouse:

1. Integration of data from distributed and differently structured databases, which facilitates a global overview and comprehensive analysis in the data warehouse. Periodically, one imports data from enterprise resource planning (ERP) systems and other related business software systems into the data warehouse for further processing.
2. Separation of data used in daily operations from data used in the data warehouse for purposes of reporting, decision support, analysis, and controlling.

Operational Data Store

The Operational Data Store (ODS) is a database that consolidates data from multiple source systems and provides a near real-time, integrated view of volatile, current data. An ODS differs from a warehouse in that the ODS's contents are updated in the course of business, whereas a data warehouse contains static data.

Data Access

Access to data falls into two major categories:

Online Analytical Processing (OLAP): Decision support software allows the user to quickly analyze information that has been summarized into multidimensional views. Traditional OLAP products, also known as multidimensional OLAP, or MOLAP, summarize transactions into multidimensional views ahead of time. User queries on these types of databases are extremely fast because the consolidation has already been done. OLAP places the data into a cube structure that can be rotated by the user, which is particularly suited for financial summaries, as shown in Figure 6.3.

Online Transaction Processing (OLTP): Online transaction processing means that master files are updated as soon as transactions are entered at terminals or received over communications lines. It also implies that confirmations are returned to the sender. They are considered real-time systems.

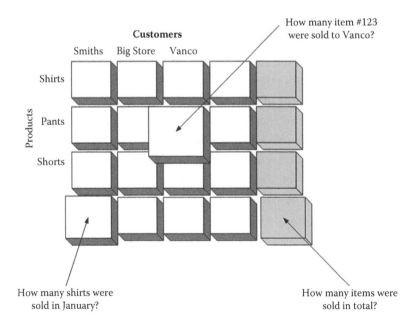

FIGURE 6.3
OLAP cube.

Replication

Replication is used to keep distributed databases up to date with a central-source database. Replication uses a database that has been identified as a central source and reproduces the data to distributed target databases. As more and more data is being made available to the public over the Internet, replication of select data to locations outside the firewall is becoming more common.

Replicated data should be accessed by applications in a read-only mode. If updates were allowed on replicated data, data would quickly become corrupted and out of sync. Updates should be directed to the database access tier in charge of updating the authoritative source rather than to a replicated database.

Replication services are available from most relational database vendors for their particular products.

RESOURCE MANAGEMENT

Resource management provides the operational facilities for managing and securing an enterprise-wide, distributed data architecture. It provides a common view of the data, including definitions, stewardship, distribution, and currency, and it allows those charged with ensuring operational integrity and availability the tools necessary to do so. Research needs to be done for all components in this category.

Security becomes an increasingly important aspect as access to data and information expands and takes on new forms such as web pages and dynamic content. The security policy needs to be examined to ensure that (a) it provides for the new types of databases and the new data types and (b) it can be enforced given the move to distributed data and Internet access.

The Data Warehouse

A data warehouse is something you do, not something you buy. A successful data warehouse does not have an end. Regardless of the methodology, warehousing environments must be built incrementally through projects that are managed under the umbrella of a data-warehousing program.

Most of the benefits of the data warehouse will not be realized in the first delivery. The first project will be the foundation for the next, which will in turn form the foundation for the next. Data warehousing at the enterprise level is a long-term strategy, not a short-term fix. Its cost and value should be evaluated across a time span sufficient to provide a realistic picture of its cost-to-value ratio.

The following seven components make up the enterprise data warehouse architecture. These components offer a high level of flexibility and scalability for the enterprise wishing to implement a business intelligence solution.

Source Systems

A data-source system is the operational or legacy system of record whose function it is to capture the transactions of the business. Source systems should be thought of as outside the data warehouse, because we have no control over the content and format of the data. The data in these systems can be in many formats, from flat files to hierarchical and RDBMS, etc. Other sources of data may already be cleansed and integrated and available from operational data stores.

Data Staging Area

The data staging area is the portion of the data warehouse restricted to extracting, cleaning, matching, and loading data from multiple legacy systems. The data staging area is the back room and is explicitly off limits to the end users. The data staging area does not support query or presentation services. A data-cleansing tool may be used to process data in the staging area to resolve name and address misspellings and the like, as well as resolve other data-cleansing issues by use of fuzzy logic.

Data Warehouse Database

The warehouse is no special technology in itself. The data warehouse database is a relational data structure that is optimized for distribution. It collects and stores integrated sets of historical, nonvolatile data from multiple operational systems and feeds them to one or more data marts. It becomes the one source of the truth for all shared data.

Data Marts

The easiest way to conceptually view a data mart is that a mart needs to be an extension of the data warehouse. Data is integrated as it enters the data warehouse from multiple legacy sources. Data marts then derive their data from the central data warehouse source. The theory is that no matter how many data marts are created, all the data is drawn from the one and only version of the truth, which is the data contained in the warehouse. Distribution of the data from the warehouse to the mart provides the opportunity to build new summaries to fit a particular department's need. The data marts contain subject-specific information supporting the requirements of the end users in individual business units. Data marts can provide rapid response to end-user requests if most queries are directed to precomputed, aggregated data stored in the data mart.

Extract Transform Load

Data Extraction-Transformation-Load (ETL) tools are used to extract data from data sources, cleanse the data, perform data transformations, and load the target data warehouse and then again to load the data marts. The ETL tool is also used to generate and maintain a central metadata repository and support data warehouse administration. The more robust ETL tools integrate with OLAP tools, data-modeling tools, and data-cleansing tools at the metadata level. Appendix 10 (available on the CRC Press website for download at http://www.crcpress.com/product/isbn/9781482249941) provides a good set of checklists for selecting and integrating a metadata repository.

Business Intelligence (BI)

BI provides the tools required by users to specify queries, create arbitrary reports, and analyze their own data using drill-down and OLAP functions. Putting this functionality in the hands of the power users allows them to ask their own questions and gives them quick and easy access to the information they need. However, one tool does not fit all. The BI tools arena still requires that we match the right tools to the right end user.

Metadata and the Metadata Repository

A repository is itself a database containing a complete glossary for all components, databases, fields, objects, owners, access, platforms, and users within the enterprise. The repository offers a way to understand what information is available, where it comes from, where it is stored, the transformation performed on the data, its currency, and other important facts about the data.

The repository describes the data structures and the business rules at a level above a data dictionary. However, metadata has taken on a more visible role among day-to-day knowledge workers. Today it serves as the main catalog or the map to a data warehouse. The central metadata repository is an essential part of a data warehouse. Metadata can be generated and maintained by an ETL tool as part of the specification of the extraction, transformation, and load process. The repository can also capture the operational statistics on the operation of the ETL process.

DATA STORAGE STRUCTURES

There are a variety of techniques and tools that enable the organization to best organize data for a variety of uses.

ROLAP: Relational On-Line Analytical Processing (ROLAP) tools extract analytical data from traditional relational databases structures. Using complex SQL (structured query language) statements against relational tables, ROLAP is able to create multidimensional views on the fly. ROLAP tends to be used on data that has a large number of attributes, where it cannot be easily placed into a cube structure.

MOLAP: Multidimensional On-Line Analytical Processing (MOLAP) is specially designed for the purpose of user understandability and high performance. A multidimensional database uses a dimensional model instead of a relational model. A dimensional model is a star schema characterized by a central fact table, as shown in Figure 6.4. One fact table is surrounded by a series of dimension tables. Data is joined from the dimension points to the center, providing a so-called star. The fact table contains all the pointers to its descriptive dimension tables plus a set of measurements of facts about this combination of dimensions.

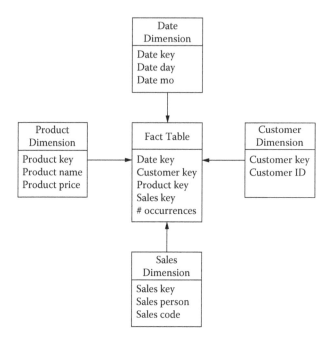

FIGURE 6.4
A dimensional model.

HOLAP: Hybrid On-Line Analytical Processing (HOLAP) tools use the best features of multidimensional and relational databases. Relational databases are best known for their flexibility. Until recently, relational databases were weak in their ability to perform the same kind of multidimensional analysis that the multidimensional databases are specifically optimized for. The introduction of hybrid relational systems with enhanced abilities to manipulate star schemas has increased the OLAP capabilities to the relational world. Hybrid tools provide high performance for both general-purpose end users and power users.

WOLAP: Web-enabled OLAP.

CUBE: In a multidimensional database, a dimensional model is a cube. It holds data more like a 3-D spreadsheet rather than a traditional relational database. A cube allows different views of the data to be quickly displayed. The ability to quickly switch between one slice of data and another allows users to analyze their information in smaller meaningful chunks, at the speed of thought. Use of cubes allows the user to look at data in several dimensions, e.g., attendance by department, attendance by attendance codes, attendance by date, etc.

EXTRACTION, TRANSFORMATION, AND LOAD

Transforming data is generally performed as part of the preparation before data is loaded into the data warehouse and data marts. Understanding the business usage of this information and the specific business questions to be analyzed and answered are the keys to determining the transformations necessary to produce the target data mart.

ETL tools are used to extract data from operational and external source systems, transform the data, and load the transformed data in a data warehouse. The same tool is used to extract and transform the data from the warehouse and distribute it to the data marts. When a schedule is defined for refreshing the data, the data-extraction and -transformation schedule must be carefully implemented so that it both meets the needs of the data warehouse and does not adversely impact the source systems that store the original data.

Extraction is a means of replicating data through a process of selection from one or more source databases. Extraction may or may not employ some form of transformation. Data extraction can be accomplished through custom-developed programs. However, the preferred method uses vendor-supported data-extraction and -transformation tools that can be customized to address particular extraction and transformation needs as well as use an enterprise metadata repository that will document the business rules used to determine what data was extracted from the source systems.

Data is transformed from transaction level data into information through several techniques: filtering, summarizing, merging, transposing, converting, and deriving new values through mathematical and logical formulas. These all operate on one or more discrete data fields to produce a target result having more meaning from a decision-support perspective than the source data. This process requires understanding the business focus, the information needs, and the currently available sources. Issues of data standards, domains, and business terms arise when integrating across operational databases.

Cleansing data is based on the guideline of populating the data warehouse with quality data, i.e., data that is consistent; that is of a known, recognized value; and that conforms with the business definition as expressed by the user. The cleansing operation is focused on determining those values that violate these rules and—through either a rejection or transformation process—bring the data into conformance.

Data cleansing standardizes data according to specifically defined rules; eliminates redundancy to increase data-query accuracy; reduces the cost associated with inaccurate, incomplete, and redundant data; and reduces the risk of invalid decisions made against incorrect data.

Good Data Management Practices

Data management is an integral function in most large organizations. It must be rigorously performed and maintained. The rapid and expansive development of information management technologies has opened the door to a vast world of information that can be processed and analyzed with increasing speed and complexity. Ensuring that information (and the interpretations derived from it) is accurate is the key challenge for successful data management. Sound data management involves a series of actions that must be clearly defined, clearly understood, and diligently followed.

The achievement and maintenance of data integrity depend on several key data management roles within the organization: data/project sponsors, data stewards, data and database administrators, and system administrators. Each of these roles is discussed in the following section.

Data Management Roles

Table 6.3 displays the relationship matrix between data management functions and personnel's corresponding roles. It is quite possible for roles to require both content knowledge and technical skills. As we move across the matrix from data sponsorship to system administration, the required skills gradually shift from content in nature (program management level, data-content level) to more highly technical in nature (systems, database management, GIS skills, etc.).

Each of these roles is described in the following subsections.

Data Sponsor

The data sponsor is an advocate for a particular information activity such as a spatial data set or application. The person in the organization representing this role has a vested interest in the information activity and provides an appropriate level of support to ensure its success. The data sponsor normally has decision authority (at the management level) and approves resources available to the project.

TABLE 6.3

Relationships of Data Management Functions and Roles People Play

	Roles				
Functions	**Data Sponsor**	**Data Steward**	**Data Admin.**	**DB Admin.**	**System Admin./ Support**
Development requirements	C	C	C/T	T	T
Identification enforcement standards		C	C/T	T	
Design implementation		C	C/T	T	T
Quality control data integrity		C	C/T	T	T
Backup and recovery			C/T		T
Data sharing		C	C/T	T	T
Change management; change analysis		C	C/T		
Connectivity			C/T		T
Input and update		C	C/T		
Security			C	T	T
Metadata			C/T	T	
Training		C	C/T		

C = primarily *content* knowledge required.
T = primarily *technical* knowledge required.
C/T = both *content* and *technical* knowledge required.

Sponsor duties include:

1. To review project plans and assess relevancy to corporate information needs. The sponsor must inform management about the scope and effect of the project and its impact on the organization.
2. To serve as an advocate for the project. This advocacy role is not finished with the successful implementation of a data set or application; it continues through evaluation and support of required future developments related to changing information needs due to technological advancements.
3. To collaborate in setting goals and priorities.
4. To ensure that staffing, funds, and other resources are available, in addition to making sure that the appropriate data management roles are assigned and fulfilled.
5. To review the project's progress and use of resources.

Sponsor coordination responsibilities include:

1. Project sponsors must coordinate with counterparts at the leadership-team level on budget and staffing issues. Implicit in this task is ensuring that adequate resources are available for the project.
2. Coordination is required at the planning level to ensure that priorities are clarified and that the project can proceed with the allotted resources.
3. The sponsor also coordinates with the roles of data steward, data administrator, and database administrator at project initiation and periodically during the project life cycle.
4. Sponsors coordinate with higher level counterparts in the program area that the projects fall within.

Other sponsor requirements include:

1. Every project must have clearly defined sponsorship.
2. Sponsorship is an ongoing responsibility that does not end with a project's implementation; this role extends through the project life cycle as well. Prior to beginning an information activity, a commitment to this responsibility must be comprehended and accepted.

Data Steward

Effective resource management requires data that is current, accurate, and readily available. To achieve this goal, responsibility for effective data management must be assigned to data stewards from top to bottom within the organization. Data automation and data sharing have increased the necessity for accurate and immediate data accessibility. It is the data steward's role that is essential to meeting these requirements.

Data steward duties include:

1. The development of procedures and standards that ensure the data is both acceptable and accurate in the applicable program area. It is imperative that only data relevant to the organization's mission is collected, and that the data is of sufficient quality. This also includes

functioning as a liaison with the users of the data. The data steward must be assertive in asking for input when defining and managing corporate data sets.

2. The implementation of data standards. Stewards must define how the standards will be applied to the resource(s) or program(s).
3. The development of new standards when necessary. This includes maintaining state-of-the-art knowledge of existing data standards for the program.
4. The development of quality assurance and quality control plans. Examples of this include data gathering, updates, and sampling protocols for alphanumeric databases and database edit rules.
5. To check data and databases to address the needs of others who use and share the data.
6. To initiate data-sharing and -exchange agreements, where necessary.
7. To follow the life-cycle management/project planning and configuration-management procedures in an application's development.
8. To determine user training needs and the resources necessary for user training (specific to the data and applications).
9. To determine data/application update needs and points of implementation. Included in this task is establishing periodic update cycles (either specific dates or frequency of updates) when relevant.
10. To establish and maintain data/application documentation, e.g., user manuals, data dictionaries, and metadata.
11. To serve as a point of contact for data or application.
12. To define access and security requirements for data/applications.
13. To comply with map accuracy standards where applicable.

Data steward coordination responsibilities include:

1. To coordinate with counterparts within the program area.
2. To coordinate with the user community of the data/application.
3. To coordinate with the data administrator, database administrator, and data sponsor roles.

Data Administration

Data administration is responsible for the management of data-related activities. Two levels of data administration activities exist: system and project.

System-level functions deal with management issues, including planning, developing data standards (in conjunction with data stewards), developing policies, establishing data-integrity procedures, resolving data-conflict issues, and managing data-resource-related DBMS.

At the system level, data-administration policies ensure careful management of data both at creation and during use. This management practice is necessary to maintain data integrity, maximize data use, and to minimize costs associated with data management and collection.

At the physical management level, we intentionally classify the database administrator (DBA) as a subcomponent of the data administrator role. The DBA role differs from the data administrator role in that the DBA supports the development and use of a specific database system. The DBA role must fulfill the following tasks: defining user requirements, developing data models, training and consulting, establishing and monitoring data integrity, monitoring database usage, and controlling database changes.

Data administrator duties include:

1. Implement a program of data administration that meets the organization's vision with respect to consistency, shareability, and quality of data. This must reflect the business management requirements of the organization.
2. Develop strategies, policies, procedures, standards, guidance, and assistance needed for effective data administration.
3. Help to facilitate maximum data-sharing capability and to eliminate data-definition redundancies by promoting a common description and representation of data. Cooperation with data stewards is necessary to accomplish this task.
4. Promote data-collection strategies to ensure that data is collected at the source, and that key data-collection surveys meet identified integration and business needs.
5. Establish and support strategies governing access, retention, and disposition of data.
6. Establish a communication program with customers and suppliers of information resources.
7. Maintain a repository of active sponsors and stewards for all information activities and components. Also must ensure that stewardship responsibilities are properly established and maintained for the shared components.
8. Establish and support corporate strategies for data administration.

9. Promote a shared data environment that is both flexible and responsive to the changing business needs of the organization.

10. Establish an integrating framework (enterprise data model) and work with development projects to ensure compatibility with the framework. The enterprise data model will consist of a collection of models ranging from high-level strategic planning views through the implementation of shared databases.

11. Develop data- and function-modeling standards and procedures.

12. Develop and enforce standards for maintaining corporate data.

13. Participate in the review of all software releases to ensure compliance with data-administration policy, procedures, and standards.

14. Facilitate the change-management process for all corporate data.

15. Ensure that data-administration standards comply with government and industry standards while also providing for information exchange and operational compatibility.

16. Ensure compliance with metadata policy and facilitate the maintenance of official metadata records.

17. Facilitate customer access to metadata.

18. Promote data security. This task most notably includes identifying security requirements and assisting the identification of data-security procedures and policies.

Data administrator coordination responsibilities include:

1. The data administrator coordinates with the DBA, data stewards, program area leads, project managers, and application developers by providing education, technical support, reviewing feedback, and developing good working relationships throughout the enterprise.

2. The data administrator role serves as an internal consultant to help employees, managers, and developers locate and retrieve data that meets their information needs. This consultation helps provide leverage to the organization's data investment.

3. The data administrator role serves as a coordination point between the various data stewards. By providing this type of coordination, both data integration and standard consistency are maintained throughout the organization.

Database Administration

The focus of this section is the database administration subcomponent of data administration. It should be noted that the duties of the data administrator and the database administrator may overlap; these duties can be performed by one or more persons in the organization.

Both the DBA, who utilizes a technical perspective, and the data steward, who utilizes a content perspective, must work together to build a framework that promotes and provides several data management functions. In simplest terms, the DBA is responsible for the database framework and all transactions (inputs and updates) associated with the data set.

At the physical (project) level, the DBA must focus on the detailed needs of the individual users and applications. The database-development aspect of data management shoulders the bulk of the responsibility for developing data models and database implementation. Data development involves the analysis (planning), design, building, maintenance, documentation, and monitoring aspect.

Database administration duties include:

1. Formulates a conceptual model of the database in conjunction with the system-level data-administration requirements. As a result, the DBA must be identified/assigned at a project's earliest stages to provide a background and establish the project's scope needed in the model.
2. Works closely with the system administrator to ensure that the physical environment is conducive to design and development, e.g., identifying appropriate physical space, networking, and access criteria.
3. Coordinates the development and implementation of procedures that will ensure data consistency, integrity, and quality with the data steward.
4. Builds a data structure conducive to an enforcement of standards as developed at the system level of data administration and by data stewards. Although the ultimate responsibility for identification of standards related to the data and processes resides with the data steward, it is the responsibility of the DBA to build a data structure conducive to the enforcement of these standards.
5. Ensures that data structures are suitable for analysis and application development. Performs database tuning to ensure efficient input, update, and retrieval of data.

6. Monitors the data set/application use and routinely reports back to the data steward regarding the use of a particular data set/application.
7. Ensures that the data set is readily available for sharing both internally and externally.
8. Coordinates the identification, assessment of impacts, strategy, and implementation of change-management procedures for a data set.
9. Implements appropriate data-security measures by aiding in the control of access at several levels. Works closely with the system administrator to ensure that this security exists at the appropriate levels (network, platform, data, and application).
10. Assesses current and new technology merit, e.g., the new technology/tool's performance, the cost ramifications of change at all levels, etc.

Database administration coordination responsibilities include:

1. DBAs must coordinate with project sponsors and data stewards to design and develop a data structure that meets their needs.
2. DBAs must coordinate with system administrators and other information support to ensure adequate physical environment and system security.
3. DBAs must coordinate the identification, impact assessment, strategy, and implementation of the change-management procedures for the data set.

System Administration and System Support

System administrator duties include:

1. Assesses existing computer resources and identifies additional needs
2. Develops guidelines and offers consultation for optimal computer configurations
3. Determines the online storage capacity, computer memory, and server, workstation, PC, and X-terminal configuration for the processing and management of data
4. Monitors computer resources and makes recommendations for changes to the system
5. Ensures that the systems are kept running and maintained with the latest technology

6. Loads data onto the system and ensures its security. Provides security for corporate data via access control
7. Provides access for maintenance of corporate data
8. Performs scheduled backups of the data
9. Archives historical data

Coordination responsibilities include:

1. Coordinates with the data administrator and database administrator to understand the nature and size of the data sets that will be worked with
2. Coordinates with the data administrator and the DBA to ensure that backups and archives are performed when necessary
3. Works with the data administrator, DBA, and data stewards to ensure needed security and data access
4. Coordinates with all individuals involved in the process to ensure that the systems are meeting project and organizational needs

DATA MANAGEMENT RESPONSIBILITIES

Data management consists of the functions listed in Table 6.4. The data management functions are defined as follows:

1. *Development and management requirements*: Development and management requirements refer to management leadership's commitment toward the process of data development and data management. To be successful, management leadership must be totally involved and prepared to commit people, time, and financial resources to the projects and their associated tasks they are sponsoring—not to mention using intelligent foresight during a project's resource analysis. It is important to make your resource specialists and managers available when the important issues are defined and when working through analysis and data requirements. Although this may be a

TABLE 6.4

Data Management Functionality

Data Management Functions	
A	Development and management requirements
B	Identification and enforcement standards, design, and implementation
C	Data and mapping standards
D	Quality control, data integrity, and backup and recovery
E	Data sharing
F	Change management and impact analysis
G	Connectivity
H	Input and update
I	Security
J	Metadata
K	Training

repetitive process, taking place at the planning stages of identifying information needs and continuing throughout the life of the project, it is imperative to a project's proper development.

The actual event of defining "development and management requirements" is quite common; it occurs every time the details of a project are defined. For the purposes of this discussion, we are focusing specifically on defining the level of involvement of the spatial/associated-natural-resource data component of project planning.

2. *Identification and enforcement standards, design, and implementation*: Identification standards simply are guidelines to help maintain data collection/updates, definitions, and validation protocols. Enforcement standards are guidelines to help ensure that the identification standards are followed. Both functions are based on the outcomes of the development and management requirement phases described in item 1.

Successful implementation of data management depends on intelligent up-front data design, e.g., following up on standards agreements, constructing a data model, and setting up the actual system. The actual implementation should always follow the physical design process.

3. *Data and mapping standards*: To ensure that your databases, data entry forms, acceptable codes, applications, etc., are all shareable, consistent, and scientifically sound, data standards should be designed in advance. Given the large amount of data processing, it

should be apparent that data-collection standards are essential for data integrity.

4. *Quality control, data integrity, and backup/recovery*: Before data can become corporate or shared, the appropriate mapping standards and data-definition standards must be complied with via quality control.

   Another important procedure that must be performed regularly, especially when a project or corporate data set reaches a significant milestone, is data backup. Data backup protects the project's progress from any unanticipated system failures or user errors by saving it to the proper media and archiving it. To ensure real-time data integrity, recovery contingencies must also be in place.

5. *Data sharing*: Sharing data is essential to most projects; multiple users must have access to the same data to make this type of data processing effective. Before data sharing can occur, the data, metadata, projection, and format must all be integrated. Data sharing has direct links with data security because certain users will have different types of access, depending on their needs or update responsibilities. Connectivity is also implicit in data sharing, which is discussed under item 7.

6. *Change management and impact analysis*: Impacts from data-standard changes or technological changes (hardware/software upgrades) must be anticipated and planned for. The possible ramifications on certain end users, organizations, and applications must be accounted for during a project's planning.

7. *Connectivity*: Connectivity is how data is shared and distributed in a networked architecture. User requirements determine the scale of connectivity that is required; these requirements may or may not be apparent to the user community.

8. *Input and update*: The actual collection, input, and update of data may take place in several different locations and several different steps. The technical side of data sharing has to do with the various data types: Different types of data require different approaches to updating. Static data is usually low maintenance, whereas dynamic data is usually high maintenance (monitored by the specialist, data steward, and the database administrator). Update cycles are largely dependent on the dynamic/static nature of the data. Input and update protocols must be developed so that data stewards have standard methodologies to follow.

9. *Security*: A number of security levels exist in a multiple-user interface: network, platform, and data. Security levels are based on user requirements both internal and external to applications (e.g., databases). To help implement security access levels, a review process should be established.

Network security pertains to the different levels of security throughout the computer network and with firewall(s) management. Platform security relates directly to access privileges according to the platform(s) you are operating on (e.g., IBM, DG, Prime, PCs, and associated operating systems). Here is where the issue of data access restrictions appear—normally set by the system administrator. Because data security is application specific, data stewards must determine the ownership requirements, and DBAs must then implement the requirements (e.g., RWE [read, write, execute], RW, or R access).

10. *Metadata*: Metadata management requires proper documentation throughout the life cycle of any data set. Technically, metadata is data about data. Although similar, data dictionaries do not apply to this definition.

11. *Training*: Appropriate training is imperative for those collecting data, those entering data, those designing database(s), and certainly for those persons involved in the data management process. A certification processes for some roles can be very valuable to ensure that consistent, sound, and accurate data is being collected and entered into the corporate database.

GUIDELINES

These guidelines are intended to provide a guide in the evaluation, selection, design, construction, and implementation of a data warehouse.

Guideline 1: Information is valued as an asset, which must be capable of being shared.

1. A policy pertaining to information stewardship will have to be developed. This entails determining responsibility for accuracy,

access authorization, historical trails, manipulation approval, definitions, and integrity relationships.

2. Information and its value must be identified by its current keepers. It must be authenticated and documented. Stewardship must be identified or assigned. The metadata must be capable of being universally available so that the data contained within can be leveraged by all who are authorized to use it.

3. A mechanism will be required to maintain identified metadata information that can be listed, categorized, and show stewardship, level of privacy/security, and location of information. There is a need for unified metadata information management to make it accessible for all agencies.

4. Supporting policies will need to be established for security, privacy, confidentiality, and information sharing. This requires the development of data-use agreements.

5. Data will need to be structured for easy access and management by adopting enterprise data standards.

6. Identified data should be used from existing sources and not recaptured by new development.

7. Standards should be adopted to provide more global sharing capabilities.

8. Management tools will be required to maintain and manage a metadata repository.

9. Change-control procedures will need to be defined and adopted to ensure that the metadata repository is current.

10. Methodology will be needed to publish and disseminate information on the data available for sharing.

11. Creation of an enterprise data model will be required.

12. Policy and procedures will need to be established to maintain timely and accurate enterprise-wide geographic information.

13. Policies for service-level agreements will need to be defined to determine the availability and level of service.

14. Enterprise-wide systems will be needed to support the creation, storage, and retrieval of documents, images, and other information-rich objects that are used within processes or are exchanged with external organizations and constituents.

Guideline 2: The planning and management of the enterprise-wide technical architecture must be unified and have a planned evolution that is governed across the enterprise.

1. A unified approach will require a change in cultural attributes.
2. Normal evolution will require prioritization and reprioritization across all IT initiatives.
3. Dependencies must be maintained.
4. The architecture must be continually reexamined and refreshed.
5. Short-term results vs. long-term impact must be constantly considered.
6. Establishing enterprise architecture takes time and involves a lot of change.
7. Make sure that the chosen architecture has a broad range of capabilities to handle vast needs and best-of-breed solutions in the marketplace (Internet and PDAs and kiosk).
8. Planning for retirement must be considered for obsolete and nonstandard products.
9. Retraining of staff moving from obsolete technologies will be required.
10. In-house software engineers, data architects, DBAs, and warehouse experts will need to be developed and trained.

Guideline 3: Architecture support and review structures shall be used to ensure that the integrity of the architecture is maintained as systems and infrastructure are acquired, developed, and enhanced.

1. A structured project-level review process and authority will be needed to ensure that information systems comply with the IT architecture and related standards.
2. Processes incorporating the guidelines of this (technical) architecture must be developed for all application procurement, development, design, and management activities.
3. This compliance process must allow for the introduction of new technology and standards.
4. Conceptual architecture and technical domain guidelines should be used as evaluation criteria for purchasing as well as developing software.
5. Negotiation at the enterprise level will be needed to handle an increase in compliant systems.

6. An open mind will be needed when reviewing for compliance and the possible need to broaden the existing architecture or to consider possible exceptions.
7. Phase-out plans will need to be developed.
8. An inventory of who is using what architectures will be required.

Guideline 4: Organizations should leverage a data warehouse and data marts to facilitate the sharing of existing information. This data warehouse will contain the one single version of the truth.

1. Data warehousing must become a core competency of IT.
2. Data warehousing requires and supplies configuration standards; these standards will need to be developed and maintained.
3. End-user tools must be provided to relieve the burden on programmers to provide this functionality.
4. End users must become more knowledgeable about the information available to them. This can be accomplished by increasing end users' awareness of and knowledge about the tools they need to access and analyze this information.
5. The processes and procedures refreshing the data warehouse will require high levels of reliability and integrity.
6. Warehousing is not meant to replace shortcomings in transaction applications. Guidelines on maintaining data and data retention will need to be developed.
7. Not all requests for data are simple in nature and appropriate for end-user tools. Not all data will be available to all users.
8. End users should be able to access the data without knowledge of where it resides or how it is stored.
9. Data warehouse architecture design will require an integrated design effort to provide usefulness. The full potential of a data warehouse will not be realized unless there is full participation throughout the enterprise.
10. The user community must be made aware of the (un)timeliness of information.

Guideline 5: IT systems should be implemented in adherence with all security, confidentiality, and privacy policies and applicable legal and regulatory requirements.

1. The IT systems will need to identify, publish, and keep the applicable policies current.
2. Data elements will need to be secured.
3. Access control will have to be categorized, but this need may vary depending on the data and the audience.
4. Compliance to policies will have to be monitored.
5. The organization will have to make the requirements for security, confidentiality, and privacy clear to everyone.
6. Education on issues of privacy and confidentiality will have to become a routine part of normal business processes.
7. The capabilities of data access will have to be audited.
8. There should be an understanding that part of the stewardship role interprets security, confidentiality, and privacy.
9. All access requests for data that is not publicly available should be made to the steward of the data.
10. There must be a means to publish and implement changes to the status of data's access requirements.

Guideline 6: The enterprise architecture must reduce integration complexity to the greatest extent possible.

1. The number of vendors, products, and configurations in the state's environment will need to be reduced.
2. The enterprise must maintain configuration discipline.
3. The architecture will, in some instances, sacrifice performance and functionality.
4. The architecture will rely on components supplied by vendors, which will make the enterprise more vulnerable.
5. The cost of vendor dependency will need to be factored in when figuring the total cost of ownership.
6. Determination of "the greatest extent possible" includes consideration of how reducing complexity can negatively impact the ability to provide critical client services.

Guideline 7: Consider reuse of existing tools and infrastructure before investing in new solutions

1. Software license agreements and system development contracts should be written to allow for reuse across the enterprise.

2. Areas that provide clear advantages and businesses cost savings are likely to require quick adaptation.

Guideline 8: Systems must be designed, acquired, developed, or enhanced such that data and processes can be shared and integrated across the enterprise and with partners.

1. IT staff will need to consider the impacts on an enterprise-wide scale when designing applications.
2. IT staff will need a method for identifying data and processes that need integration, when integration should take place, who should have access to the data, and cost justification for integration.
3. It will be necessary to coordinate, maintain, and arbitrate a common set of domain tables, data definitions, and processes across the organization.
4. Overintegration can lead to inefficient data management processes.
5. The use of a metadata repository will be required.
6. Enterprise integration teams composed of dedicated enterprise data architects and applications architects will be required to assist in integration efforts.
7. Stewardship review of integration efforts will be required.
8. There will be a need to evaluate the practicality of any integrated project before development.

Guideline 9: New information systems will be implemented after business processes have been analyzed, simplified, or otherwise redesigned as appropriate.

1. An agreed-upon business reengineering process will be required.
2. It will be necessary to identify the business need for data.
3. The legal requirement for retention of data will need to be determined.
4. New technology will be applied in conjunction with business process review.
5. Business processes will need to be optimized to align with business drivers.
6. Additional time and resources will have to be invested in analysis early in the systems' life cycle.

7. Organizational change will be required to implement reengineered work processes.
8. Implementation of new systems may require regulatory or legislative change.

Guideline 10: Adopt a total cost-of-ownership model for applications and technologies that balances the costs of development, support, training, disaster recovery, and retirement against the costs of flexibility, scalability, ease of use, and reduction of integration complexity.

1. This will require looking closely at technical and user training costs, especially when making platform or major software upgrades during the lifetime of the system.
2. Designers and developers will have to take a systemic view.
3. Individual IT components will have to be selectively suboptimized.
4. There will be a need to develop a cost-of-ownership model.
5. A method of coordinated retirement of systems must be developed.
6. Budget issues for staffing and training will need to be considered.
7. A cost structure will have to be developed for providing access to shared information.
8. Funding will have to be provided for data costs that are not billable or recoverable.
9. Permanent, reliable funding mechanisms will need to be established for developing enterprise-wide geographic information such as aerial photography, satellite imagery, transportation, and hydrographic data layers.

Guideline 11: Infrastructure and data access will employ reusable components across the enterprise, using an *n*-tier model.

1. Component management will need to become a core competency.
2. Development of a culture of reuse will be required.
3. Design reviews will become crucial.
4. Data marts will need to be modularized without making components too small or too simple to do useful work.

Guideline 12: The logical design of application systems and databases should be highly partitioned. These partitions must have logical boundaries established, and the logical boundaries must not be violated.

1. Applications will need to be divided into coded entities (e.g., presentation, process, and data access).
2. For databases, there will be a need to develop competency in partitioning horizontally and vertically; this will result in more but simpler tables and views. Design reviews must ensure that logical boundaries are kept intact. Data management responsibilities will be increased for DBAs.
3. An increase in the analytical skills of project analysts will be required to determine when partitioning takes place based on expected data and/or access requirements.

Guideline 13: Online transaction processing (OLTP) should be separated from data warehouse and other end-user computing and Internet access.

1. Data marts represent a type of configuration standard for physical partitioning.
2. Data warehousing and data marts will need to become core competencies of IT.
3. Business and IT will need to agree on the purpose and objective of the data warehouses.
4. Data redundancy will be necessary.
5. Data marts will not reflect the most current data.
6. It will not always be necessary or even desirable to physically partition data, such as when there is a low scalability requirement.

Guideline 14: IT solutions should use industry-proven, mainstream technologies.

1. Criteria for vendor selection and performance measurement will need to be established.
2. Criteria to identify the weak vendors and poor technology solutions will need to be established.

3. Migration away from existing weak products in the technology portfolio will be required.
4. The number of solution choices will be limited.
5. There will be a need to respond as changes in technology occur.

Guideline 15: Priority should be given to products adhering to industry standards and open architecture.

1. Criteria will have to established to identify standards and the products using them.
2. IT organizations will need to determine how they will transition to this mode.
3. Establishment of priorities will reduce some solution choices.

Guideline 16: An assessment of business-recovery requirements will be mandatory when acquiring, developing, enhancing, or outsourcing systems. Based on that assessment, appropriate disaster-recovery and business-continuity planning, design, and testing will take place.

1. Systems will need to be categorized according to business-recovery needs (e.g., business critical, noncritical, not required).
2. Alternative computing capabilities will need to be in place.
3. Systems should be designed with fault tolerance and recovery in mind.
4. Plans for work-site recovery will need to be in place.
5. Costs may be higher.
6. Data must be capable of online backups to provide 24 × 7 availability.

Guideline 17: The underlying technology infrastructure and applications must be scalable in size, capacity, and functionality to meet changing business and technical requirements.

1. Scalability must be reviewed for both upward and downward capability.
2. Scalability may increase the initial costs of development and deployment.
3. The scalability requirement will reduce some solution choices.

SUMMARY

Oracle's database and data management product sets requires IT to fully understand not only the technology of the product set chosen, but how to build, align, manage, and secure that data.

7

Application Development

Oracle has a wide variety of application development tool sets capable of working with their Oracle database and other product sets. As you can see in Figure 7.1, Oracle provides support for most programming languages, in one way or another. Probably the most popular of Oracle's programming offerings is Java, as you can see on the right side of Figure 7.1 and in Table 7.1.

One of the more popular development environments is NetBeans, an integrated development environment (IDE). It's easy enough for a novice programmer, but it also provides some robust capabilities for more advanced programmers, as shown in Figure 7.2. NetBeans IDE is a free and open-source IDE for application development on Windows, Mac, Linux, and Solaris operating systems. The IDE simplifies the development of web, enterprise, desktop, and mobile applications that use the Java and HTML5 platforms. The IDE also offers support for the development of PHP and C/C++ applications.

JDeveloper is another freeware IDE supplied by Oracle Corporation. It offers features for development in Java, XML, SQL, PL/SQL, HTML, JavaScript, BPEL, and PHP. JDeveloper covers the full development life cycle, from design through coding, debugging, optimization, and profiling to deploying. With JDeveloper, Oracle has aimed to simplify application development by focusing on providing a visual and declarative approach to application development in addition to building an advanced coding environment. Oracle JDeveloper integrates with the Oracle Application Development Framework (Oracle ADF), an end-to-end Java EE-based framework that further simplifies application development.

The core IDE exposes an application programming interface (API) that other teams in Oracle use to build extensions to JDeveloper. BPEL, Portal, Business Intelligence, and other components of the Oracle

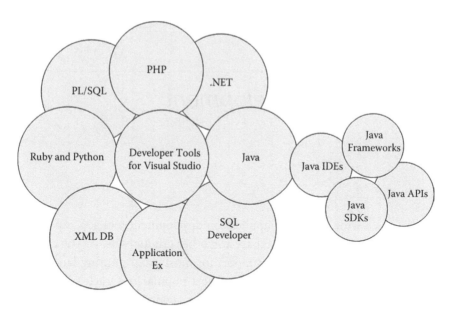

FIGURE 7.1
Oracle's application development tool set.

platform all build their design-time tools on top of JDeveloper. The same IDE platform also serves as the basis of another Oracle product, SQL Developer, which Oracle Corporation promotes specifically to PL/SQL and database developers.

Oracle Application Express (Oracle APEX, previously named Oracle HTML DB) is a software development environment running inside the Oracle Database. Oracle Application Express is free of charge and can be run inside Oracle Database Express Edition (also a free product). During installation of Oracle Database Express Edition, Oracle APEX is installed by default; however, Oracle APEX can be installed in any of the other Oracle Database Editions for free. If Oracle APEX is running inside Oracle Database Express Edition, the functionality is limited by the limitation of Oracle Database Express Edition, e.g., CPU limit (memory limit). Using only a web browser, an inexperienced programmer can use APEX to build complex web applications from scratch.

Oracle SQL Developer is an IDE for working with SQL in Oracle databases. Oracle Corporation provides this product free; it uses the Java Development Kit. Oracle SQL Developer supports Oracle products and a variety of third-party plug-ins that users may deploy to connect to non-Oracle databases. Oracle SQL Developer works with IBM DB2, Microsoft

TABLE 7.1

Oracle Java Offerings

Type	Tool	Description
Java IDEs	Java JDeveloper	Oracle JDeveloper is a free integrated development environment that simplifies the development of Java-based SOA and Java EE applications. JDeveloper offers complete end-to-end development to Oracle Fusion Middleware and Oracle Fusion Applications with support for the full development life cycle.
	NetBeans	Quickly and easily develop desktop, mobile, and web applications with Java, HTML5, PHP, C/C++, and more. NetBeans IDE is free, open source, and has a worldwide community of users and developers.
	Oracle Enterprise Pack for Eclipse 12c	Oracle Enterprise Pack for Eclipse (OEPE) 12.1.2.1.1 for Eclipse Kepler simplifies the utilization of Oracle Fusion Middleware Technologies in the development of applications with unparalleled features and user experience.
Java Frameworks	Oracle ADF	Oracle ADF is an end-to-end Java EE framework that simplifies application development by providing out-of-the-box infrastructure services and a visual and declarative development experience.
	Oracle TopLink	Oracle TopLink delivers a proven standards-based enterprise Java solution for all of your relational and XML persistence needs based on high performance and scalability, developer productivity, and flexibility in architecture and design.
	EclipseLink	The EclipseLink project delivers a comprehensive open-source Java-persistence solution addressing relational, XML, and database web services
	JavaFX	JavaFX 2 is the next step in the evolution of Java as a rich client platform, shortening development time and easing deployment of data-driven business and enterprise client applications.

(Continued)

TABLE 7.1 (CONTINUED)

Oracle Java Offerings

Type	Tool	Description
Java APIs	Java TV	Provides a performant, mature platform for TV and media-based client devices, enabling the development of compelling, interactive Java applications for Blu-ray Disc players, TVs, set-top boxes, and more.
	Java Card API	The Java Card Platform provides an open, interoperable environment enabling the development and deployment of portable trusted identity services to individuals and personal devices.
Java SDKs	Java SE JDK	JDK (Java Development Kit): For Java developers. Includes a complete JRE plus tools for developing, debugging, and monitoring Java applications.
		Server JRE (Server Java Runtime Environment): For deploying Java applications on servers. Includes tools for JVM monitoring and tools commonly required for server applications, but does not include browser integration (the Java plug-in), auto-update, or an installer.
		JRE (Java Runtime Environment): Covers most end-user needs. Contains everything required to run Java applications on your system.
	Java Me SDK	Java for mobile devices.

Access, Microsoft SQL Server, MySQL, Sybase Adaptive Server, and Teradata databases. These tools and others are listed in Table 7.2, demonstrating the wide range of Oracle support for various environments.

Application-development tool sets are just tools. For these to work effectively, there must be a formalized process that enables the developers to make the most productive use of these tools. For the remainder of this chapter, we are going to delve into the various aspects of software engineering such that the reader can get a high-level view of how all of this is best integrated into the organization.

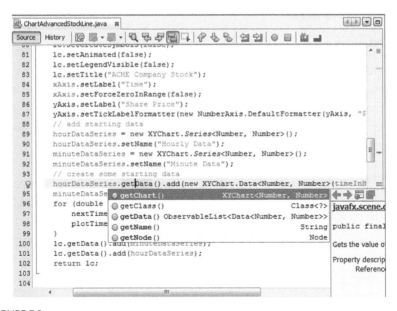

FIGURE 7.2
NetBeans interface.

TABLE 7.2

Domain-Specific Development Tools

Environment	Overview	Tools
Oracle Database and PL/SQL	Oracle offers rapid web development tools that integrate with the Oracle Database and use the PL/SQL development language to simplify development.	• Oracle Application Express • Oracle Forms • Oracle SQL Developer
Oracle Solaris and Oracle Linux	Oracle Linux is an open-source operating system available under the GNU (General Public License). Oracle Solaris provides services to run enterprise applications with massive horizontal scalability as well as mainframe-class scalability.	• Oracle Solaris Studio • Oracle Solaris • Oracle Linux
.NET	Oracle offers utilities that will help .NET developers to integrate and leverage the Oracle platform and the Oracle Database.	• Oracle Developer Tools for Visual Studio • Oracle Data Provider for .NET • Oracle Database Extensions for .NET • WebCenter WSRP Producer for .NET

PRINCIPLES OF SOFTWARE ENGINEERING

Computer systems come in all shapes and sizes. There are systems that process e-mail and systems that process payroll. There are also systems that monitor space missions and systems that monitor student grades. No matter how diverse the functionality of these systems, they have several things in common:

1. *All systems have end users.* It is for these end users that the system has been created. These end users have a vested interested in seeing that this system is doing what it is supposed to be doing correctly and efficiently. You might say that these end users have a stake in seeing that the system is successful. Sometimes these end users are referred to as *stakeholders.* There are different types of stakeholders. A good systems analyst is careful to avoid leaving stakeholders out erroneously. But this is indeed what happened when the post office started developing the automated system that you now see in use today at all post offices. This system was developed in a vacuum. What this means is that only higher level employees were involved in system development. The clerks that actually work at the windows were left out of the process. When it came time for this system to be deployed, the lack of involvement of this critical set of stakeholders almost led to an employee mutiny.

2. *All systems are composed of functions and data.* All of us like to get our payroll checks. To create a payroll check requires us to define several functions (sometimes called *processes*). For example, there might be functions for (a) obtaining employee information, (b) calculating payroll taxes, (c) calculating other deductions, and (d) printing the check. Systems analysts are not payroll clerks, nor are they accountants. A typical systems analyst does not have the information to create a payroll processing system without the involvement of stakeholders. Instead, the analyst needs to utilize several analytical techniques, including interviewing and observation, to get the details on how to perform these processes. Functions are only one-half of the equation, however. The other half is the data. Sometimes the data will already be available to the systems analyst, e.g., via a corporate database or file. Sometimes, however, the systems analyst will have to create a new database for the application. For this particular task, the analyst will usually work with a database administrator or data

administrator, as that person would have the expertise and authority to create or modify a database for use with the new or enhanced application.

3. *All systems use hardware and software.* A systems analyst has many decisions to make. The first decision is to select the platform on which to run this system: (a) PC only, (b) mainframe only, (c) client/server (i.e., PC client and mainframe or workstation server), etc. The analyst also has to decide whether or not to use any third-party software (i.e., Excel, SAP, etc.) and may even have to decide on which programming language and type of database to use.

4. *All systems are written using programming languages.* If the IT (Information Technology) department is filled with COBOL programmers, it might not be a wise decision to decide to use Java. If Java is mandatory, then the systems analyst has to plan for this by either training existing staff or outsourcing the development effort to a consulting firm. This information is contained within the requirements document, often called the *system requirements specification* (SRS).

5. *All systems should be designed using a methodology and proper documentary techniques.* There are many developmental methodologies. The two main generic categories are *structured* and *object-oriented.* The tools and techniques surrounding these methodologies are part and parcel of software engineering. A properly developed system is carefully analyzed and then designed. The first step of this process is the plan, and the next step is the SRS. The third step is the design document. Finally comes implementation, testing, and then deployment. These are some of the main steps in the software-development life cycle (SDLC).

Software Developer

I started out in this field as a programmer. In those days (several eons ago), there were real boundaries between the different types of jobs one could do. If you were a programmer, you didn't do analysis work and vice versa. In fact, most analysts back then knew very little about programming.

That's all changed but, typically, you still start out as a programmer and then the sky's the limit. A programmer is a person who knows one or more programming languages (e.g., Java, C++, etc.). The programmer's job is to read a programming specification, which is usually written by the systems analyst, and then translate that specification into program code.

In most companies, the programmer works within a project team that is managed by a project leader who, in turn, is managed by a project manager. Each project team has one or more programmers and probably one or more systems analysts. The programmer works on the code and seldom, if ever, works with the end users. The systems analysts, on the other hand, work directly with the end users to develop the requirements and specification for the system being designed.

While a programmer can lack all the social graces because few outsiders deal with this person, the system analyst is on the front lines. The analyst needs to be articulate, friendly, and a good listener. The system analyst must also have the capability of paying a great deal of attention to detail and be creative in coming up with techniques for uncovering hidden information. For example, when developing the FOCUS system, a financial system used by the New York Stock Exchange, I had to uncover hundreds of mathematical formulas that could be used to analyze the financial forms. I also had to design dozens of screens that could be utilized efficiently by the end users. Instead of my designing the screens (this was pre-Internet days), I turned the end users loose with a word processing programmer and asked them to list the information they wanted to see and where they wanted to see it. This is called JAD or *joint application development*.

When I first starting working for the New York Stock Exchange, I was responsible for building a computer system that processed a series of financial forms (like your tax forms) that were required to be filled out by the various member firms of the stock exchange. These forms contained hundreds of financial items.

My job as an analyst was to work with the people in the regulatory department who understood how to process these forms. These were the end users. Our job was hard, as the financial forms were complex. The end users were accountant types with vast experience in interpreting these forms. The reason for looking at these forms at all was to determine whether the firm was financially healthy—a very important job.

As the systems analyst on the job, I had to meet regularly with these end users and try to pick their brains. We met several times a week to work on the project. There was lots of yelling and screaming and tons of pizza. In the end, however, we developed a document that was quite detailed in describing everything that the system—called FOCUS—was supposed to do. Once this document was complete, it was turned over to the programmers, whose job it was to turn the document into a complete working system.

As you can see from my description, I've left a few job titles out of the picture. That's because each organization is structured a bit differently. For the most part, when one develops a system, there are at least two departments involved. One is the end-user department (e.g., marketing, operations), which represents the end users, who have a need for a system to be developed or modified. The end-user department turns to the computer department—sometimes called IS (information systems) or MIS (management information systems) or IT (information technology)—to help them turn this need into a working system.

The end-user department is composed of experts who do a particular task. Maybe they are accountants, or maybe they are in marketing—they still are experts in what they do. They are managed, just like IS people, by managers. We can refer to these managers as *business managers*, just like we refer to a computer manager as an *IS manager*. While most systems analysts work directly with those that report to the business manager, the business manager still plays a critical role. We need to turn to this manager if there is some information we need from the entire department or when we need to have something done that only the business manager can direct.

SDLC: Systems Development Life Cycle

The development of computer systems has many moving parts. Each of these parts has a name, e.g., analysis, design, etc. We call the entirety of these steps a *systems development life cycle.*

Why do we call this a life cycle? A system has a life of its own. It starts out as an idea and progresses until this idea germinates and then is born. Eventually, when the system ages and becomes obsolete, it is discarded or dies. So *life cycle* is really an apt term.

The idea phase of the SDLC is the point at which the end user, systems analyst, and various managers meet for the first time. This is where the scope and objectives of the system are fleshed out in a very high-level document.

Next, a team composed of one or more system analysts and end users tries to determine whether the system is feasible. There are many reasons why systems are *not* feasible: too expensive; technology not yet available; not enough experience to create the system. These are just some of the reasons why a system will not be undertaken.

Once the system is determine to be feasible, systems analysis is initiated. This is the point when the analysts put on their detective hats and try to ferret out all the rules and regulations of the system. What are the inputs? What are the outputs? What kind of online screens will there be? What kind of reports would there be? Will paper forms be required? Will any hookups to external files or companies be required? How shall this information be processed? As you can see, there's much work to be done at this point and many questions to be answered. In the end, all of the answers to these questions will be fully documented in a requirements document.

Once all the unknowns are known and are fully documented, the systems analyst can put flesh on the skeleton by creating both high-level and then detailed designs. This is usually called a *specification* and can be hundreds of pages long. This document contains flowcharts, file and database definitions, and detailed instructions for the writing of each program.

All along the way, the accuracy of all of these documents is checked and verified by having the end users and analysts meet with each other. In fact, most approaches to system development utilize the creation of a project team that consists of both end users and IS staff. This team meets regularly to work on the project and verify its progress.

Once a complete working specification is delivered to the programmers, implementation can get under way. For the FOCUS system, we turned the specification over to a team of about 20 programmers. The systems analyst, project leader, and project manager were all responsible for making sure that the implementation effort went smoothly. Programmers coded code and then tested that code. When this first level (unit testing) of testing was done, there were several other phases of testing, including systems testing, parallel testing, and integration testing. Many companies have QA (quality assurance) departments that use automated tools to test the veracity of systems being implemented.

Once the system has been fully tested, it is turned over to production (changeover). Usually, just prior to this, the end-user departments (not just the team working on the project) are trained and manuals distributed. The entire team is usually on call during the first few weeks of the system after changeover, because errors often crop up and it can take several weeks for the system to stabilize.

Once the system is stabilized, it is evaluated for correctness. At this point, a list of things to correct as well as a wish list of things that didn't wind up in the first phase of the system is created and prioritized. The team, which consisted of technical and end-user staff, usually stays put and works on the future versions of the system.

Feasibility Study: The First Step

It never pays to just jump into developing a system. Usually, it's a good idea to do a feasibility study first. The easiest part of the feasibility study is determining whether the system is technically feasible. Sometimes, however, it might not be feasible because the company doesn't have the technical expertise to do the job. A good system analyst will go one step further and see if it's feasible to outsource the project to people that can do the job. Sometimes, you'll find that the technology is just not robust enough. For example, many years ago I wanted to deliver voice-recognition devices to the floor of the New York Stock Exchange. The technology at that time was just too primitive, so the entire project was deemed not feasible.

Adding a layer of complexity to the problem is when you discover that the project is feasible from a technical perspective but would require vast organizational changes (e.g., creation of new end-user departments). This, then, would make the project organizationally not feasible.

Finally, the project just might cost too much money. To figure this out, you will need to do a cost/benefit analysis. This will require you to figure out an estimated cost for everything you wish to do, including cost of hardware, cost of software, cost of new personnel, cost of training, etc. Then you need to calculate the financial savings for creating the new system, e.g., reduce staff by one-third, save five hours a day, etc. However, sometimes the benefits are intangible, e.g., compete with our major competitor.

Once it has been determined that the project is feasible, a project plan is created that plots out the course for the entire systems development effort, e.g., budget, resources, schedule, etc. The next step, then, is to start the actual analytical part of systems development. For that, we need to collect some information.

Information-Gathering Channels

One of the first things you will do when starting a new project is gather information. Your job is to understand everything about the department and proposed system you are automating. If you are merely modifying an existing system, you are halfway there. In this case, you will review all of the system documentation, the system itself, and the end users to ferret out the changed requirements.

How can you make sense out of a department and its processes when you don't know anything about it? One of the things you do is act like a detective and gather up every piece of documentation you can find. When I built the FOCUS system, I scrounged around and managed to find policy manuals and memos that got me part of the way toward understanding what these people did for a living. Other sources of information include reports used for decision making, performance reports, records, data capture forms, web sites, competitors sites, and archive data. But passive review is seldom enough. The next step is to be a bit more active and direct.

The first thing you can do is interview end users. For our FOCUS project, while I had already created a project team consisting of tech people and end users, I decided that it would be worthwhile to interview a representative sampling of people working in different jobs that all touched the process to be automated.

You can't interview someone without preparation. This consists of first understanding all that you can about the job and person being interviewed, and then preparing a set of questions for this person.

Sometimes an interview is insufficient to meet your needs. Your subject may not be able to articulate what he or she does. The next step, then, is to observe the person on the job.

I've done much work in the artificial-intelligence arena, where observation is a large part of the systems analysis process. One of the case histories that people in the field often talk about is one concerning the building of a tax expert system.

At one end of a large table sat a junior accountant. A large number of tax books were piled in front of the junior accountant. At the other end sat some of the most senior tax accountants at the firm. There was nothing piled in front of them. In the center of the table sat the system analysts, armed with a video recorder. The interviewer was armed with a script that contained a problem and a set of questions. The task at hand was for the junior accountant to work through the problem guided by the experts. The experts had nothing to refer to—just what was in their memories. Thus they were able to assist the junior accountant in solving the problem while the video camera recorded the entire process.

Direct observation can only be done selectively—a few people at the most. Another technique, which will let you survey a broad number of people at one time, is the questionnaire. Building a questionnaire requires some skill. There are generally two types of questions:

Open-ended
1. What are the most frequent problems you have in buying books from a book store? _____
2. Of the problems listed above, what is the single most troublesome? _____

Closed
1. The tool is used as part of the program development cycle to improve quality. How important is the tool?

   1 2 3 4 5 (circle appropriate response, where 5 is the highest score)

A good questionnaire will probably be a combination of both types of questions. It's also important to (a) make sure that you format your questionnaire for easy readability (lots of white space and even spacing), (b) put all the important questions first (in case they don't finish the survey), and (c) vary the type of question so that they don't just circle 5s or 1s all the way down the page.

Diagramming or Modeling the System

There are a wide variety of techniques you can use to diagrammatically describe your problem and its solution, and there are a wide variety of tools that can assist you in drawing these diagrams. One of the diagrammatic techniques is flowcharting, and the tool of choice is Microsoft Visio.

One of the most practical tools is the data flow diagram (DFD), as shown in Figure 7.3. DFDs are quite logical, clear, and helpful when building systems—even web-based systems. All inputs, outputs, and processes are recorded in a hierarchical fashion. The first DFD, referred to as DFD 0, is often the system from a high-level perspective. Child DFDs get much more detailed. Figure 7.3 is a snippet of a real online test system. It's a rather complicated system that lets people take tests online. This particular DFD shows the data flow through the log-in process. The rectangular boxes (e.g., D5) are the data stores. Notice that D5 is an online cookie. D1, on the other hand, is a real database. It's a relational database, and this is one particular table. The databases and their tables are defined in a data dictionary. The square box is the entity (i.e., test taker) and can be a person, place, or thing. The other boxes are process boxes. Process 1.1 is the process for Get Name, and there will be an associated child DFD labeled

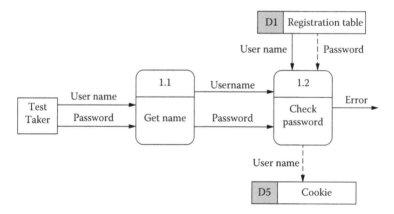

FIGURE 7.3
Data flow diagram (DFD).

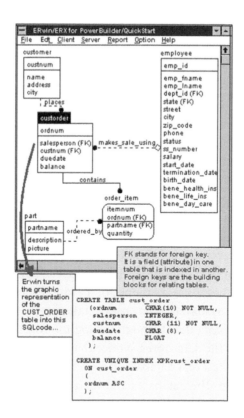

FIGURE 7.4
Entity relationship diagram (ERD).

"1.1 Get Name." The term *1.1 Get Name* will also appear in a process dictionary that will contain a detailed specification for how to program this procedure.

Other modeling tools include:

Entity relationship diagram: An ERD is a database model that describes the attributes of entities and the relationships among them. An entity is a file (table). Today, ER models are often created graphically, and software converts the graphical representations of the tables into the SQL code required to create the data structures in the database, as shown in Figure 7.4.

State transition diagram: A STD describes how a system behaves as a result of external events. In Figure 7.5, we see the effects of a person reporting a pothole.

Data dictionary: The data dictionary is a very organized listing of all data elements that pertain to the system. This listing contains some very specific information, as shown in Figure 7.6. It should be noted that there are many variations in the formats of data dictionaries.

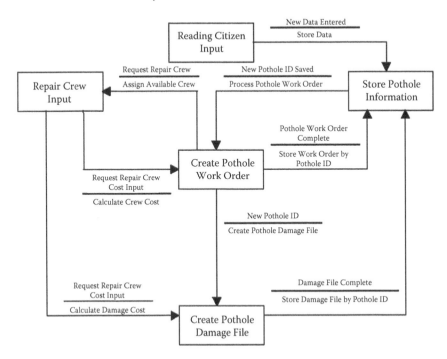

FIGURE 7.5
State transition diagram (STD).

Name:	Pothole
Aliases:	None
Where used/How used:	Pothole information is the main input (Pothole Submission) and output (Fixed Pothole Data) of the whole system (see level 0 of the ERD).
Content Description:	
Pothole ID = Ten digit number Address = Sixty Characters City = Thirty Characters State = Two Characters Zip = Nine Characters Location = Ten Characters District = One digit number Repair Priority = Two digit number Repair Crew ID = Two digit number Repair Time = Hours or Days Status = Five Characters Material Cost = Dollar amount Total Cost = Dollar amount Description = Two Hundred and Fifty Characters	
Supplementary Description:	
Location possible values: "curb," "middle," "left side," "right side" District possible values: North = 1, South = 2, East = 3, West = 4 Repair Priority possible values = 1 to 10 Status possible values: "Open" or "Closed"	

FIGURE 7.6
Data dictionary.

Process specification: The PSPEC describes the what, when, where, and how of the program in technical terms. It describes just how the process works and serves to connect the DFD to the data dictionary. It uses pseudocode (sometimes called *structured English* or *program definition language* [PDL]) to explain the requirements for programming the process to the programmer. The following is an example:

```
Process #1
Name Logon
Number: 1
Name: Logon
Description: Registered test takers will logon to their
account with their username and password through this
```

```
process. Once they register, they will be able to take
the test.
Input data: User name from the test taker, password
from the test taker, user name from the Registration
table, password from the Registration table
Output data: User name to the cookie
Type of process: Validation
Process logic:
Get user name and password from the user
If correct then
        Allow the user to take the test
else
        Produce an error
endif
```

Other ways of representing process logic are:

- A decision table
- A decision tree
- A mathematical formula
- Any combination of the above

Class diagrams: Those analysts working on an OO (object-oriented) system will utilize OO tools and diagrammatic techniques. One of these is a class diagram that is drawn using Unified Modeling Language (UML). A class diagram is shown in Figure 7.7.

The class called automobile
- Motor
- Four wheels

PARENT

inheritance ↓ Derived class

The class called sports car
- Inherits motor
- Inherits four wheels
- Fast rpm
- Sleek design

CHILD (extra features)

FIGURE 7.7
Class diagram.

Developmental Methodologies

The Software Engineering Institute, which is part of Carnegie Mellon located in Pittsburgh, Pennsylvania, is famous for a framework that describes software process maturity. A summary of the five phases appears below. Read this while keeping in mind that most organizations, sadly, are at Stage 2 or 3.

Stage 1: *Initial*, which is characterized by processes that
- Are ad hoc
- Have little formalization
- Have tools informally applied

Key actions to get to next step
  - Initiate rigorous project management, management oversight, and quality assurance

Stage 2: *Repeatable*, which is characterized by processes that
- Have achieved stability with a repeatable level of statistical control

Key actions to get to next step
  - Establish a process group
  - Establish a software-development process architecture
  - Introduce software engineering methods and technology

Stage 3: *Defined*, which is characterized by processes that
- Have achieved foundation for major and continuing progress

Key actions to get to next step
  - Establish a basic set of management processes to identify quality and cost parameters
  - Establish a process database
  - Gather and maintain process data
  - Assess relative quality of each product and inform management

Stage 4: *Managed*, which is characterized by processes that
- Show substantial quality improvements
- Are coupled with comprehensive process measurement

Key actions to get to next step
  - Support automatic gathering of process data
  - Use data to analyze and modify the process

Stage 5: *Optimized*, which is characterized by processes that
  • Demonstrate major quality and quantity improvements
  Key actions to get to next step
    – Continue improvement and optimization of the process

Companies that have achieved a Stage 2 process maturity or higher make use of methodologies to ensure that the company achieves a repeatable level of quality and productivity. There are many methodologies available for use. Some of these are vendor driven, i.e., they are used in conjunction with a software tool set.

In general, methodologies can be categorized as follows. It should be noted that one methodology can be used in conjunction with another methodology:

Waterfall method: This is a phased, structured approach to systems development. The phases include requirements feasibility analysis, system design, coding, testing, and implementation. Please note that there are variations of these stated phases. Usually, each phase is performed sequentially, although there is some potential for overlap. This is the methodology that is used most often in industry.

Iterative (prototyping): Most of this approach is used to replace several of the phases in the SDLC. In the SDLC approach, the time to market, so to speak, can be months (sometimes years). During this time, requirements may change, and the final deliverable, therefore, might be quite outmoded. To prevent this from happening, it is a good idea to try to compress the development cycle to shorten this time to market and provide interim results to the end user. The iterative model consists of three steps: (1) listen to customer; (2) build/revise a mock-up; (3) let customer test-drive the mock-up and then returns to step 1.

Rapid application development (RAD): This is a form of the iterative model. The key word here is *rapid*. Development teams try to get a first pass of the system out to the end user within 60 to 90 days. To accomplish this, the normal seven-step SDLC is compressed into the following steps: business modeling, data modeling, process modeling, application generation and testing, and turnover. Note the term *application generation*. RAD makes use of application generators, formerly called CASE (computer-assisted software engineering) tools.

Incremental model: The four main phases of software development are analysis, design, coding, and testing. If we break a business problem into chunks or increments, then we can use an overlapping, phased approach to software development. For example, we can start the analysis of increment one in January, increment two in June, and increment three in September. Just when increment three starts up, we are at the testing stage of increment one and the coding stage of increment two.

Joint application development (JAD): JAD is more of a technique than a complete methodology. It can be utilized as part of any of the other methodologies discussed here. The technique consists of one or more end users who are then folded into the software development team. Instead of an adversarial software-developer–end-user dynamic, the effect is to have the continued, uninterrupted attention of the person(s) who will ultimately be using the system.

Reverse engineering: This technique is used to (1) understand a system from its code, (2) generate documentation base on the code, and (3) make desired changes to the system. Competitive software companies often try to reverse engineer their competitor's software.

Reengineering: Business goals change over time. Software must change to be consistent with these goals. Reengineering utilizes many of the techniques already discussed here. Instead of building a system from scratch, the goal of reengineering is to retrofit an existing system to new business functionality.

Object oriented: Object-oriented analysis (OOA), object-oriented design (OOD), and object-oriented programming (OOP) are very different from what we've already discussed. In fact, you will need to learn a whole new vocabulary as well as new diagramming techniques.

Agile: Agile software development is a group of software development methods based on iterative and incremental development, where requirements and solutions evolve through collaboration between self-organizing, cross-functional teams. It promotes adaptive planning, evolutionary development and delivery, and a time-boxed iterative approach while also encouraging rapid and flexible response to change. It is a conceptual framework that promotes foreseen tight interactions throughout the development cycle.

The book *Agile Manifesto* introduced the term in 2001. Since then, the Agile Movement, with all its values, principles, methods, practices, tools, champions, practitioners, philosophies, and cultures, has significantly changed the landscape of the modern software engineering and commercial software development in these Internet times. Interestingly, the agile methodology, in the form of a book on extreme programming from agile guru Kent Beck, has gained a cult following as a management bible for its simple leadership ideas.

The Agile Manifesto (http://agilemanifesto.org/) states:

> We are uncovering better ways of developing software by doing it and help-ing others do it. Through this work we have come to value:
>
> **Individuals and interactions** over processes and tools
>
> **Working software** over comprehensive documentation
>
> **Customer collaboration** over contract negotiation
>
> **Responding to change** over following a plan

The Agile Manifesto is based on 12 principles:

1. Customer satisfaction by rapid delivery of useful software
2. Welcome changing requirements, even late in development
3. Deliver working software frequently (weeks rather than months)
4. Working software is the principal measure of progress
5. Sustainable development, able to maintain a constant pace indefinitely
6. Close, daily cooperation between business people and developers
7. Face-to-face conversation is the best form of communication
8. Projects are built around motivated individuals, who should be trusted
9. Continuous attention to technical excellence and good design
10. Simplicity—the art of maximizing the amount of work not done—is essential
11. Self-organizing teams
12. Regular adaptation to changing circumstances

System Design

Most of the models we've discussed previously fall under the structured rubric (save for the OO model). The requirements document—or SRS (systems requirement specification)—is written for a broad audience and reflects this structured technique. Usually it is provided not only to IT staff, but to the end users as well. In this way, the end users are able to review what they've asked for as well as the general architecture of the system. Once approved, the system now must be designed. The system specification, here called the SDS (systems design specification), contains a very finite level of detail—enough so that programmers will be able to code the entire system. This means that the SDS must contain:

- Information on all processes
- Information on all data
- Information about the architecture

You have to start somewhere. That somewhere is usually the very highest level of a design. There are three logical ways to do this:

Abstraction: This permits you to concentrate at some level of generalization without regard to irrelevant low-level details. This is your high-level or logical design.

Stepwise refinement: This is a successive decomposition or refinement of the specifications. In other words, you move from the high level to the detailed, from the logical to the physical.

Modularity: This means that you know a good design when you see a compartmentalization of data and function.

Look again at the DFD in Figure 7.4. That DFD was not the first in the series. The very first DFD would have been DFD 0, which is equivalent to the high level of detail from which it is recommended that you start from. Here you can see the logical components of the system. Underneath the 0 level we start to get more detailed and more physical. At these lower (or child) levels, we start specifying files and processes.

The design document that you create will rarely look the same from one organization to another. Each has its own template and its own standard diagramming tool (e.g., Visio vs. SmartDraw) and its own diagramming format (e.g., flowcharts vs. UML [uniform modeling language] vs. DFDs).

Where the requirements document is high level, the specification is much more detailed. It is, after all, a programming specification. For the most part, the specification document for the testing system we've discussed included: (a) a general description of the system, (b) its users, (c) its constraints (i.e., must run on a PC), (d) the DFDs or other format, (e) the data dictionary, (f) the process dictionary, and (g) a chart (e.g., Gantt chart) showing the tasks that need to be done. The purpose of this specification (usually called a *spec* by those in the field) is to give the programmers a manual from which they can code. If it's a good spec, the programmers shouldn't need to come back to you time after time to get additional information.

Object-Oriented Methodologies

OO systems development follows the same pattern as structured systems development. First you must analyze your system OOA. Next you design the system using OOD. Finally, you code the system using OOP techniques and languages (e.g., C++, Java).

OO techniques may have some similarity to traditional techniques, but the concept of OO is radically different from what most development people are used to. This methodology revolves around the concept of an object. An object is a representation of any information that must be understood by the software. Objects can be:

- *External entities*: printer, user, sensor
- *Things*: reports, displays
- *Occurrences or events*: alarm, interrupt
- *Roles*: manager, engineer, salesperson
- *Organizational unit*: team, division
- *Places*: manufacturing floor
- *Structures*: employee record

The easiest way to think of an object is just to say it is any person, place, or thing.

One of the important features of OO is the reusability of its objects. A well-coded object is often thought of as a black box. What this means is that the programmer should be able to glue together several objects to create a working system. The programmer shouldn't have to know too much about any of these objects. Does anyone remember playing with Lego blocks as a child? It was easy to create incredible things such as bridges and buildings. That was because each of the blocks was easily connected to all other blocks. It's the same with objects (see the definition of *encapsulation* in the following list).

First, some OO definitions:

Class: In object technology, a user-defined data type that defines a collection of objects that share the same characteristics. An object, or class member, is one instance of the class. Concrete classes are designed to be instantiated. Abstract classes are designed to pass on characteristics through inheritance.

Object: A self-contained module of data and its associated processing. Objects are the software building blocks of object technology.

Polymorphism: Meaning many shapes. In object technology, the ability of a generalized request (message) to produce different results based on the object that it is sent to.

Inheritance: In object technology, the ability of one class of objects to inherit properties from a higher class.

Encapsulation: In object technology, making the data and processing (methods) within the object private, which allows the internal implementation of the object to be modified without requiring any change to the application that uses it. This is also known as *information hiding*.

Take another look at Figure 7.7. Here we have a class called *automobile*. This class has several attributes in common. One is that this thing has a motor. Another attribute is the fact that an automobile (usually) has four wheels. In an OO system, you can create derived classes from the parent class. Notice the nice, shiny red sports car. This is the derived class called *sports car*. It also has a motor and four wheels that it *inherits* from the parent class. But in this derived class we have some additional attributes: fast rpm, and sleek design. The sports car is the *child* of the *parent* class named *automobile*. So we can say "every convertible is an automobile" but not "every automobile is a convertible."

To develop an OO application, one must define classes. If you know anything about OO programming languages such as C++, all variables within a program are defined as some type of data. For example, in C and C++, a number is defined as a type called *integer*. When we define a class in a programming language, it is defined as a type of class, as shown here:

```
//Program to demonstrate a very simple example of a class
called DayOfYear.
#include <iostream.h>
//This is where we define our class. We'll call it DayOfYear
//It is a public class. This means that there are no
restrictions
//on use. There are also private classes.
//The class DayOfYear consists of two pieces of data: month
and day and
//one function named output ()
class DayOfYear
{
public:
void output();
int month;
int day;
};
```

Designing OO systems requires the use of different modeling and definitional techniques that take into account the idea of classes and objects. UML is the standard for modeling OO software. Figure 7.7 showed a sample class diagrammed using UML. Contained within a typical SDS are numerous diagrams (models):

- Class diagrams
- Object models
- Package diagrams, which show how the classes are grouped together
- Collaboration diagrams, which show how the classes collaborate or work with each other

Testing

When you tie many programs together, you have a system. It is not uncommon for a system to have thousands of lines of code. All of this code must be tested. The very first level of testing is at the programmer's desk. This is where the programmer works with whatever tools are available to make sure that everything works.

When a group of programmers work together, their project manager might think it a good idea that a walk-through be held. This is when the team gets together and examines the code as a group to find flaws and discuss better ways to do things. Usually this isn't done. One reason is that programmers don't like to do this. Another reason is that it's very time consuming.

You can consider the *unit testing* a programmer does at his or her own desk, meaning the testing of a unit of work (a program). When several programs have to interact together, another type of test that you might want to perform is *integrating testing*. This is a test to determine if the separate parts of the system work well together. For example, let's say Program 1 creates a file that contains a student file, and Program 2 then processes that student file. If Program 1 makes a mistake and creates the student file incorrectly, then Program 2 will not work.

A *system test* tests the complete system. All of the inputs are checked; all of the outputs are checked; and everything in between is checked. If there is another existing system, a parallel test is done. *Parallel* is a good term for this, because to do this you must run both system in tandem and then check the results of both for similarities and differences.

Finally, acceptance testing is done. This means that you run a test and the end user either agrees or disagrees with the test and approves or disapproves it.

In any case, testing is a lot of work. Many people are involved, including the end users and, usually, a quality assurance (QA) department. QA folks spend all of their time writing testing scripts (i.e., a list of things to test for) and then running those scripts. If they find an error, they send a report to the programmer, who then fixes it.

QA usually uses testing tools to assist with this massive job. These tools assist with the creation of scripts and then automatically runs those scripts. This is especially helpful when doing stress testing—testing to see how well the system works when many people are using it at the same time.

Testing is usually not performed in a vacuum. An analyst or manager prepares a test plan that details exactly what must be tested and by whom. The test plan contains the testing schedule as well as the intricate details on what must be tested. These detailed plans are called *test cases* and form the basis for the test scripts that are used by the programmer or the QA staff member, usually in conjunction with a testing tool.

A sample test case that would appear in a test plan is presented here. This would be turned into a script for use by the testers.

1.1.1 Test Case: Accounting: Payment

1.1.1.1 Description: The purpose of this test is to determine if a representative of the service care provider can enter a payment receipt within the accounting subsystem.

1.1.1.2 Required Stubs/Drivers: The accounting subsystem will be invoked with particular attention to the Payment class.

1.1.1.3 Test Steps

1. The service care provider must successfully log into the system.
2. The service care provider must invoke the Accounting user interface to enter the payment receipt.
3. The service care provider must enter a payment receipt and press the button to commit the transaction.

1.1.1.4 Expected Results

Test Success

1. A subsequent query indicates the customer's balance reflecting the recent payment.
2. A successful message is displayed.

Test Failure

1. The customer's balance does not reflect the payment receipt.
2. The customer's balance reflects an incorrect amount that is a result of faulty logic within the program.

Oracle has a wide variety of testing tools, such as its Application Testing Suite. This is a comprehensive, integrated testing solution that ensures the quality, scalability, and availability of your web applications, web services, packaged Oracle Applications, and Oracle databases.

This integrated, full life-cycle solution enables you to define and manage your application testing process, validate application functionality, and ensure that your applications will perform under load. With Application Testing Suite, you can deploy your web applications and web services in less time while maximizing the efficiency of your testing team.

Application Testing Suite comprises the following tightly integrated products:

1. *Oracle Functional Testing*: Automated functional and regression testing of web applications
2. *Oracle Functional Testing Suite for Oracle Applications*: Functional and regression testing of Oracle packaged applications
3. *Oracle Load Testing: Scalability*: Performance and load testing of web applications
4. *Oracle Load Testing Suite for Oracle Applications*: Scalability, performance, and load testing of Oracle packaged applications
5. *Oracle Test Manager*: Test process management, including test requirements management, test management, test execution, and defect tracking

Installation

When you have a very small system, you can just put it online (direct). If your system is larger, then there are several ways to approach installing (implementing) the system. If there is an existing system that you are going to replace, then you can install the new system in a parallel mode. This means that you run both systems at the same time for a period of time. Each day, the end users check the outputs. Once they feel comfortable, turn the old system off.

Many companies run multiple servers with the same system running on each server. One good way to install a system is to install it on a single server first, see how it runs, and then install it on another server. This is called a *phased approach*.

Documentation

One day, all of the programmers who wrote the original system will leave. If there is not adequate documentation, then the new programmers will not understand how to work on the system. I recently worked on a project (Internet gambling for a foreign country) where the programmer did not have any documentation at all. The system was written in C++ and ASP. There were hundreds of programs. It was almost impossible to figure out which program ran first! So, you really do need to have system documentation.

It is also critical to have some documentation for the end users. You've all seen the manuals that come with software that runs on your PC. Look at the manual that comes with Visio and imagine yourself as the end user for this software. If you write a system, you will need to write a manual for your end users.

Finally, you will need to train your end users to use the system. When I worked for the New York Stock Exchange, we brought in a tool that permitted our end users to use a 4th Generation Language (4GL) to do their own queries against the system's database. We needed to train these end users to use the 4GL productivity. Instead of writing and teaching a course ourselves, we hired an expert who did it for us.

Maintenance

Many, many years ago I worked with a project leader who wanted to play with a new toy. At that time, databases were just coming into vogue. The project leader decided to create a database for a new system. The problem was that this particular system didn't need this particular database. The system was written, but as a result of the horrid choice of databases, it never ran well. In fact, it bombed out all the time.

After a year of problems, management decided that the system needed to be fixed. And fix it we did. This is called *corrective maintenance*—modifying an existing system so that it works correctly. There are lots of reasons why maintenance is done.

One reason we're all familiar with this is because of security and viruses. Systems people frequently make modifications to software because of problems such as this. I know some casino gaming programmers who had to suspend programming new features into the system to take care of the Code Red worm. This is an example of preventive maintenance.

Most often, the reason for maintenance is simply to improve the system. Let's say that the end-user casino decides to add a new game to the system, or a new data field is added to a database or a new report is required. All of these are examples of maintenance for improvement purposes.

Some organizations have two types of programmers. One type usually works on new software, and the other type is stuck with maintenance. This isn't often done anymore, because maintenance programmers are usually an unhappy lot and, subsequently, their turnover rate is quite high.

All systems need to be managed. You can't just make changes to a system willy-nilly. The way you control what happens to a system is to continue holding meetings with your end users and developing a prioritized list of changes and additions that they want you to make. Occasionally, a change might come in from a person who is not on the end-user committee. To handle these requests, system personnel usually make use of a standard change-request form. This form contains information such as desired change, reason for change, screen shots of the existing screen that needs to be changed (if applicable), and more, depending on the organization. Such changes usually have to authorized by the end user's management before it is sent to the computer department.

Once the change request comes to the computer department, if it's simple and there's some spare time, the modification is scheduled immediately. Usually, however, it is added to a prioritized list of things to do. Once it reaches the top of the list, the same SDLC steps used during development are used during maintenance. In other words, you need to determine whether the modification is feasible, determine its cost, develop a specification, etc.

Training

Once the system is installed, the end users will require some training. There are various ways to achieve this, which can range from in-house training to CAI (computer-assisted instruction).

Once the end users are trained, they'll need some support on a day-to-day basis. First, as already discussed, they'll need a manual so they can look up answers to questions. Some systems do not use paper manuals. Instead, everything is embedded in a help file. If the manuals are insufficient, then the company might want to do what most companies are doing and fund and staff a help desk. Sometimes people in end-user departments rely on a person within their department who has become an expert at using the system. This person is usually referred to as the *resident expert.*

SUMMARY

In this chapter, we reviewed Oracle's developmental tool suites. We then focused on a broad array of systems-development issues and methodologies. Just keep in mind that a tool without a robust process is like a car without an engine.

8

Fusion

Oracle Fusion is really three separate entities: the architecture, the middleware, and the applications, as shown in Figure 8.1. Oracle Fusion Architecture provides an open architecture ecosystem, which is service- and event-enabled. Many enterprises use this open, pluggable architecture ecosystem to write Oracle Fusion applications, or even third-party applications, on top of Oracle Fusion Middleware.

Oracle Fusion Architecture is based on the following core principles:

- *Model driven*: For applications, business processes, and business information
- *Service- and event-enabled*: For extensible, modular, flexible applications and processes
- *Information-centric*: For complete and consistent, actionable, real-time intelligence
- *Grid ready*: Must be scalable, available, secure, and manageable on low-cost hardware
- *Standards based*: Must be open and pluggable in a heterogeneous environment

Oracle Fusion Applications are built on top of the Oracle Fusion Middleware technology stack using Oracle's Fusion Architecture as a blueprint. Oracle Fusion Architecture is not actually a product, and can be used without licensing it from Oracle.

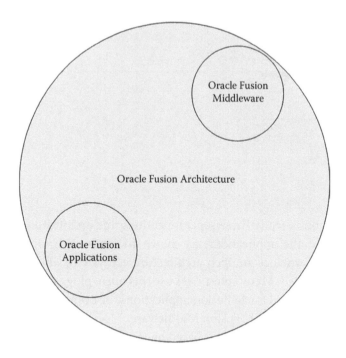

FIGURE 8.1
Oracle Fusion.

MIDDLEWARE

Oracle Fusion Middleware (OFM, also known as Fusion Middleware) consists of several software products from Oracle Corporation. OFM spans multiple services, including Java EE and developer tools, integration services, business intelligence, and business process management, as shown in Figure 8.2. OFM depends on open standards such as BPEL (Business Process Execution Language), SOAP (Simple Object Access Protocol), XML (Extensible Markup Language), and JMS (Java Message Service).

OFM provides software for the development, deployment, and management of service-oriented architecture (SOA). It includes what Oracle calls "hot-pluggable" architecture, designed to facilitate integration with existing applications and systems from other software vendors such as IBM, Microsoft, and SAP AG.

Some of these products have been discussed in previous chapters, so you will hopefully get the sense of Oracle's overlapping product lines. Table 8.1 provides more descriptive details on each of the Oracle Fusion components.

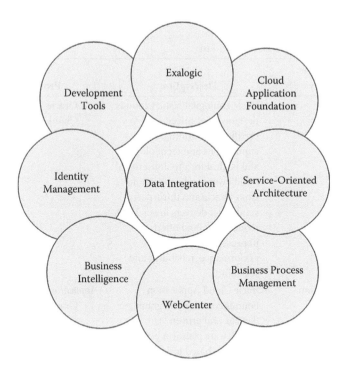

FIGURE 8.2
Oracle Fusion Middleware.

Most notable is the emphasis on SOA. Oracle SOA Suite enables system developers to set up and manage services and to orchestrate them into composite applications and business processes. With Oracle SOA Suite's hot-pluggable components, organizations can easily extend and evolve their architectures instead of replacing existing investments.

Services are unassociated, loosely coupled units of functionality that are self-contained. Each service implements one action, such as submitting an online application for an account, retrieving an online bank statement, or modifying an online booking or airline ticket order. Within a SOA, services use defined protocols that describe how services pass and parse messages using description metadata.

Underlying and enabling all of this requires metadata in sufficient detail to describe not only the characteristics of these services, but also the data that drives them. Programmers have made extensive use of XML in SOA to structure data that they wrap in a nearly exhaustive description-container. Analogously, the Web Services Description Language (WSDL) typically describes the services themselves, while the SOA protocol describes

TABLE 8.1

Oracle Fusion Middleware Product List

Middleware Category	Description	Product List
Exalogic	Oracle Exalogic Elastic Cloud is designed, optimized, and certified for running Oracle applications and technologies and is ideal for mission-critical middleware and applications from Oracle and third-party vendors. It delivers lower TCO, reduces risk, and offers unprecedented levels of performance, reliability, and scalability.	• Oracle Exalogic Elastic Cloud
Cloud Application Foundation	Oracle Cloud Application Foundation is an integrated, flexible, and proven middleware platform built on standards-based technologies for portability, efficiency and lower TCO. It brings together key industry-leading technologies: Oracle WebLogic Server for Java EE; Oracle Coherence In-Memory Data Grid; Oracle Tuxedo for C/C++/COBOL; Oracle Virtual Assembly Builder; and Oracle Traffic Director for load balancing capabilities. Oracle Cloud Application Foundation provides you with choice across conventional systems and cloud environments. It is optimized to run on Oracle Exalogic Elastic Cloud for on-premise cloud deployments and is available on third-party clouds for increased flexibility and scalability.	*Application servers*: • Oracle WebLogic Server • Oracle GlassFish Server • Oracle Tuxedo *In-memory data grid*: • Oracle Coherence *Web servers*: • Oracle Web Tier • Oracle iPlanet Web Proxy Server and Web Servers • Oracle Internet Application Server *Cloud foundation*: • Oracle Virtual Assembly Builder • Oracle Traffic Director • Java Cloud Services

(Continued)

TABLE 8.1 (CONTINUED)

Oracle Fusion Middleware Product List

Middleware Category	Description	Product List
Data Integration	Gain pervasive, continuous access to trusted data with high performance and low TCO. Oracle data integration provides a complete and integrated solution with real-time and bulk data movement, transformation, data quality, data services, and data federation.	• Oracle Data Integrator Enterprise Edition • Oracle GoldenGate • Oracle Enterprise Data Quality
Service-Oriented Architecture	Oracle SOA transforms complex application connectivity into agile and reusable service-based application integration to speed time to market, increase agility, and lower costs.	• Oracle SOA Suite • Oracle Service Bus • Oracle BPEL Process Manager • Oracle B2B Integration • Oracle Event Processing • Oracle Business Activity Monitoring • Oracle Business Rules • Oracle Enterprise Repository • Oracle API Gateway • Oracle SOA Management Pack, Enterprise Edition
Business Process Management	Oracle BPM Suite provides the ability to optimize business processes that span multiple systems, applications, and functional groups in an iterative and agile fashion. It offers a unified enterprise-class platform to design and automate business processes for better visibility, more control, and an excellent customer experience.	• Oracle Business Process Management Suite 11g • Oracle Process Accelerators

(Continued)

TABLE 8.1 (CONTINUED)

Oracle Fusion Middleware Product List

Middleware Category	Description	Product List
WebCenter	Oracle WebCenter is the engagement platform powering exceptional experiences. It connects people and information by bringing together the most complete portfolio of portal, web experience management, content, and social and collaboration technologies into a single integrated product suite.	• Oracle WebCenter Content • Oracle WebCenter Portal • Oracle WebCenter Sites • Oracle WebCenter Social
Business Intelligence	Oracle provides the most complete, open, and integrated business intelligence solution available, with a complete range of best-in-class BI capabilities, including enterprise reporting, ad hoc query and analysis, dashboards, and scorecards.	• Oracle Business Intelligence Tools and Technology • Oracle Exalytics In-Memory Machine • Oracle Endeca Information Discovery • Oracle Real-Time Decisions • Oracle Essbase
Identity Management	Oracle offers a complete identity management platform that enables enterprises to improve security, enforce compliance, lower administration costs, and leverage extreme scalability with tightly integrated components that speed deployment and simplify user identity administration and access management.	• Oracle Access Management • Oracle Identity Governance • Oracle Directory Services • Oracle Identity and Access Management

(Continued)

TABLE 8.1 (CONTINUED)

Oracle Fusion Middleware Product List

Middleware Category	Description	Product List
Development Tools	Oracle offers the industry's most complete and integrated set of tools for application development, database development, and business intelligence to support any development approach, technology platform, or operating system.	• Java IDEs • Java Frameworks • Java APIs • Java SDKs • Oracle BI Publisher • Oracle Data Integrator • Oracle Reports • Oracle Application Express • Oracle Forms • Oracle SQL Developer • Oracle Solaris Studio • Oracle Solaris • Oracle Linux • Oracle Developer Tools for Visual Studio • Oracle Data Provider for .NET • Oracle Database Extensions for .NET • WebCenter WSRP Producer for .NET

the communications protocols. SOA depends on data and services that are described by metadata that should meet the following two criteria:

1. The metadata should be provided in a form that software systems can use to configure dynamically by discovery and incorporation of defined services, and also to maintain coherence and integrity. For example, metadata could be used by other applications, like a catalog, to perform autodiscovery of services without modifying the functional contract of a service.

2. The metadata should be provided in a form that system designers can understand and manage with a reasonable expenditure of cost and effort.

The purpose of SOA is to allow users to combine fairly large chunks of functionality to form ad hoc applications built almost entirely from existing software services. The larger the chunks, the fewer are the interfaces required to implement any given set of functionality. However, very large chunks of functionality may not prove sufficiently granular for easy reuse. Each interface brings with it some amount of processing overhead, so there is a performance consideration in choosing the granularity of services.

SOA as an architecture relies on service orientation as its fundamental design principle. If a service presents a simple interface that abstracts away its underlying complexity, then users can access independent services without knowledge of the service's platform implementation.

The main benefit of SOA is to allow simultaneous use and easy mutual data exchange between programs of different vendors without additional programming or making changes to the services. These services are also reusable, resulting in lower development and maintenance costs and providing more value once the service is developed and tested. Having reusable services readily available also results in quicker time to market.

There are no industry standards relating to the exact composition of a service-oriented architecture, although many industry sources have published their own principles. Some of these principles include the following:

- *Standardized service contract*: Services adhere to a communications agreement, as defined collectively by one or more service-description documents.
- *Service loose coupling*: Services maintain a relationship that minimizes dependencies and only requires that they maintain an awareness of each other.
- *Service abstraction*: Beyond descriptions in the service contract, services hide logic from the outside world.
- *Service reusability*: Logic is divided into services with the intention of promoting reuse.
- *Service autonomy*: Services have control over the logic they encapsulate.
- *Service statelessness*: Services minimize resource consumption by deferring the management of state information when necessary
- *Service discoverability*: Services are supplemented with communicative metadata by which they can be effectively discovered and interpreted.
- *Service composability*: Services are effective composition participants, regardless of the size and complexity of the composition.

- *Service granularity*: This is a design consideration to provide optimal scope and the appropriate granular level of the business functionality in a service operation.
- *Service normalization*: Services are decomposed and/or consolidated to a level of normal form to minimize redundancy. In some cases, services are denormalized for specific purposes, such as performance optimization, access, and aggregation.
- *Service optimization*: All else being equal, high-quality services are generally preferable to low-quality ones.
- *Service relevance*: Functionality is presented at a granularity recognized by the user as a meaningful service.
- *Service encapsulation*: Many services are consolidated for use under the SOA. Such services often were not planned to be under SOA.
- *Service location transparency*: This refers to the ability of a service consumer to invoke a service regardless of its actual location in the network. This also recognizes the discoverability property (one of the core principle of SOA) and the right of a consumer to access the service. Often, the idea of service virtualization also relates to location transparency. This is where the consumer simply calls a logical service while a suitable SOA-enabling runtime infrastructure component, commonly a service bus, maps this logical service call to a physical service.

APPLICATIONS

Oracle Fusion Applications (OFA) is a set of software applications from Oracle Corporation. It is distributed across various product families, including financial management, human capital management, customer relationship management (CRM), supply chain management, procurement, governance, and project portfolio management.

OFA were announced shortly after Oracle's US$18 billion acquisition spree of PeopleSoft, JD Edwards, and Siebel Systems in 2005. OFA were envisioned and pitched as an enterprise resource planning (ERP) suite—a combination of features and functionalities taken from Oracle E-Business Suite, JD Edwards, PeopleSoft, and Siebel product lines. The suite is built on top of the OFM technology stack, which leverages the service-oriented architecture capabilities of Oracle Fusion Architecture. Oracle Fusion is

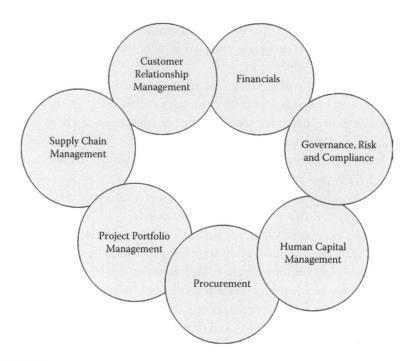

FIGURE 8.3
Oracle Fusion Applications.

essentially an ERP software that offers complete business solutions for all the wings of enterprise, as shown in Figure 8.3. Table 8.2 provides a list of Oracle Fusion applications, including a description and list of products within each category.

Note the CRM application. While Siebel's product line certainly influenced Oracle's Fusion CRM, the company does market the Oracle Siebel CRM solution separately, as shown in Table 8.3. The same is true for the PeopleSoft applications, as shown in Table 8.4.

As you can readily see, Fusion middleware and applications span tens of dozens of applications. It is quite possible to utilize Oracle (or other vendor) applications and services in all areas of an organization's business. Prior to disbanding the IT department altogether, it is worthwhile to consider what, when, and why one should forgo internal development and procure a vendor's products and services. Thus, for the remainder of this chapter, we will consider procurement.

TABLE 8.2

Oracle Fusion Applications

Application Category	Description	Product List
Customer Relationship Management	Oracle Sales Cloud drives smarter sales by helping reps to sell more, managers to know more, and companies to grow more. Oracle Sales Cloud combines a mobile-first strategy for sales reps and managers with powerful analytics and forecasting, customer insights, and seamless integration with marketing and partners for increased revenue.	• Oracle Sales Cloud
Financials	Oracle's Fusion Financial Management is a complete and integrated financial management solution that sets the foundation for good governance and consistent growth while helping today's fast-growing and dynamic organizations make better decisions, increase efficiency, reduce costs, and continuously innovate. Only Oracle combines the best of the best capabilities across Oracle's financial solutions to deliver a comprehensive solution that arms finance professionals with the right information at the right time, increases productivity, and accelerates business performance. Oracle Fusion Financial Management Cloud will bring power to your people and is your software as a service financial-management solution available by subscription. A complete set of enterprise cloud services ensures customer success before, during, and after enablement.	*Financials*: • Fusion Financial Management • Fusion Expenses • Fusion Advanced Collections *Fusion accounting hub*: • Accounting Integration Platform • Reporting Platform *Financial reporting and analytics*: • Fusion Financial Reports Center • Oracle Transactional Business Intelligence • Oracle Financial Analytics

(Continued)

TABLE 8.2 (CONTINUED)

Oracle Fusion Applications

Application Category	Description	Product List
Governance, Risk, and Compliance	Oracle Fusion Governance, Risk, and Compliance (GRC) provides a complete enterprise GRC platform that gives you the power to discover unified intelligence for insight into the status of all GRC activities across the enterprise; to manage end-to-end support for cross-industry and industry-specific GRC processes; and to enforce best-in-class automated controls that work across multiple business applications.	*Risk & financial governance:* • Enterprise GRC Manager • Financial Governance • GRC Intelligence *Advanced controls:* • Transaction Controls Governor • Configuration Controls Governor • Preventive Controls Governor *Access & segregation of duties (SOD) controls:* • Application Access Controls Governor
Human Capital Management	Oracle's Fusion Human Capital Management (HCM) enables you to develop a global foundation for human-resources data and improved business processes. Fusion HCM delivers a robust set of best-in-class human-resources functionality that enables you to increase productivity, accelerate business performance, and lower your cost of ownership. Oracle HCM Cloud will bring power to your people and is your software-as-a-service HCM solution available by subscription. A complete set of enterprise cloud services ensures customer success before, during, and after enablement.	*Global core human capital management:* • Fusion Benefits • Fusion Global Human Resources • Fusion Global Payrol • Fusion Global Payroll Interface • Fusion Workforce Lifecycle Manager *Workforce service delivery:* • Fusion Network at Work • Fusion Workforce Directory Management *Talent management:* • Fusion Goal Management • Fusion Performance Management • Fusion Talent Review • Fusion Workforce Compensation

(Continued)

TABLE 8.2 (CONTINUED)

Oracle Fusion Applications

Application Category	Description	Product List
		• Oracle Taleo Recruiting Cloud Service • Oracle Taleo Learn Cloud Service *HR analytics*: • Fusion Transactional Business Intelligence for Human Capital Management • Fusion Workforce Predictions
Procurement	Oracle Fusion Procurement, a key component of Oracle Fusion Applications, helps you spend smarter. With Oracle Fusion Procurement you can practice smarter negotiation, smarter buying, and smarter collaboration.	• Oracle Fusion Sourcing • Oracle Fusion Purchasing • Oracle Fusion Procurement Contracts • Oracle Fusion Supplier Portal • Oracle Fusion Self Service Procurement
Project Portfolio Management	Oracle Fusion Project Portfolio Management (PPM) dramatically improves the way project-driven organizations and project professionals work. Oracle Fusion PPM provides access to information and collaboration between team members to enable efficient and effective project management while ensuring smarter business decisions. Project-driven organizations benefit from its ground-up design with the user experience in mind: helping customers keep pace, keep score, and deliver extraordinary business and project insight.	• Oracle Fusion Project Performance Reporting • Oracle Fusion Project Contracts • Oracle Fusion Project Control • Oracle Fusion Project Costing • Oracle Fusion Project Billing • Oracle Fusion Project Integration Gateway

(Continued)

TABLE 8.2 (CONTINUED)

Oracle Fusion Applications

Application Category	Description	Product List
Supply Chain Management	Fusion Supply Chain Management (SCM) applications are next-generation applications that build upon Oracle's best-of-breed SCM product suite to address today's newest business challenges. Fusion SCM applications can transform your business operations by delivering: a single view for order, supply, and fulfillment plans across the entire enterprise; an embedded Global Order Promising solution to normalize supply and demand information across disparate fulfillment systems; a unified and accurate product definition that is harmonized within and across the enterprise value chain, as well as comprehensive inventory and cost management capabilities.	• Oracle Fusion Distributed Order Orchestration • Oracle Fusion Product Hub • Oracle Fusion Inventory and Cost Management • Oracle Fusion Procurement

PROCUREMENT

Making the Outsourcing Decision

Outsourcing is a three-phased process:

Phase 1: Analysis and evaluation
Phase 2: Needs assessment and vendor selection
Phase 3: Implementation and management

Phase 1: Analysis and Evaluation

In order to understand the services that need to be outsourced, organizational goals need to be identified, particularly the core competencies.

TABLE 8.3

The Siebel Product Set

Product Area	Siebel Product
Siebel Sales	• Siebel Sales
	• Oracle CRM On Demand Sales
	• Mobile and Handheld
	• Sales Analytics
	• Siebel Collaboration
	• Quote and Order Capture
	• Microsoft Exchange Server
	• Partner and Channel Management
Quote and order capture	• Siebel Dynamic Catalog
	• Siebel Product and Pricing Analytics
	• Siebel Dynamic Pricer
	• Siebel Product and Catalog Management
Enterprise marketing	• Siebel eMail Marketing
	• Oracle Marketing Analytics
	• Siebel Web Marketing
	• Siebel Events Management
	• Siebel Loyalty Management
	• Siebel Campaign/Dialogue Management
	• Siebel Marketing Resource Management
Contact center and service	• Siebel Contact Center
	• Siebel Contact Center and Service Analytics
	• Oracle CRM Call Center On Demand
	• Siebel Field Service
	• Siebel Help Desk
	• Siebel Mobile Solutions
	• Siebel Warranty Management
Self-service and e-billing	• Oracle Self-Service E-Billing
	• Siebel E-Commerce
	• Oracle iStore
	• Siebel E-Support
Partner relationship management	• Siebel Partner Analytics
	• Siebel Partner Portal
	• Siebel Partner Manager
CRM technology	• Siebel Application Deployment Manager
	• Siebel Application Response Measurement
	• Siebel CRM Desktop
	• Oracle Fusion Middleware Siebel Best Practice Center

(Continued)

TABLE 8.3 (CONTINUED)

The Siebel Product Set

Product Area	Siebel Product
	• Siebel Handheld
	• Siebel Remote and Mobile Web Client
	• Siebel Server Sync
	• Siebel Task-Based UI
	• Siebel Test Automation
	• Siebel Wireless

Once the goals and core competencies are identified, information related to these activities is gathered to compare the cost of performing the functions in-house with the cost of outsourcing them. This enables the company to answer nonfinancial questions such as, "How critical are these functions/activities?" or "What are the dependencies on these activities?" or "Will this activity become a mission-critical activity?" This will help organizations reach decisions about whether or not to outsource. Long-term cost and investment implications, work morale, and support should also be considered.

Phase 2: Needs Assessment and Vendor Selection

The objective of this phase is to develop a detailed understanding of the needs of the organization and the capabilities of possible solution providers. In this phase, a request for a proposal (RFP) is developed and delivered to applicable vendors. The RFPs need to be structured in a manner to facilitate assessment and comparison of the various vendors. The RFP should contain the complete requirements, the problem that needs to be resolved, desires, etc. A clearly structured and documented RFP also helps vendors understand and evaluate what a company is looking for and assists them in assessing whether they can provide the required service.

When evaluating the vendor proposals, the organization should look not only at the technological capability of the vendor, but also at factors such as the vendor's financial stability, track record, and customer-support reputation. Contacting the vendor's existing and previous clients would give the organization a good idea about the vendor's abilities. A matrix,

TABLE 8.4

PeopleSoft Products

Product Area	PeopleSoft Product
Human capital management	• Global Core Human Capital Management • Workforce Management • Workforce Service Delivery • Talent Management
Financial management	• Asset Lifecycle Management • Credit-to-Cash • Financial Control and Reporting • Financial Analytics • Governance, Risk, and Compliance • Procure-to-Pay • Travel and Expense Management • Treasury Management • Additional Applications for Financial Services • Additional Applications for Public Sector
Supplier relationship management	• Catalog Management • eProcurement • eSettlements • eSupplier Connection • Financials • Procurement and Spend Analytics • Purchasing • Services Procurement
Enterprise services automation	• Project Portfolio Management • Project Analytics • Program Management • Resource Management • Proposal Management • Project Costing • Project Discovery • Billing • Contracts • Expenses • Grants
Supply chain management	• Customer Order Management • Supply Chain Planning • Supply Chain Warehouse • Inventory and Fulfillment Management

(Continued)

TABLE 8.4 (CONTINUED)

PeopleSoft Products

Product Area	PeopleSoft Product
PeopleTools tools and technology	• Application Development
	• Integration
	• Life-Cycle and Administration
	• PeopleSoft Interaction Hub
	• Platforms and Engineered Systems
	• Security

such as the one shown in Table 8.5, can be used to aid in the decision-making process.

1. Choose or develop the criteria for comparison and the weight (importance) of each
2. Select the alternatives to be compared
3. Generate scores—for each comparison, the product should be evaluated as being better (+), the same (S), or worse (–)
4. Compute the total score

Four scores will be generated: the number of plus scores, minus scores, the overall total, and the weighted total. The overall total is the number of plus scores, minus the number of minus scores. The weighted total is the scores times their respective weighting factors, added up. The totals should not be treated as absolute in the decision-making process, but as

TABLE 8.5

Pugh Matrix

Criterion	Weight	Concepts (Step 2)
(Step 1)	:	Generate score (step 3)
	:	
:		:
:		:
Total +		
Total –		
Overall total		Generate totals (step 4)
Weighted total		

guidance only. If the two top scores are very close or very similar, then they should be examined more closely to make a more-informed decision.

Once a vendor is selected, the organization needs to make sure that a fair and reasonable contract, beneficial to the organization, is negotiated. It is imperative that the organization clearly define service levels and the consequences of not meeting them. Both parties should make sure that they understand the performance measurement criteria.

Phase 3: Implementation and Management

The final phase in the outsourcing decision process is the implementation. During this phase, a clear definition of the task needs to be identified, and establishing a time frame would be very helpful. Mechanisms need to be established to monitor and evaluate performance during the vendor's developmental process. This is important, even after implementations, to make sure that the outsourced tasks are being delivered by the vendor as they are supposed to be delivered. The ability to identify, communicate, and resolve issues promptly and fairly will help the company achieve mutual benefits and make a relationship successful.

Depending on the size of the outsourcing contract, the manager responsible for the program's delivery and integration may be responsible for all of the process or only some. These are the horizontal and vertical factors of outsourcing management. A manager of the horizontal process is often involved in the decision to outsource, and is then responsible for defining the work, selecting and engaging the vendor, and managing the delivery and completion of the program. This manager normally handles all day-to-day negotiations. With larger programs, particularly those on a global scale, there is often a decision taken at senior levels to outsource. A negotiation team is appointed to work through the complex agreements, usually under strict confidentiality, until the agreement is finalized and announced. It is then the role of the manager of the vertical component to implement and manage the ongoing program. Part of this role is the interpretation of the agreement and identification of areas not covered by the agreement.

Procurement Planning

Procurement planning, which encompasses the outsourcing decision, should be every bit as rigorous as project planning. Once you've made a decision to go outside the organization, a procurement plan should be created. While all companies do things differently, there are still some very common elements in a procurement plan. A sample plan will be described in this section.

Description of the Project

The description provides an overview of the proposed procurement request. The project itself should be described. At a minimum, the project plan should be referenced. Those practicing configuration management will have the benefit of a standardized policy for configuration identification. The policy for configuration identification incrementally establishes and maintains the definitive current basis for control and status accounting of a system and its configuration items (CIs) throughout their life cycles. The configuration-identification process ensures that all processes have common sets of documentation as the basis for developing a new system or modifying an old one. Hence, a project plan in this environment would have a unique identifying number and would be easily referenced.

The description should also indicate whether the project requires commercial off-the-shelf (COTS), modified off-the-shelf (MOTS), or custom software development. The percentage of each should be calculated.

Other questions that should be answered by this section are:

1. Does the project require integration, or is the project a stand-alone system with minimal integration?
2. What is the system maintenance strategy?
3. Which databases or legacy systems are required to be used or created?

Market Research

Market research, which is a marketing term, is related to the research one typically does when performing a feasibility study. Research needs to be done to determine what is available on the market. Who are the vendors and what are their products or services? It is advisable to request meetings with customers of each product, preferably in a related industry. At a minimum, you will want to conduct a reference check detailing your findings, as shown in Table 8.6.

TABLE 8.6

Reference Check Statements

Bidder Name:	Did the Response Meet Expectations?					
	RC1		RC2		RC3	
Statement	Yes	No	Yes	No	Yes	No
1 Effectiveness of contractor collaboration with the on-site project manager						
2 Ability of contractor to facilitate discussions with other stakeholders						
3 Ability of the contractor to integrate easily with other project staff						
4 Overall satisfaction with contractor method of introducing issues/problems encountered on project						
5 Speed in which contractor brought forward identified issues						
6 Did contractor bring forward feasible solutions at the same time they presented issues or problems?						
7 Was the assignment of staff personnel stable?						
8 Were deliverables timely and in conformance with contract specifications?						
9 What was your overall satisfaction with contractor?						

Most importantly, you will want to assess the stability of the vendor company itself. How long has the company been in business? Is it in danger of being acquired or merged with another company? You then need to request a price estimate from interested bidders/sources.

The procurement plan should describe this effort in terms of the approach to the market survey, the functional requirements of the products/services to be acquired, the prospective sources, and the competitive environment.

Acquisition Methodology Steps

In this section of the procurement plan, the proposed acquisition methodology should be described.

- Describe why this will be a competitive or noncompetitive bid. If consultants are being used, explain why in-house staff can't be used.
- Describe how sources for competition will be sought, promoted, and sustained throughout the acquisition. If competition is not contemplated or achievable, discuss the basis of that decision. Justify why the requirement(s) cannot be modified to take advantage of competition.
- Describe the proposed procurement steps. For example, a request for proposal (RFP) can be structured using all or a combination of a request for information (RFI) as well as conceptual, technical, draft, and final proposal methodologies.
- Discuss key deliverables, including management plans and reports that will be used to monitor the contractor's performance.
- For the best value solicitations, describe the evaluation factors and values (percent or points) assigned for the functional/technical requirements. As shown in Table 8.7, the evaluation factors must be based on functional requirements.
- Discuss the evaluation factors and scoring methodology. If appropriate, include additional scoring or evaluation worksheets as appendices, as shown in Tables 8.8 and 8.9. Discuss mandatory and desirable requirements and indicate whether reference checks will be performed. If weighted scores are used, indicate how the weighted score is computed and how the weighting is applied. Indicate why the weights were chosen, as shown in Table 8.10.

TABLE 8.7

Sample Evaluation Factors and Values

Evaluation Factor	Value Assigned (e.g., % or points)
Development and conversion	45%
Training tasks and deliverables	25%
VC costs	30%

TABLE 8.8

Mandatory Requirements

Reqmt #	Description of Requirement	Score

TABLE 8.9

Weighted Desirable Requirements

Reqmt #	Description of Requirement	Weight	Score	Weighted Score

TABLE 8.10

Scoring Values

Score	Description
0	*No value*: Fails to address the component or the bidder does not describe any experience related to the component.
1	*Poor*: Minimally addresses the component, but one or more major considerations of the component are not addressed. Low degree of confidence in the bidder's response or proposed solution.
2	*Fair*: The response addresses the component adequately, but minor considerations may not be addressed. Acceptable degree of confidence in the bidder's response or proposed solution.
3	*Good*: The response fully addresses the component and provides a good quality solution. Good degree of confidence in the bidder's response or proposed solution.
4	*Very good*: All considerations of the component are addressed with a high degree of confidence in the bidder's response or proposed solution.
5	*Excellent*: All considerations of the component are addressed with the highest degree of confidence in the bidder's response or proposed solution. The response exceeds the requirements in providing a superior solution.

Procurement Risk Management

This section describes methods to protect the company's investment and ensure adequate contractor performance. Protections might include:

1. Payment holdbacks
2. Performance bond requirements
3. Warranty provisions
4. Liquidated damage provisions

Like anything else in project management, procurement risks must be managed. One of the most popular techniques is to include language in the statement of work (SOW) requiring that the acceptance of deliverables for the company will pay the vendor's invoice. The vendor should be required to take timely and appropriate measures to correct or remediate the reason(s) for nonacceptance and demonstrate that the vendor has successfully completed the scheduled work for each deliverable before payment is made.

Contract Management Approach

In this section of the procurement plan, the project's specific approach, tools, and processes should be described, including:

1. Contract-management plan
2. Issue and action-item process
3. Problem-tracking process
4. Status-reporting process
5. System-acceptance process
6. Invoice process
7. Deficiency-management process
8. Dispute-resolution process
9. Deliverables-management process

Describe the tools used to manage the contract, contractual requirements, and deliverables. The status-reporting approach, including written reports and meetings, should also be documented. Discuss how meetings minutes, issues, and action items are recorded, tracked, and resolved. Detail specific approaches to monitoring and managing contractor performance and how performance problems and issues will be resolved, including the dispute process and payment withholds/liquidated damages.

Perhaps the best way to manage risk is to prevent problems from happening in the first place. Keeping a tight rein over outsider contracts is critically important. Status meetings, walk-throughs, quality assurance, and other software-engineering and project-management techniques should be used.

SUMMARY

Procurement in many organizations is a hit-or-miss affair. CIOs need to recognize that this is an important aspect of the project, as selecting the correct vendor (and solution) can make or break a project. The process of procurement management needs to be standardized, as does the process of project management. In all cases, a procurement plan should be created that details the steps taken to research and then select the most cost-effective technologies or services.

Procuring any product or service requires the organization to review the licensing company's metrics and restrictions. For a good handle on how all of this relates to Oracle, I urge you to review OMT-CO's excellent overview entitled, "The Licensing of Oracle Technology Products— Compliance, Metrics, Licensing Restrictions," which can be found at http://omtco.eu/references/oracle/the-licensing-of-oracle-technology-products-compliance-metrics-licensing-restrictions/.

Index